CONTROVERSY
The birth control debate 1958–1968

CONTROVERSY

The birth control debate 1958-1968

AMBROGIO VALSECCHI

With an introduction by Gregory Baum, O.S.A.

Translated by

Dorothy White

CORPUS BOOKS
Washington—Cleveland

CORPUS PUBLICATIONS

Editorial Offices   *Sales & Distribution*
1330 Massachusetts Ave., N.W.   2231 West 110th Street
Washington, D.C. 20005   Cleveland, Ohio 44102

Originally published as *Regolazione delle nascite. Un decennio di riflessioni teologiche*, ©1967, Queriniana, Brescia, 1967

First published this edition, 1968
© Translation, 1968, Geoffrey Chapman Ltd

Library of Congress Catalog Card Number : 68-58720

49904

This book is set in 11 on 12 point Imprint

Made and printed in Great Britain

CONTENTS

	Preface	vii
	Introduction by Gregory Baum, O.S.A.	ix
I	The debate begins—the problem of the pill: 1957–1958	1
II	Discussion about progestational drugs: 1959–1963	9
III	A new aspect of the problem of the pill: 1964–1965	37
IV	The discussion about other contraceptive methods	72
V	The teaching of the Second Vatican Council	119
VI	The various positions assumed since the Council	153
	Conclusion	205
	Appendix A: The Encyclical *Humanae Vitae*	213
	Index of modern authors	231

PUBLISHER'S NOTE

After this book had gone to press, Pope Paul VI issued his encyclical on birth control, *Humanae vitae*. With the author's permission the book now contains the English text of the encyclical and an Introduction by Gregory Baum, O.S.A.

PREFACE TO THE FIRST ITALIAN EDITION

MORE than ten years have gone by since the summer of 1957 and the appearance of the first books or articles by Catholic theologians on the subject of the use of the 'pill': a new contraceptive method had been suggested and Christian moralists were obliged to pronounce upon it. Since then the problem of methods of birth control—of 'the pill', first of all, but later on of every other contraceptive method—has fully occupied the attention of moral theologians. This may perhaps have been the question most widely and seriously debated during the last ten years. The twenty thousand or more pages which we have been able to read, and which we review in this book, are a proof of this. And in ten years the positions assumed by moral theologians have been radically altered entailing grave, or even dramatic, modifications which no one would ever have dared to imagine when the discussion began.

We have tried to offer a summary of this debate. Taking for granted the right and duty to regulate births (which Pope Pius XII had already asserted and which was to find most authoritative acknowledgment in the doctrine of 'responsible parenthood' formulated by the Council) we have been able to concentrate on the various stages of the debate on the legitimacy of the various means used to obtain this end. As we see, the subject under review is somewhat circumscribed but the area for research was so vast that some limit had to be set. Moreover, this specific problem, besides being in itself of enormous practical importance, has called into play a whole complex of principles which have a determining influence on the solution of many other moral questions.

Two observations must be made here. First of all, we beg the forgiveness of those authors, among the many from whom we have quoted, whose thought we may perhaps have misunderstood or even distorted. Our intention has almost always been to present the various points of view without in every case taking sides, but rather leaving the discussion itself to bring about a considered judgment. Nevertheless, we may have been guilty of some error or partisanship, and if this has been the case we apologize now. Secondly, we are well aware that the sphere in which we have been working is that of doctrinal information: in all that regards practical and pastoral conduct we shall, as will be seen, be guided by the instructions promised by Pope Paul VI, which we still await.

Theological Seminary
Venegono Inferiore
September 1967

INTRODUCTION

ECCLESIOLOGICAL COMMENTARY ON THE ENCYCLICAL *HUMANAE VITAE* BY GREGORY BAUM O.S.A.

The publication of Pope Paul VI's encyclical on birth control was accompanied by events unprecedented in recent Church history. A large number of theologians all over the world publicly declared that they were unable to give an unqualified assent to the encyclical. All Catholic theologians readily accept the fundamental principle of the encyclical, namely the inseparable unity between love and fertility in human sexuality; all Catholic theologians apply this principle to the general orientation of married life and demand that married people engage in the twofold quest of seeking greater mutual love and of becoming better parents. But many Catholic theologians have been unable to follow the encyclical in the application of this fundamental principle to every single act of sexual intercourse in marriage. They have reaffirmed the conviction, acquired over the last few years by studying the issue and listening to the witness of married couples, that if a marriage is orientated towards love and children in general, then there may well be situations where contraceptive sexual intercourse is permissible and good.

The Special Nature of the Dissent

Two things are remarkable about this dissent. First, it is based on theological reflection. Whenever papal teachings were criticized and even rejected in the past this happened through scholars, or men in public office, or the secular community as a whole. The grounds for such rejections were usually non-theological. The present dissent from the papal teaching on birth control is unique inasmuch as it is based on Catholic theological principles or, in the case of the many lay people who have joined the theologians, on lessons learnt from Christian experience.

The second remarkable fact about the wide-spread dissent is that it took place within the structure of authority. It was not an act of rebellion! The theologians acknowledged the divinely

appointed ministry of the hierarchy in general and the papal
primacy of teaching and jurisdiction in particular. They acknowledged the right and duty of the pope to teach even on matters
of rational (non-revealed) morality. The theologians insisted,
however, that in case of an authoritative, non-infallible teaching,
Catholics are free to dissent when they have sufficient objective
and tested grounds for doing so. The Catholic tradition provides
for this freedom.

This remark is in need of further explanation. Catholic
theological literature has distinguished between two kinds of
assents. Faith is an assent, created by the Spirit, to the divine
Word proclaimed by the Church. Faith is unconditional. Faith
is grounded on the veracity of the God who speaks. At the same
time the Church is commissioned to teach even beyond the area
of divine revelation. In this area her teaching is by nature always
non-infallible. How is this authoritative teaching of the Church
to be received? Catholic theological literature has called the
assent due to non-infallible teaching 'religious assent' or
'obedience of mind and heart'. This vocabulary has been adopted
in the papal documents themselves.[1] We find this vocabulary
confirmed by Vatican II.[2] A Catholic acknowledges with external
and internal religious obedience the teaching of popes and
bishops, even when they do not exercise their infallible teaching
office. But what is this religious assent? It is not an act of faith.
Because its object is non-infallible and hence could possibly be
wrong, the assent is always conditional. Its formal basis is the
trust that the Magisterium of the Church is guided by the Spirit
in its official teaching. Because of this trust Catholics are certain
that in general, in the majority of cases, the official teaching is
correct; but nothing in the dogma of the Church assures them that
occasionally, in exceptional cases, the official teaching may not
be mistaken.[3] For this reason Catholic theological literature has
said that the religious assent owed to the Church's authoritative,

---

[1] Cf. Pius IX's letter to the Archbishop of Munich in 1863 (Denz. 1684),
Pius X's motu proprio *Praestantia Scripturae* in 1907 (Denz. 2113), Pius XI's
encyclical *Casti Connubii* in 1930 (AAS, 1930, 580), and Pius XII's encyclical
Humani Generis in 1950 (Denz. 2313).

[2] Constitution on the Church, section 25.

[3] Cf. Ch. Journet, *L'Eglise du Verbe Incarné*, vol 1, Paris, 1955, pp 447–57.
(English translation available.)

non-infallible teaching is conditional: i.e. there are conditions under which it is licit for a Catholic to dissent from an official position.

A number of bishops, according to the Catholic press, have denied this right to dissent. Such a denial, however, leads inevitably to contradiction. To deny the right to dissent either means that a non-infallible teaching can never be wrong (and this is a contradiction for a position is called non-infallible precisely because there is no guarantee that it is always true) or means that while a non-infallible position may be wrong ecclesiastical obedience demands that we say it is right (and this would be preposterous).

A great number of theologians all over the world have expressed their dissents in articles, in brief statements to the press, in conversations on radio and television. A highly significant statement of dissent was produced by a large group of American theologians. The original statement was signed by about 100 men and women teaching theology. Since then the statement has been signed by more than 500 men and woman belonging to the Catholic scholarly community in the United States of America. Here is the text.

As Roman Catholic theologians we respectfully acknowledge a distinct role of hierarchical Magisterium in the Church of Christ. At the same time Christian tradition assigns theologians the special responsibility of evaluating and interpreting pronouncements of the Magisterium in the light of the total theological data operative in each question or statement. We offer these initial comments on Pope Paul VI's encyclical on the regulation of birth.

Many positive values concerning marriage are expressed . . . However, we take exception to the ecclesiology implied and the methodology used by Paul VI in the writing and promulgation of the document: they are incompatible with the Church's authentic self-awareness as expressed in and suggested by the acts of the Second Vatican Council itself. The encyclical consistently assumes that the Church is identical with the hierarchical office. No real importance is afforded the witness of the life of the Church in its totality; the special witness of many Catholic couples is neglected; it fails to acknowledge the witness of the separated Christian churches and ecclesial communities . . . Furthermore, the encyclical betrays a narrow and positivistic notion of papal authority, as illustrated by the rejection of the majority view presented by the commission established to consider the question,

as well as by the rejection of the conclusions of a large part of the
international Catholic theological community.

Likewise, we take exception to some of the specific ethical
conclusions contained in the encyclical. They are based on an
inadequate concept of natural law: the multiple forms of natural
law theory are ignored and the fact that competent philosophers
come to different conclusions on this very question is disregarded
. . . Other defects include: overemphasis on the biological aspects
of conjugal relations as ethically normative; undue stress on
sexual acts and the faculty of sex viewed itself apart from the
person and couple; a static world view which downplays the
historical and evolutionary character of humanity in its finite
existence . . . ; unfounded assumptions about 'the evil
consequences' of methods of artificial birth control; indifference to
the Second Vatican Council's assertion that prolonged sexual
abstinence may cause 'faithfulness to be imperilled and its
quality of fruitfulness to be ruined'; an almost total disregard for
the dignity of millions of human beings brought into the world
without the slightest possibility of being fed and educated decently.

In actual fact, the encyclical demonstrates no development over
the teaching of Pius XI's *Casti Connubii*, whose conclusions
have been called into question for grave and serious reasons.
These reasons, given a muffled voice at Vatican II, have not been
adequately handled by the mere repetition of past teaching.

It is common teaching in the Church that Catholics may dissent
from authoritative, non-infallible teachings of the Magisterium
when sufficient reasons for so doing exist. Therefore, as Roman
Catholic theologians, conscious of our duty and our limitations,
we conclude that spouses may responsibly decide according to
their conscience that artificial contraception in some circumstances
is permissible and indeed necessary to preserve and foster the
values and sacredness of marriage.

It is our conviction also that true commitment to the mystery
of Christ and the Church requires a candid statement of mind at
this time by all Catholic theologians.[4]

These extraordinary events accompanying the publication of
the papal encyclical demand the reflection of the Catholic ecclesi-
ologist. What is the meaning of this crisis of authority?

The Shift at Vatican II

To understand the present crisis we must study the shift in

---

[4] *Commonweal*, Aug. 23, 1968.

the understanding of the papal Magisterium that occurred at Vatican II.

After Vatican Council I (1870) which had defined the doctrine of papal infallibility, a certain theological tendency in the Church, often encouraged from on high, vastly enlarged the claims of the Magisterium, in particular of the papal Magisterium, beyond the strict definition. While Vatican I restricted papal infallibility to solemn teaching (*ex cathedra* pronouncements), there was a tendency in theological literature to attribute infallibility to the ordinary teaching of the pope or at least, without going that far, to assign to this teaching such a central role in the Church that neither bishops nor theologians were allowed to qualify it. The pope became almost the sole authoritative teacher in the Church. Moreover, while traditionally infallibility had to do with the proclamation of divine revelation, a certain theological tendency enlarged the area of infallibility to include doctrines loosely connected with divine revelation, human wisdom and rational morality. Many authors understood the expression *doctrina de fide et moribus*, outlining the area of infallibility, as referring to the entire area of belief and the entire area of the moral life. Actually the doctrine on faith and morals refer to Christ's teaching what we must believe (faith) and what we must practice (morals). Doctrine on faith and morals are the *credenda* and *facienda* of the Christian gospel.

At Vatican II this tendency to widen the claims of the papal Magisterium was reversed. No systematic treatment of the Magisterium was undertaken, but a number of significant events took place during the Council that revealed the new orientation. The first draft of the Constitution on the Church, prepared by a preconciliar commission under the direction of the Roman Curia, had attempted to confirm the trend of widening papal teaching authority. The first draft contained two chapters, one on the Magisterium and the other on obedience, which revealed the highly juridical conception of the Church current in Roman thinking and assigned an extraordinarily elevated place to the papal Magisterium in the Church. While the draft did not claim infallibility for the Ordinary Magisterium of the pope, it did assert a kind of practical infallibility: echoing a remark of Pius XII, the draft laid down that after the Ordinary Magisterium had taught on a controverted subject, the matter was no longer open to the discussion of theologians. The draft gave the pope such a central position as teacher that other bishops—leave alone theologians—were unable to participate in the Magisterium of the Church. The draft, moreover, revealed the tendency to widen the area of the Church's infallibility that developed in the theological literature over the last century.

It is well known that the first draft of the conciliar document on the Church was rejected by the Council. It was criticized as juridical, monarchical and triumphalistic. A new draft was composed by a commission elected by the Council. This second draft, as well as the final version, approached the mystery of the Church in a new way. Church is people of God. All the gifts of Christ to the Church, including her sacramental and hierarchical gifts, must be understood in this perspective.

The new draft did not deal with the Magisterium as such. The special effort of this new draft was to set down the collegiality of bishops. While reaffirming papal primacy in the Church, Vatican II taught that the pope is not alone in teaching and policy-making: he is accompanied in this by the bishops of the Church, successors of the apostles.

At an ecumenical council, such as Vatican II, the bishops are teachers and legislators with the pope, who calls, chairs and approves the meeting; but even when no council is being held, the pope cannot teach or rule in such a way as to exclude the bishops from collegial co-responsibility in teaching and policy-making for the universal Church. The relation of pope and bishops cannot be reduced to an easy formula. While on the one hand the pope can exercise his primacy in canonical or legal independence from the bishops, the bishops on the other have an authority to participate in the universal teaching and policy-making that is not derived from the pope but from their own office. There is an inevitable tension between pope and episcopate in the exercise of the Magisterium.

This tension was acknowledged and lived out courageously at the Council itself. But since the bishops of the Church were trained in a system where their only mode of participation was one of unqualified obedience, the tension between the centre and the various parts of the Church, acknowledged by Vatican II, has not yet become part of the Church's life. The present crisis may be a beginning. While these lines are being written no episcopal conference has yet expressed itself on the recent papal encyclical.[5]

Vatican II confirmed the teaching of Vatican I in regard to papal infallibility and papal primacy in general. The Council, however, limited infallibility to divine revelation.[6] In other words, it corrected the widening trend of the first draft. The conciliar document also placed the teaching of the pope in the context of the episcopal college.[7] Here again the trend of the first draft was corrected. Vatican II acknowledged the central role of the Ordinary Magisterium of the papacy as well as the special role of bishops to teach with authority. It confirmed the traditional expression that Catholics owe 'religious assent of mind and will' to the authoritative, non-infallible teaching.[8] However, the sentence that after such teaching Catholic theologians can no longer discuss the issue, was left out. We read in the official commentary (Expensio Modorum) that some bishops demanded a clarification of this religious assent. They desired that the conditional character of this assent be explained. This was a delicate subject. The conciliar document had already changed the entire orientation of the first draft and reduced two chapters on Magisterium and obedience to a few lines in the new draft. The whole issue of authority could not be discussed at Vatican II. The official commentary simply states that the bishops who wish to know the limits of this religious assent should consult theological authors.[9]

[5] According to a report in the London Times of Sept. 2 the Belgian bishops published a document in which they grant freedom of conscience in regard to birth control.

[6] Constitution on the Church, section 25: 'The infallibility . . . extends as far as the deposit of revelation extends, that must be religiously guarded and faithfully expounded.'

[7] In the second (corrected) draft of the Constitution on the Church a sentence on the pope's Ordinary Magisterium was appended to the section dealing with the Magisterium of the bishops. In the third draft and and the final version, this sentence was inserted in that part of the section that deals with the Ordinary Magisterium of bishops. The official explanation supplied with the text specifies that this change was made to place the papal Magisterium into the context of the teaching of the entire episcopate. Cf. G. Baum, Commentary on the Constitution on the Church, Paulist Press (English publishers: Darton, Longman and Todd), on chapter 3.

[8] Constitution on the Church section 25.

[9] Cf. Expensio Modorum to chapter 3, p. 42.

The Constitution on the Church applied other correctives to the juridical, monarchical and triumphalistic understanding of the Magisterium. It clearly acknowledged that the Spirit guides the Church through every one of her members.[10] While the apostolic hierarchy has the authority to shift the insights and test the charisms of the Christian people and hence to formulate the authentic teaching of the Church, there remains a certain tension between the hierarchical and charismatic elements in the Church. The hierarchical relation between pope, bishops, people, theologians, and other teachers cannot be reduced to a perfect juridical formula: tensions remain. Since Vatican II has acknowledged the pilgrim character of the Church and hence ignorance, sin and mistakes in her earthly life,[11] it is possible to infer that these tensions are the indispensable ways in which the entire Church is brought into greater fidelity to the divine Word.

The Magisterium Corrected

The tensions between the hierarchial and charismatic elements have been an essential part of the Church's experience over the last hundred years. While the Magisterium tends to insist that its teaching has never changed, the historian of doctrine finds that the outstanding characteristic of the papal Magisterium over the last hundred years is the fact that it has changed on so many issues.

Perhaps the most significant case to be remembered is that of religious liberty. When the Catholic liberals of the nineteenth century first advocated the separation of Church and State as an ideal and consequently defended the principle of religious liberty, the Roman Magisterium rejected their view. Several papal documents condemned the principle of religious liberty. Here is

---

[10] *Constitution on the Church*, section 12.

[11] *Constitution on the Church:* 'The Church is at the same time holy and always in need of purification, continually following the way of penance and renewal' (sec. 8); 'Moving forward through trial and tribulation, the Church is strengthened by the power of God's grace . . . that in the weakness of the flesh she may not waver from perfect fidelity . . . and never cease to renew herself' (sec. 9). Decree on Ecumenism: 'Christ summons the Church, as she goes her pilgrim way, to that continual reformation of which she always has need, insofar as she is an institution of men here on earth . . . If in various times and circumstances deficiencies . . . in church discipline or the formulation of church teachings have occurred . . . these should be set right at the opportune moment and in the proper way' (sec. 6).

the famous sentence from Pius IX's encyclical *Quanta Cura* (1864): 'From the completely false conception of social rule they did not hesitate to promote that erroneous opinion, especially injurious to the Catholic Church and the salvation of souls, called by our Predecessor Gregory XVI insane raving, namely that freedom of conscience and of worship is the proper right of each man, and that this should be proclaimed and asserted in every rightly constituted society.'[12] Because of the juridical and monarchical structure of the Church in the nineteenth century and in the early part of the twentieth, public dissent from the official position was almost impossible. Catholics dissented from the papal teaching nonetheless. Only towards the middle of the twentieth century did theologians challenge the papal teaching openly. At Vatican II, after considerable struggle, the Catholic Church finally endorsed the principle of religious liberty.[13] Religious liberty is the right of every man and a just society should protect and promote the religious liberty of its members.

At the beginning of the twentieth century the Biblical Commission, created by Pope Pius X, issued decrees that were to resolve difficult problems of biblical scholarship in an authoritative manner.[14] Some solutions imposed by the Biblical Commission were wrong. Yet Pius X demanded that the decrees be acknowledged by an obedience of mind and will.[15] Because of the authoritarian understanding of the hierarchical office, the scholars who could not accept the official teaching were obliged to leave the Catholic Church. Yet even then the tension between the hierarchical and the charismatic remained in the Church. Biblical scholars slowly worked towards a revision of the official positions. Already Pius XII's encyclical *Divino Afflante Spiritu* (1943) overcame the fundamentalism espoused by the papal Magisterium of the past and encouraged a more open approach of biblical scholarship. In the fifties and, more especially, in the sixties during the Vatican Council, the new approach received its final approval. The decrees of the Biblical Commission remain with us as reminders of the errors contained in official teaching and of the

[12] Denz. 1690, cf. 1613.

[13] *Declaration on Religious Freedom.*

[14] For references see Denzinger, Index alphabeticus, under 'Commissio de Re Biblica'.

[15] Pius X's motu proprio *Praestantia Scripturae*, Denz. 2113.

inevitable tension between authority and free inquiry in the Church.

We shall look briefly at a third example, the attitude of the official Church to the ecumenical movement. Pope Pius XI's encyclical *Mortalium Animos* (1928) condemned the movement for Christian unity as leading to indifferentism and confusion. In this encyclical Pius XI did not acknowledge with a single word the existence of an authentic Christianity outside the Roman Church. He did not acknowledge the presence of Christ among other Christians. Yet Catholic theologians continued to concern themselves with the ecumenical movement. The tension between the hierarchical and charismatic was high in this area for over two decades. Thanks to Pope John the ecumenical movement was eventually approved in the sixties. The teaching of Vatican II's Decree on Ecumenism reversed the teaching of previous popes on the subject. Today the Catholic Church acknowledges other Christians as Christians and other Churches as communities of salvation.

Tension Between Institution and Charisma

A reflection on these three examples reveals the tension between the Roman Magisterium and other parts of the Church. It also reveals the suffering the authoritarian ways of the Magisterium caused to far-sighted people in the Church as well as the great harm this manner of teaching has inflicted on the Catholic Church as a whole.

In this century, especially over the last decades, the distance between the Roman teaching and the theology taught in other parts of the Church has widened. The reasons for this are the claims the Roman Magisterium makes for itself: it tends to regard itself as self-sufficient. It does not willingly acknowledge that it is in need of being taught by the wisdom produced by the Spirit in the whole Church. The Roman theological schools are isolated from the world-wide intellectual community. Many men holding high positions in the Roman Curia are, by their style of life as princes of the Church, prevented from sharing in the life of the universal human community. They do not participate as equals in discussions, in research projects, in pastoral work, and in conversations with ordinary people in various parts of the world.

The clothes they wear symbolize their desire to belong to another century and another world.

The distance between the Roman teaching and doctrinal development in the rest of the Catholic Church was brought out dramatically at Vatican Council II. Most of the first drafts, prepared under the supervision of the Roman Curia, were rejected by the Council. The new drafts with a new doctrinal orientation were opposed by a minority of bishops, among whom the Roman Curia played a considerable part. The Vatican Council demonstrated that the Roman theological tradition is no longer representative of universal Catholic teaching.

By introducing the principle of collegiality in the Church, Vatican II reversed the trend that has isolated the Roman teaching. Decentralization and participation have become the ideals of the Catholic Church—at least on paper. Yet the documents emanating from Rome since Vatican II have not reflected the collegial spirit nor the widening of the theological perspective. The men in the Curia who oppose the Dutch Catechism are precisely those who opposed the doctrinal renewal at Vatican II. Some Roman decisions of recent years have affirmed papal authority in a monarchical way. Some Roman documents speak in terms of an out-dated neo-scholastic theology which is no longer taught in the rest of the Church. It is in this context that the controversy over the papal encyclical *Humanae Vitae* must be understood. The public dissent brought into the open an ecclesiastical tension that had gone on for some time in a hidden way. In this dramatic manner outside the collegial system, the papal Magisterium may find itself subject to modification and correction. One may hope that this will lead to a more collegial manner of teaching in the future.

The papal position on birth control, we note, was never permitted to enter the collegial process. It was withdrawn from discussion at the Vatican II. Some bishops managed to open up the subject and advocate a wider approach to it. The conciliar document dealing with marriage and family limitation reflected a contemporary theological approach. It left open the question of means; but when at the last minute Pope Paul tried to insert into the text a remark that would have endorsed the traditional papal position, the competent conciliar commission refused to comply. The general tendency of the Council went in the other direction.[16]

The issue, moreover, was not put on the agenda of the Synod of Bishops. The papal commission, extended several times, and eventually comprising several bishops, produced a majority report that advocated the change of papal teaching and admitted the morality of contraception. The Lay Congress, meeting in Rome in 1967, expressed itself almost unanimously in favour of changing the papal teaching. The public reaction to the encyclical *Humanae Vitae* records that a highly centralized and non-collegial teaching no longer functions in the Catholic Church.

The Catholic people belong to diverse cultural environments and hence have different experiences of moral values. It is questionable whether in such a situation a uniform set of moral norms can be proposed in the Church. The evaluation of birth control depends in part on the state of women in society, on the acknowledged role of sexuality, on the place assigned to personal conscience, and on other factors of social life. Since people seek unity, common responsibility and the development of life in ways that depend in part on the society in which they live, the self-identical call of the gospel to follow Jesus makes demands on them which are, in fact, non-identical. Since the Catholic Church is universal and simultaneously belongs to many cultures and ages, a certain pluriformity within the unity of faith is quite inevitable. The present crisis over the papal encyclical brings to light the need for greater pluriformity in unity of the Catholic Church.

---

[16] Cf. G. Baum, 'Birth Control, What Happened?' *Commonweal*, Dec. 24, 1965.

I

THE DEBATE BEGINS—THE PROBLEM OF THE PILL:
1957–1958

THE debate we are about to examine began with the problem of
the 'pill', that is, with the use of those various synthetic products
(derived from progesterone and testosterone and frequently
combined with the use of an oestrogen) which may also have the
effect of causing sterility in a woman by preventing the process
of ovulation.[1]

I. *The first studies*

The discussion began in America where, as soon as scientific
research (particularly that undertaken by G. Pincus and J.
Rock) pointed out the very real possibility that the new products might
be used as contraceptives, the first accounts and studies of the
moral problem appeared in four articles (the first a very short one)
which were published between July 1957 and August of the
following year:

F. J. Connell, C.SS.R., 'The contraceptive pill', *The American
Ecclesiastical Review* 137 (1957), pp. 50–1.

W. J. Gibbons, S.J., 'Antifertility drugs and morality', *America*
98 (1957), pp. 346–8.

W. J. Gibbons, S.J.—T. K. BURCH, 'Physiologic control of
fertility: process and morality', *The American Ecclesiastical
Review* 138 (1958), pp. 246–77.

J. J. Lynch, S.J., 'Progestational Steroids: some moral problems',
Linacre Quarterly 25 (1958), pp. 93–9.

In his brief article Connell distinguishes two different ethical
criteria by which contraceptive treatment must be judged. If its

[1] The medico-scientific aspects of the problem (which chiefly concern the
process by which ovulation is inhibited and the clinical effects of the treatment)
do not interest us here and are presumably already well known. Cf. the clear
and up to date account by G. BONOMI, *Le pillole anticoncettive*, Rome, Editoriale
Idea, 1965, 91 pp., and the article by G. B. GARBELLI, 'I progestativi nella
regolazione delle nascite: la situazione dal punto di vista medico', *La Scuola
Cattolica, Supplemento* 93 (1965), pp. 141*–156*. In English, cf. *Control of
ovulation*, ed. C. A. VILLEE, Oxford, Pergamon Press, 1961, 251 pp.

purpose is therapeutic (for example, that of alleviating severe menstrual pains) it is licit, on the basis of the principle of 'double effect', even if at the same time it delays or prevents ovulation. It is illicit if its purpose is directly contraceptive because 'any direct and positive interference in the processes of human generation, whether before, during or after copulation, is a transgression of the law of God'.[2]

Gibbons' point of view is the same and was already expressed in his article in *America* (December 1957) and then more amply treated, in co-operation with Dr Burch, in *The American Ecclesiastical Review* of the following April. This author considers every therapeutic use of progestatives to be licit (for example, in order to cure a predisposition to miscarriage, or amenorrhoea or other irregularities of the female cycle) but illicit their deliberate use as contraceptives. In the former case he refers not only to the principle of 'double effect' but also to that of the 'total good', which justifies every mutilation considered necessary for the good of the whole organism; the latter use, on the contrary, is an illicit deliberate sterilization. He says that the deliberate suspension of ovulation for contraceptive purposes constitutes an unjustifiable interference with the generative function: even if the effect is produced physiologically and not by surgery, and may be only temporary, this does not alter the fundamental moral question.[3]

With even greater reason he considers illicit every use of the new progesterone products if their effect—as seems to be the case with some—is to prevent the implantation of the fertilized egg by altering the uterine endometrium (in which case they would cause abortion) or if their effect is to obstruct, by modification of the vaginal or cervical acidity, the vitality and penetrative power of the spermatozoa. These products would then be real and actual 'contraceptives' even if taken orally.

But the Jesuit demographer has also something new to add.

[2] The author seems to consider legitimate also the use of progestational drugs to regularize the female cycle, and more particularly (but the medical aspect is somewhat uncertain) in order to reduce the number of the fertile days, in every cycle, to the exact limits which would be observed in a normal cycle of 28 days.

[3] To support this affirmation the authors quote the Holy Office Decree of 1940 against sterilization, 'whether permanent or temporary', which 'is forbidden by natural law': *A.A.S.* 32 (1940), 73.

First of all, he clearly affirms that, in spite of the illegitimacy of their possible use as contraceptives, the anovulants do not cause any interference with sexual activity, which they allow to develop freely. Therefore they cannot be compared with the common physical or chemical contraceptive means which alter the natural process of copulation. In the second place, Gibbons proposes a new line of argument which Connell had perhaps intuitively discerned: the use of progestational drugs 'to regularize the female cycle', in order to make more safe the use of the Ogino-Knaus method. The author observes that doctors are not in agreement as to whether irregular and unexpected ovulations are to be considered pathological, and so he does not pass definite judgment on the permissibility of using progestational drugs to correct these irregularities. For example, may a woman by their means prevent ovulation until the day when, according to her calculations, it ought to take place? However, the manner in which the author puts this question seems to indicate that he considers this method permissible, provided that treatment of this sort is intended only for purposes of regulation and not for the prevention of conception.

Lynch's article (August 1958) is simpler because it seems to ignore the problems we have referred to.[4] It restricts itself to applying to the new drugs the principle of double effect, and concludes, on the one hand, that they are entirely illicit if they are used with the intention of sterilizing the woman whereas, on the other hand, they are licit when used therapeutically, and he carefully specifies the occasions for such use (in amenorrhoea, oligomenorrhoea, menorrhagia, metrorrhagia and dysmenorrhoea). The author writes more particularly of the progestational therapy of certain female types of functional sterility: the total suppression of ovulation for several months which is obtained in this way cannot in his opinion be considered as a true sterilization, because it is intended to obtain what is known as the 'ovulation rebound', that is, a more efficient ovulatory activity and fertilization capacity

---

[4] Lynch's point of view had already been expressed at a congress held a short time previously by the Catholic Thealogical Society of America and published later on in the records: 'Moral aspects of pharmaceutical fertility control', in *Proceedings of the Thirteenth Annual Convention of the Catholic Theological Society of America*, 1958 (June), pp. 127-38. We have not yet been able to study this article.

when the cure is suspended; moreover, one cannot speak correctly of sterilization when the person thus treated is known already to be sterile.

From America the discussion passed to Europe, and more precisely to Belgium and Holland, where two moral theologians, Janssens and van Kol (the former in June and the latter in October 1958), took up the same subject and examined it more closely, showing a remarkable similarity of views.

> L. Janssens, 'L'inhibition de l'ovulation est-elle moralement licite?', *Ephemerides Theologicae Lovanienses* 34 (1958), pp. 357–60.
> A van Kol, S.J., 'Progestatieve hormoon-praeparaten: enkele opmerkingen vanuit moraaltheologisch standpunt', *R. Kathol. Artsenblad* 37 (1958), pp. 323–31.

Referring to Gibbon's first article, Janssens accepts without demur the legitimacy of the therapeutic use of the new products and adds to these licit uses that which is intended to correct anomalies of the female cycle. He observes that these are, for example, present during the period of the menopause, which is frequently preceded by a series of very irregular cycles (sometimes anovulatory), an anomaly which can legitimately be corrected by opportune treatment with progestogens. In such cases one would merely be confirming a state of sterility which should naturally be present during the menopause but which, because of its uncertainty, has a serious effect upon the woman's psycho-somatic equilibrium. In the same way, the author reasons, the treatment with progestational drugs is licit also when it is placed at the service of the natural mechanism which suppresses ovulation during lactation. This mechanism, especially in the conditions in which we live in our 'highly developed' countries, may for some unknown reason fail to function, and so the spacing of births which it should naturally produce may be frustrated: in that case recourse to anovulants merely ensures a sterility which nature already desires.

The eminent moral theologian of Louvain says nothing about the deliberately contraceptive use of progestogens: he is concerned only with what he considers their legitimate use. On the other hand, van Kol's article once more categorically declares this use to be illicit, saying that this is 'a modern form of direct sterilization, contrary to the doctrine of the Church, clearly formulated in the Holy Office Decree dated 22 February 1940'. Instead, he declares that interventions with a therapeutic purpose are licit, and especially those intended to regularize the cycle, 'in order to facilitate a well motivated periodical continence'. As regards their use in the pre-menopause period and especially during lactation, van Kol expresses some reserves with regard to Janssens's position, considering that from the medical point of view the presumed pathological character of ovulation at that time has not been proved. But he does not dare to reject the opinion of a moral theologian of such acknowledged authority.

So we come to Pius XII's speech, delivered 12 September 1958 (published in *A.A.S.*, 4 October, the last of his pontificate). There are, however, two more articles to which we must refer. Although written after the Pope's speech, their authors show no sign of having read it for they make no reference to it. These two articles appeared in Reviews in December 1958.

J. Connery, S.J., 'Notes on Moral Theology', *Theological Studies* 19 (1958), pp. 549–51.
P. Palazzini, 'Controllo delle nascite', *Studi Cattolici* 9 (1958), pp. 58–64.

Connery agrees with Gibbons in considering this treatment licit in cases of abnormal irregularities of the female reproductive cycle. But he goes further and considers permissible the use of progestational drugs even only in order to reduce every cycle to the normal 28 days and to cause ovulation punctually on the fourteenth day. In fact, the author confesses that he does not know whether this is medically possible (we know that this is quite impossible with progestational drugs) but if it could be effected he does not see in this conduct any danger of sterilization. 'Sterilization consists not in regulating ovulation but in suppressing it.' He then declares that he is inclined to agree with Janssens about the period of lactation, although he considers that this question (for the same reasons as those put forward by van Kol) has yet to be more closely examined.

Palazzini thinks very much along the same lines, and he quotes long passages from Janssens. The Roman moralist condemns as illicit the deliberately contraceptive use of drugs but admits their therapeutic use and he admits also intervention during the pre-menopause period. He raises no objection to the administration of progestational drugs during lactation. He admits however to feeling certain doubts about the possibility of harmful effects (perhaps even long deferred) from the new treatment, and it is this doubt which hampers moral theologians in their attempt to form a judgment.

II. *Pius XII's intervention*

The result of the first studies made of this subject is already sufficiently clear. Almost all the authors agree in rejecting the deliberately anti-ovulatory use of progestational drugs, which they deem to be direct sterilization: Janssens alone is silent about this. All agree in justifying their therapeutic use (concerning which an interesting discussion is now taking place) on the grounds of the two principles of double effect and total good. The therapeutic use, moreover, is enlarged to include interventions aiming at the regulation of the female cycle, at least when the irregularities in question are of a pathological nature. But the opinion is being put forward that it is licit to administer progestational drugs also in order to effect what nature herself requires but which for some unknown reason she seems unable to procure. For example, it seems licit (to Janssens, Connery, Palazzini and, with certain reserves, to van Kol) to use progestational drugs to ensure that there is no ovulation during lactation, and Connery agrees to their being used to regularize all the cycles and bring about ovulation at a fixed time (but this use does not seem practicable from the medical point of view). In any case the authors observe that the administration of the new products, which serve purposes licit in themselves, cannot be called intrinsically wrong.

Now we come to Pius XII's discourse, delivered on 12 September 1958 to the Seventh International Congress of Hematology. Referring explicitly to the principle of double effect, the Pope recognises the legitimacy of the various therapeutic uses of the pills but strongly condemns (not without a stern rebuke to moral theologians who might think differently) all uses which are deliberately anti-ovulatory. We quote the relevant passage:

'Is it licit to prevent ovulation by means of pills used as remedies for irregularities of the uterus and of the organism although this medication, by preventing ovulation, also renders fecundation impossible? Is this permitted to the married woman who, despite this temporary sterility, desires to have relations with her husband? The answer depends on the person's intention. If the wife accepts this medication not with a view to preventing conception but solely on the advice of a physician, as a necessary remedy for a malady of the uterus or of the ogranism, she is causing an indirect sterilization which is permissible, according to the general principle concerning actions having a double effect. But a direct, and therefore an illicit, sterilization is caused whenever ovulation is arrested in order to preserve the uterus and the organism from the consequences of a pregnancy which they are not able to support.'

So far nothing has emerged which is new or different from what transpired from the moral discussion we have already reported. But we must point out the following passages in the Pope's speech in which, in somewhat obscure terms, he seems to refer briefly (in order to condemn it) to the use of progestogens in order to treat incidental natural defects. He says:

'It is necessary likewise to reject the opinion of many physicians and moralists who permit the use (of the pills) whenever a medical indication renders too early a conception undesirable, or in other similar cases which it will not be possible to mention here; in these cases the employment of the drugs has as its end the prevention of conception by preventing ovulation; it is therefore a case of deliberate sterilization.

'To justify it they quote at times the moral principle which is in itself correct but wrongly interpreted: "licet corrigere defectus naturae" they say (it is permissible to correct natural defects), but since in practice it suffices, in order to use this principle, merely to have a reasonable probability, they contend that here it is a case of correcting a natural effect. If this principle had unqualified validity, doctors could without hesitation make use of the drug method to stop the transmission of a defective heredity. But it is necessary to consider by what means the natural defect is corrected and to take care not to violate in any respect the moral principle involved.'[5]

[5] cf. *A.A.S.* 50 (1958), 734. The original was in French.

These assertions by the Pope seemed at least to one commentator to be pronounced in opposition also to the opinion expressed by Janssens concerning the period of lactation, during which the progestogen would be in fact used to assist a normal natural process. Of the three commentators who, as far as we know, published their replies in the months which followed, it was van Kol who expressed this point of view. The other two seemed to consider the question still left open, and did not read this opposition into Pius XII's words. Tesson considered that the Pope's speech, when 'studied attentively', did not condemn as illicit an intervention aimed at 'regularizing the hormonal activity of the pituitary gland', even if this entailed some interference with ovulation, and Furlong, who in his comments on the Pope's speech offered a summary of previous studies, quoting Gibbons, Janssens, Lynch and Tesson, restricted himself to hoping that the moralists would be able to 'draw correct practical conclusions' from the Pope's statements. We add a biographical note of these three articles and with them close this first period of the controversy we are examining:

E. Tesson, 'Derniers enseignements de Pie XII aux medecins. Nouvelles methodes anticonceptionelles', *Etudes* 299 (1958), pp. 245–8.

F. Furlong, S.J., 'Tres allocutiones ultimae Pii Papae XII de medicina. De sterilizatione pharmaceutica', *Periodica de re morali, canonica, liturgica* 47 (1958), pp. 294–9.

A. van Kol, S.J., 'Regeling van de ovulatie, Paus Pius XII over het gebruik van "progestatieve hormoon-praeparaten" ', *Nederlandse Kathol. Stemmen* 55 (1959), pp. 1–8.

II

DISCUSSION ABOUT PROGESTATIONAL DRUGS:
1959–1963

In reality the intervention of Puis XII had no determining effect on the course of further discussion, one way or another. Obviously the moralists concerned with the problem knew what he had said, and frequently gave it most careful consideration, but the differences between their points of view, it has rightly been pointed out,[1] are not due to different interpretations of the Pope's words but to different ways of approaching the problem itself.

In those years 1959–1963 everyone was in agreement in condemning the deliberately anti-ovulatory use of the progestational pills. But meanwhile various arguments went on, enlarging and defining their licit uses (for therapy, for regulation of the female cycle, etc.) or discussing in a more general way the many different situations or circumstances in which progestational treatment may be permitted or even recommended, despite its anti-ovulatory effect. The literature is vast, and the list of titles here indicated is but a selection; on this subject theologians have written at length in all the principal languages.

I. *Bibliography, in the principal languages*

Certainly the most numerous studies are in English, especially in America—and it is not difficult to group them under certain headings. First of all, we must refer to the information offered in the review published every year by the American Jesuits: *Theological Studies*, in which, while dealing with the most significant work in this field, the two reviewers Lynch and Farraher have been able to express their own opinions. We give the series

---

[1] cf. W. van der Marck, O.P., 'Fruchtbaarheidsregeling. Poging tot antwoord op een nog open vraag', *Tijdschrift voor theologie* 3 (1963), p. 392. We shall discuss the whole article later on.

of these 'Notes', indicating the pages in each bulletin which concern our subject.

J. J. Lynch, S.J., 'Notes on Moral Theology', *Theological Studies* 20 (1959), pp. 239–40; 21 (1960), pp. 231–2; 22 (1961), pp. 256–60; 23 (1962), pp. 239–47.

J. J. Farraher, S.J., 'Notes on Moral Theology', *ibid.*, 21 (1960), pp. 599–603; 22 (1961), pp. 626–32; 24 (1963), pp. 79–85.

Then we must mention the longer and more original articles which appeared in five theological reviews. In the United States, there appeared in *The American Ecclesiastical Review* some clarifications signed by the Redemptorist Connell (who had been the first to raise the problem and in this very review) and in the *Homiletic and Pastoral Review* an article by the Jesuit McCormick. In Ireland O'Callaghan's views were published, accompanied by some critical notes by Dr Acland, in *The Irish Theological Quarterly*. There was also a series of short but significant articles in the English *Clergy Review*, all written by McReavy, and in Australia a group of contributions, sometimes presented as answers to questions of conscience, appeared in *The Australasian Catholic Record*:

F. J. Connell, C.SS.R., 'The sale of contraceptives', *The American Ecclesiastical Review* 140 (1959), 120–3; *The morality of ovulation rebound: ibid.*, 143 (1960), 203–5; *An abortive pill: ibid.*, 146 (1962), 59–61.

R. A. McCormick, S.J., 'Antifertility pills', *Homiletic and Pastoral Review* 62 (1962), pp. 692–700. Also by the same author, 'Family size, rhythm and the pill', in *The problem of population. Moral and theological considerations*, Notre Dame, University Press, 1964, pp. 58–84.

D. O'Callaghan (and J. D. Acland), 'Fertility control by hormonal medication', *The Irish Theological Quarterly* 27 (1960), pp. 1–15, pp. 337–9; 28 (1961), pp. 155–9. ACLAND's notes are on pp. 332–3 and 155–6. O'CALLAGHAN expounds his theses again in the pamphlet, *Moral principles of fertility control*, Dublin (Clonmore and Reynolds), London (Burns and Oates), 1960, p. 40. See also by the same author 'Family regulation: the Catholic view', *The Irish Theological Quarterly* 30 (1963), pp. 163–9 (pages 167–9 are of special interest).

L. L. McReavy, 'Oral Contraceptives', *The Clergy Review* 44 (1959), pp. 431–5; 'Protein diet and fertility', *ibid.*, 45 (1960), pp. 482–4; 'Contraceptive pills and non-consummation', *ibid.*, 45 (1960), pp. 686–8 (cf. 46 (1961), pp. 54–5); 'Why direct temporary sterilization is wrong', *ibid.*, 45 (1960), pp. 741–3; 'Pharmaceutical birth prevention', *ibid.*, 46 (1961), pp. 103–6; 'Use of steroid drugs to regularize menstrual cycles', *ibid.*, 46 (1961), pp. 746–50.

N. Crotty, C.P., 'The moral issues in hormonal control of fertility', *The Australasian Catholic Record* 38 (1961), pp. 102–13; Th. Connolly, 'Further observations on the use of fertility drugs', *ibid.*, 38 (1961), pp. 179–94. See also some answers to questions of conscience given in *ibid.*, 38 (1961), pp. 140–6 (J. Madden), 40 (1963), pp. 35–44 (Th. Connolly), 40 (1963), pp. 211–14 (J. Madden).

There were also some thoughtful articles, written more for the general reader, published in reviews not strictly theological in character:

J. O'Donnell, S.J., 'Moral concepts of progestational therapy', *Georgetown Medical Bulletin* 14 (1961), pp. 330–3.

P. M. Loftus, 'Theological aspects of the contraceptive pills', *Catholic Medical Quarterly* 14 (1961), pp. 97–103.

G. Healy, S.J., 'Anovulant pills', *Philippine Studies* 9 (1961), pp. 495–504.

H. E. Di Christina, 'God or Man in birth control?', *The Priest* 17 (1961), pp. 331–5.

Finally we must refer to the very frank and ample treatment of the problem by the Jesuit moral theologians J. Ford and G. Kelly who wrote many of the books referred to above:

J. C. Ford, S.J., G. KELLY, S.J., *Contemporary Moral Theology: II. Marriage Questions*, Cork, The Mercier Press, 1963, pp. 338–77 (chap. 16: 'Sterilizing drugs').

Theological writings in Flemish and Dutch are very numerous and have marked originality. First of all the Franciscan Delille, in the light of Pius XII's doctrine, surveys the whole problem as far as it is known to us today:

A. Delille, O.F.M., 'Verhindering van ovulatie en procreatie bijzonder in het licht van de leer van Pius XII', *Sacerdos* 27 (1959–60), pp. 277–93, 405–22; cf. also *ibid.*, 28 (1960–61), pp. 310 11.

Other studies followed, of a specifically theological character, among which must be mentioned particularly those by Anciaux, Professor at the Major Seminary of Malines and Heggen, Professor at the Roermond Seminary. So far we have not been able to see the last long article referred to, so we do not know whether it is in line with the new trends of thought.

F. Neirynck, 'Regeling van de ovulatie', *Collationes Brugenses et Gandavenses* 6 (1960) 130–4.

P. Anciaux, 'Gerboorteregeling en hormoonpraeparaten. Morele aspecten der behandelingen met progestatieve stoffen', *Collectanea Mechliniensia* 30 (1960), pp. 5–18. This appears also in French: 'Régulation des naissances et thérapies hormonales. Aspects moraux des traitements à base de substances progestatives', *Saint-Luc médical* 32 (1960), pp. 67–80. By the same author see also, written in more general terms: 'Verandert de huwelijksmoraal? Pastorale beschouwingen bij een groeicrisis', *Collectanea Mechliniensia* 31 (1961), pp. 113–33.

F. J. Heggen, 'Een moraal—theologische waardering van progestatieve hormoonpraeparaten', *Analecta van het bisdom Roermond* 43 (1963), pp. 164–80.

E. R. Proesmans, C.SS.R., 'Het inhibiren van de ovulatie', *Sacerdos* 31 (1963–64), pp. 278–85, 548–61.

Finally we must record the numerous contributions to this field of study offered by the Dutch Catholic medical review, the *Roomsch-Katolieke Artsenblad*, the latest of which, by Beemer, Professor of Moral Theology at the Major Seminary of Warmond, and by Dr Hillen, anticipate in some respects the new turn the discussion took towards the end of 1963.

H. Fortmann, 'Het gezin, gezien vanuit de openbaring', *R.-Kathol. Artsenblad* 38 (1959), pp. 305–8. Also: *Katholieke standpunt ten opzichte van het probleem van bevolking en geboortebeperking*, *ibid.*, 39 (1960), pp. 47–50.

H. Rottinghuis, 'De problematiek der geboortebeperking', *ibid.*, 39 (1960), pp. 183–95.

A van der Wey, O.Carm., 'Enkele actuele vragen over onfeil-baarheid', *ibid.*, 39 (1960), pp. 242–4.

Th. C. J. Beemer, 'Beïnvloeding van de vruchtbaarheid door de progestatieve hormoonpraeparaten, moraaltheologisch bes-chouwd', *ibid.*, 42 (1963), pp. 7–12 (with notes by H. J. Savalle, 'Enkele dedachten en vragen bij het artikel van Professor Dr Th. Beemer in het Januarinummer van dit blad', *ibid.*, 42 (1963), pp. 147–9).

F. J. M. Hillen, 'Ovulateremming en gezinsregeling', *ibid.*, 42 (1963), pp. 253–63.

The most significant contributions in French also come from Belgium. We give a brief list: the first two articles are by doctors and the third, very ample and informative, is by a theologian. We mention also the Laënnec Centre of Studies in Lyons and the pages in which Lestapis treats this problem, in his famous work on birth control. Apart from scattered notes here and there, there are to our knowledge no other publications dedicated to this problem in French literature, in spite of the wealth of writings on general questions of conjugal morality, including that of birth control.

R. de Guchteneere, 'Les inhibiteurs de l'ovulation', *Saint-Luc médical* 31 (1959), pp. 10–22.

J. Schockaert, 'L'inhibition de l'ovulation', *ibid.*, pp. 231–49.

M. Thiéffry, S.J., 'Stérilization hormonale et morale chrétienne', *Nouvelle Revue Théologique* 83 (1961), pp. 135–58. See also by the same author: 'Aspects moraux des traitements inhibiteurs de l'ovulation', Laënnec Centre of Studies, in *La régulation des naissances*, Paris, P. Lethielleux, 1961, pp. 175–9.

S. de Lestapis, S.J., *La limitation des naissances*, Paris, Spes, 1959, pp. 179–82.

Häring was the first to bring up this subject and discuss it, in the German language, in a brief article of general interest, and he followed this up with other articles, all written in the period we are now studying.

B. Häring, C.SS.R., 'Verantwortete Elternschaft: aber wie?', *Theolo-gischer Digest* 2 (1959), pp. 153–9. Also 'Naturgemäss-gottgewollte verantwortete Elternschaft', *Ehe und Familie*, No. 15 ('Moderne Ehe und Kinderzahl') Vienna 1962, pp. 77ff.; another article written at this time will be referred to later on (p. 19).

But the most penetrating studies are those by Fuchs, Professor at the Pontificia Università Gregoriana, and by Böckle, now Professor in the theological faculty of the University of Bonn: they are still writing on this subject. Of the former, known for his numerous works on moral theology including the field of sexual and conjugal morality, we shall quote here, for the period now under our consideration, only those studies which deal explicitly with the question of the pill.[2]

J. Fuchs, S.J., 'Nota de aliquo casu sterilizationis therapeuticae', *Periodica de re morali canonica liturgica* 50 (1961), pp. 31–8. Idem, 'Moraltheologisches zur Geburtenregelung', *Stimmen der Zeit* 170 (1962), pp. 354–71.

F. Böckle, 'Die sittliche Beurteilung sterilisierender Medikamente', *Herder-Korrespondenz* 16 (1962), pp. 470–3. Idem, 'Insemination, Sterilisation und moderne Methoden der Geburtenkontrolle, Moraltheologisches Korreferat', *Studien und Berichte der Katholischen Akademie in Bayern*, Würzburg, 1963, pp. 127–44.

Finally, the following articles written in German by theologians (cf. Weber and Demmer) and doctors (cf. Rötzer) are also concerned with the ethical aspects of the use of progestational steroids.

L. M. Weber, 'Hormonpräparat im Dienste ethisch vertretbarer Geburtenregelung', *Arzt und Christ* 7 (1961), pp. 116–20; also 'Pillen gegen Uebervölkerung?', *Schweizerische Kirchenzeitung* 129 (1961), pp. 174–5.

J. Miller, S.J., 'Moraltheologisches zu den "Unfruchtbarkeitsdrogen" ', *Oberrheinisches Pastoralblatt* 63 (1962), pp. 213–19.

L. Liebhart, 'Sterilisierende Drogen', *Theologisch-praktische Quartalschrift III* (1963), pp. 188–203. The article is introduced by a medical explanation written by J. Rötzer, 'Geburtenbeschränkung auf medikamentösem Wege', *ibid.*, pp. 175–88.

K. Demmer, M.S.C., 'Die Moraltheologische Diskussion um die Anwendung sterilisierender Medikamente. Versuch einer Uebersicht', *Theologie und Glaube* 53 (1963), pp. 415–35.

Some Italian authors also took part in the debate and we name them here in chronological order, giving particular attention

---

[2] We have quoted here the first article by Fuchs, although it was written in Latin. Fuch's position, as outlined in these articles, is the same as that expressed in his *De castitate et ordine sexuali*, 2nd ed., Rome, 1960, pp. 72–4, and more amply in the 3rd ed., Rome, 1963, pp. 93–7.

to the three moral theologians Perico, Guzzetti and Nalesso, who, in the framework of the various considerations under review, have dared to express also their own personal and qualified opinion. The brief article by Boschi, instead, makes no mention of Pius XII's intervention and is restricted to reviewing the above-mentioned article by Palazzini; Vimercati's writings also merely summarize the dispute between the moral theologians; Concetti and Montervino treat the subject very briefly:

G. Vimercati, 'Gli inibitori dell' ovulazione', *Cronache dell' I.D.I.* (monthly review of the Dermopathic Institute of the Immacolata, Rome) 14 (1959), pp. 58–60; 'Contraccettivi orali e continenza periodica', *ibid.*, 18 (1963), pp. 319–24.

A. Boschi, S.J., 'Metodi di sterilizzazione', *Perfice munus!* 34 (1959), pp. 499–502.

G. Perico, S.J., 'Sterilizzanti ormonali', *Aggiornamenti sociali* 12 (1961) pp. 279–94.

G. B. Guzzetti, 'Antifecondativi ormanali e morale', *La Scuola Cattolica* 90 (1962), pp. 234–44.

G. Concetti, 'Il metodo Pincus e la morale cattolica', *Palestra del clero* 41 (1962), pp. 824–7.

A. Nalesso, 'Qualche osservazione sulla dottrina della Chiesa intorno alla regolazione delle nascita e sulla valutazione morale dei trattamenti inibitori della ovulazione in rapporto alla regolazione stessa', *Medicina e Morale* 13 (1963), pp. 157–84 (cf. esp. pp. 173–84).

C. Montervino, 'I progestogeni: sterilizzanti ormonali', *L'amico del clero* 45 (1963), pp. 767–70.

We turn finally to the contributions in Spanish and Portuguese; wo of these are from the Argentine (Nolasco and Salvo), one from Chile (Aldunate), one from Colombia (Salazar) and two from Spain (Zalba, Professor at the Gregorian University; and Navarro who, although he wrote in February 1964, logically belongs to the previous period because he seems totally ignorant of a new trend of thought). Meanwhile, in the *Revista Ecclesiástica Brasileira* Snoek begins his series of informative notes on the discussion, which still continue:

R. L. Nolasco, 'Esterilización hormonal', *Revista de Teologia* 9 (1960), pp. 23–41.

R. Salvo, S.J., 'La moralidad del uso terapeutico de la progesterona', *Ciencia y Fe* 16 (1960), pp. 371–82.

J. Salazar, S.J., 'Empleo de noresteroides y sustancias progestacionales y la moral cathòlica', *Cathedra* 16 (1962), pp. 267–95.

J. Aldunate, S.J., 'Notas de moral con relación al uso de las píldoras anovulantes o progestagenos', *Teologia y Vida* 3 (1962), pp. 259–66. Idem, 'El uso de las pildoras anti-ovulantes despues del parto', *ibid.*, 4 (1963), pp. 40–3.

J. Snoek, C.SS.R., 'Esterilização hormonal', *Revista Ecclesiástica Brasileira* 21 (1961), pp. 988–90; 22 (1962), pp. 441–2; 'Fecundidade humana e Moral', *ibid.*, 22 (1962), pp. 701–7; 'Problemas de Moral Matrimonial', *ibid.*, 23 (1963), pp. 740–6 (cont.).

M. Zalba, S.J., 'Aspectos moral de la regulación de la natalidad', *Arbor* 56 (1963), pp. 343–69 (cf. esp. pp. 357–69).

S. Navarro, C.M.F., 'Un problema moral urgente', *Illustración del clero* 57 (1964), pp. 264–78.

We note that not all the studies here mentioned are of equal importance; some, in particular, are merely informative and are restricted to references to the various theses expounded in the most important and original texts. This explains why, in the account we are about to give of their doctrinal content, some of these names will not receive individual mention.

II. *The doctrinal content*

All the authors we have so far referred to are agreed that it is absolutely wrong to use the progestational drugs for a deliberately contraceptive purpose; the discussion has been about other uses which, because they have not this deliberate and single purpose, might eventually be considered licit. A series of new situations is now becoming the object of study and controversy, situations which are outside the range of those strictly therapeutic interventions which have already been declared permissible; this argument had begun even before Pius XII's speech.

(1) Lynch had already asserted the probable legitimacy of 'rebound therapy', on the basis of progestational drugs, which aimed at curing female sterility due to irregular endocrine activity.

In fact, from the medical point of view, it has not yet been established whether the increased fertility procured as the result of treatment with progestational drugs for a certain number of months is caused by an increased hormonal activity (called a 'rebound effect') when the gonadotrophic secretions are released after a long pause, or whether it is caused more simply by the considerable eutrophic influence which the progestational pills exercise over all the female genital organs. In any case they are remarkably effective in curing female functional sterility.

The ethical justification for this use could lie in its therapeutic intention. But it is also true that here (at least for the sake of the hypothetical 'rebound effect') the suppression of the ovulatory function is deliberately desired, if not as an end in itself, at least as a necessary condition for the hormonal reaction which is required: therefore it might be considered as an illicit direct sterilization, even when used for a legitimate and praiseworthy end. To put it simply: the good effect would be obtained by means of the evil effect. Therefore the case does not seem to lend itself to such an obvious solution, and its justification is looked for elsewhere, in the fact (as we have already seen asserted by Lynch, Salvo, Fuchs, Crotty and McCormick) that as the woman is already sterile one cannot say that she has been subjected to sterilizing treatment. It is also possible now to study the notion of direct sterilization more closely, as Connell, O'Callaghan, and above all Ford and Kelly, have done. To suspend ovulation— they observe—is not the same thing as to sterilize: sterilization means an intervention intended to cause sterility whereas in this case the woman's purpose is quite different, that of ensuring fertility; for the same reason the removal of ovaries infected with cancer is not deliberate sterilization, because the purpose of the operation is not contraceptive. What is forbidden, as deliberate sterilization, is the suppression of ovulation or the removal of the ovaries with the intention of destroying all possibilities of generation.

Therefore, although the reasons put forward vary, the use of progestational drugs for the cure of functional sterilities is generally considered permissible by all the above-mentioned moralists. However, the justification suggested by Ford and Kelly is particularly worth recording because it may lead to a less empirical and more truly ethical concept of sterilization.

(2) A second case, which also was put forward before Pius XII's speech, is when the progestational drugs are used to *regularize the female cycle*, and we have already referred to the

opinion, on the whole favourable, expressed by Connell, Gibbons, Janssens and Connery in this connection. Van Kol is less disposed to approve. Concerning this case also there is an abundant literature during the years 1959–63, and these writings show a greater knowledge of the medical aspects of the problem than did the previous publications.

The moral theologians describe two possible types of intervention intended to regularize the cycle: that which aims at establishing personal periodic regularity, thus eliminating the differences, sometimes considerable, which may be found between one cycle and another in the same woman, and that which aims at reducing every cycle in every woman to a regular average length, probably one of twenty-eight or thirty days, and also at fixing unalterably the moment of ovulation. In both these cases the method of periodic continence would be greatly facilitated by the use of progestational drugs.

We must note at once (and this is known to the moralists of this period) that neither of these processes has found precise confirmation in the medical field. As regards the second case, the 'standardization' of cycles, it is still purely theoretical, and in any case the progestational drugs are not considered to be of any use for this purpose; as for the former case, the regularization of one woman's cycles, it is true that some results may be obtained by means of these pills, but this may be a chance effect. Meanwhile it has been observed that the prolonged treatment of a woman with progestational drugs, because of a hormonal 're-bound' effect of the kind we have already described, sometimes leads to a more regular series of cycles once the treatment has ended. But these medical uncertainties do not deter the moralists from studying the cases in question in order to form an opinion about the suggestions already made, and in the expectation that medical science will render both treatments successful in the future.

Now, if we consider the medical possibility first put forward, the moral problem, here too, is mainly concerned with the interruption, deliberately procured, of the ovulatory function of the woman—although the intention is good because it aims at ensuring greater regularity of the cycle—without the possibility of invoking the justification that she is already sterile. This explains why certain authors, like Nolasco and Salvo, condemn this practice as an illicit sterilization. But others, like Lynch, Ford and Kelly, point out quite rightly that the good result effected, the regularization of the cycle, is not due so much to the suppression of ovulation as to that improvement in endocrine activity which is the direct result of this action, and which justifies it in spite of the 'accompanying' temporary sterility which it induces: therefore this case would be justified by reference to the ethical principles of double effect and the total good. In any case, this problem concerns only the medical treatment we have described.[3]

On the contrary, a more general moral problem underlies the two suggestions put forward by the moralists with regard to the regularization of the cycles, irrespective of the actual process by which this is achieved, and it is to this problem, in particular, that they devote their attention. They are debating (not always very cogently) whether this kind of action belongs to a human being's legitimate control over his own body, or whether it exceeds this and so constitutes an illicit interference in 'natural' bio-physical processes.

[3] There are in fact other medical means of regularizing the cycles with progestational preparations which do not present the above mentioned problem because they are administered during the second phase of the cycle, and therefore in the post-ovulatory period (cf. for example N. PASETTO, 'L'etere ciclopentilenolico del 17a-acetossiprogesterone nel quadro della progestinoterapia', *La Clinica Terapeutica* 3 (1962), pp. 133 ff, and the positive moral judgment pronounced by Salazar in his above-quoted article, full of medical information). The morality of these other techniques depends instead on the judgment pronounced on the more general problem, which we shall now indicate.

In 1963 the moralists examined the case of a new progestational product, *Duphaston*, which is said to be very effective in the regulation of cycles, and moreover without any anti-ovulatory effect: B. HÄRING, C.SS.R. speaks of this, 'Naturgemässe Wege verantworteter Elternschaft. Die neue Situation: das Duphaston', *Theologie der Gegenwart* 6 (1963), pp. 125–52, and also, in the following year, D. F. O'CALLAGHAN, 'A new pill: Duphaston', *The Irish Ecclesiastical Record* 101 (1964), pp. 255–8. Häring considers the use of this product to be licit and in accordance with nature. The initial optimism, however, has now progressively declined. In fact, Duphaston, produced and distributed by Philips Duphare, is merely a pure progestational steroid (6-dehydro-retroprogesterone) which is described as particularly useful from the clinical point of view because it does not give rise to those secondary effects which often follow treatment with pure progestational steroids (oestrogenic, androgenic, anabolic, or renothropic activity or masculinization etc.). It may be used, like other progestational steroids, to regularize the cycles, but here as in other cases this must be considered only as a possibility and would require a prolonged course of treatment. It is, nevertheless, quite true that Duphaston also, unlike progestatives derived from testosterone but similar to those derived from progesterone, has no anti-ovulatory effect.

This second alternative is put forward by the following writers, here listed in the chronological order of their work: Shockaert, Nolasco, Crotty (with some reserves), Thiéffry (who seems the most convinced), Perico, Guzzetti, Zalba and Navarro. They do not admit the right to interfere with the generative organs and processes when these are functioning healthily, and point out that a woman's condition is healthy even if her cycles are irregular, when she is perfectly capable of generation. In fact, no irregularity, even if considered 'anomalous' with respect to our subjective classification, constitutes in itself an objectively pathological condition, and this condition alone can justify any legitimate intervention in the generative function. These authors consider therefore that a regularization of the cycles is licit only on the hypothesis of the irregularity being pathological, that is, harmful to the health and welfare of the woman. In fact many cyclic irregularities, among those known to be treated with progestational drugs, are of this kind and in such cases a woman's right to control over her own physical powers would be justified—as it must always be—by the two classical principles of the total good and double effect.

Nevertheless several authors are in favour of the former alternative, and join those who had already adopted this line even before Pius XII's speech: among others we see Lynch, Connell, Häring, Anciaux and O'Callaghan (who are writing at the beginning of 1960 and are the most thoughtful and exact), McReavy, Fuchs, Aldunati, Snoek, Ford and Nolasco. Their arguments are sometimes founded on the imputed pathological character of all cyclic irregularities, or at least on the extreme difficulty of distinguishing, in this matter, between the abnormal and the pathological. In this sense their theoretical reasoning does not differ from that of the former group, even if it admits a greater freedom of application, but we have the impression that at other times, especially in the case of the more thoughtful writers, the argument tends to amplify itself, that is to deduce the legitimacy of eventual interventions (for purposes of regularizing the cycle) from more widely extended rights over the body and its functions. They seem to recognize these extended rights which exceed man's more restricted right to care for his health.

Therefore, whereas the remedy indicated in the former case, the so-called 'rebound therapy', led to a less narrowly physical notion of sterilization, this second case led to a more amplified and mature ethical concept of man's rights over his own body, which we shall come across again in the most recent controversies.

(3) A more profound study of the concept of sterilization and, more generally, of man's control over his physical functions (especially the generative functions) led to the consideration of a third case, which concerned the legitimacy of the use of progestational drugs *during lactation*. In favour of the legitimacy of this use were Janssens (who initiated the discussion) Connery and Palazzini; Pius XII's speech, at least as interpreted by van Kol who had already expressed his disapproval, seemed to oppose this procedure. We have now to mention numerous fresh interventions in the period we are studying.

The negative response to this proposal has been more widespread than that provoked by the previous cases. A very critical attack was launched by Nolasco, Thiéffry and Farraher, who did not hesitate to describe the procedure defended by Janssens as a true and deliberate sterilization. An examination of the actual facts, they observe, makes it very difficult to assert the 'natural' character of the absence of ovulatory activity during lactation, or at least makes it impossible to determine the 'natural' duration of this perpetual sterility: even if this should be clearly ascertained by competent medical investigations, to frustrate eventual ovulations, even if 'unnatural' during that period, would always constitute deliberate sterilization, as here no other purpose is invoked apart from that which is deliberately anti-ovulatory and contraceptive. Snoek observes that this stern criticism is difficult to answer, and other authors too, like Anciaux and Nolasco, who had pronounced favourable judgment on the procedure in the preceding case, agreed with Snoek. Zalba also gave a negative verdict.

In fact, the thoughtful replies of those moralists who defend Janssens' opinion are powerful and certainly original: we quote, as being particularly incisive, O'Callaghan (who argues with Dr Acland in the already mentioned publication *The Irish Theological Quarterly*), Ford and Kelly; they are supported by De Guchteneere, Healy, Fuchs, Weber, Salazar, Perico, Vimercati, Böckle, Demmer, Aldunati and Navarro. Their defence is twofold. First of all they point out that the mechanism which prevents the woman from ovulating in the period after the birth of a child may be called 'natural' even if medical opinions vary about its duration (from three to nine months according to the various calculations). Moreover it may be called 'natural' not only because of what should, ideally speaking, occur in order to make it possible for the female organism to make the necessary complete recovery after the birth of a child, and during a period when fundamental biological processes such as lactation are still taking place. Therefore they arrive at their second consideration: if this providential ovulatory suspension does not take place spontaneously, would the attempt to obtain it by means of progestational drugs be an illicit sterilization?

Undoubtedly it is difficult to assert that this procedure does not enter the category of direct sterilization, as it has no other immediate purpose but that of rendering the woman infertile, even if for the purpose of effecting an undeniably good result. The moralists recognize this, but also point out that this concept of sterilization is still ambiguous, or at least that not every direct sterilization for this purpose is illicit. It is illicit when it intends to deprive the woman of her 'normal' fertility, but licit when it aims at eliminating an 'excessive' fertility, extraneous and even contrary to the requirements of nature. It means suppressing 'a capacity for conception which is disordered' (Böckle). It may be said that this is a new concept of sterilization, but it is in this connection the only truly moral consideration which these authors consider acceptable: *procuratio sterilitatis a natura non intentae*', the attempt to create a sterility which nature had failed to ensure.

At this point we must face the question which has already raised its head in the previous cases: what does this 'nature' really consist of? In the case under consideration what 'excess' of fertility is really against nature? What norm should be observed, the average or most common biological procedure of that other norm which expresses the ideal order more competently? These are questions which must be answered in a later discussion.

(4) A new problem regarding the literature which appeared before Pius XII's speech is that of progestational treatment for *cyesophobia*, fear of pregnancy. This is the psychological state of a woman who, with or without objectively valid reasons, has a neurotic fear of pregnancy, a state characterized not only by this fundamental anxiety but also by a series of malaises, some of which may be grave, connected with it; these may be to do with

cardiac, respiratory, digestive or sexual activity. With regard to this last the woman may suffer from frigidity, pain in copulation, feelings of hostility towards her husband, etc. In these cases the temporary sterilization of the woman by means of progestational drugs may be of great assistance in the wider psychotherapeutic treatment which may at least partially alleviate this neurosis.

Schockaert, in the above-mentioned article, 1959, was the first to put forward the legitimacy of this intervention and his opinion, with a few emendations and reserves, seemed acceptable to Anciaux, Thiéffry, Häring, Böckle and Liebhart. Other writers however, like Fuchs, Perico (at least apparently), Snoek and Nolasco, rejected it as absolutely forbidden deliberate sterilization.

We can easily follow the reasons given by these latter writers: the treatment in question would have no other immediate purpose but that of preventing conception, a result considered necessary in order to effect a cure. Therefore this procedure cannot be justified by the principle of double effect. Nor is the principle of the total good applicable here, as in this case the sacrifice of a part (that is, of ovulatory activity) does not seem necessary to obtain a total good: it would be enough for the husband and wife to abstain from sexual relations and the same result would be obtained without any 'mutilation' being effected.

But the others consider those principles applicable also in this case; here, in fact, hormonal therapy, although having a 'side effect' of sterility, is nevertheless, in the total process of psychotherapy, a healing technique in itself and extremely useful: it therefore has a direct therapeutic influence, justified by considerations for the patients' welfare, over her neuro-psychic ailments. But we have the impression—and this is clearly seen in the writings of Fuchs—that the argument is defective because it is very difficult to deny the character of deliberate sterilization (sterility being the object of the intervention, even if considered only as a means to a good end) which the procedure assumes. Therefore, in order to justify it, one must here accept a more liberal revision of the moral concepts of sterilization and of legitimate control over bodily functions, particularly the sexual faculties. This is what Häring and Böckle try to do, as we shall better be able to see in the most recent studies of the whole question.[4]

(5) Another case under discussion, in the period we are now studying, concerns the use of pills to defer menstruation when it is likely to coincide with particularly important obligations. This would apply, for example, to the case of athletes who foresee that they will have to take part in a competition during menstruation and that they will therefore be under some disadvantage, or to the case of those who must in those particular days sit for an examination, consummate a marriage, look after guests, etc.

In reality, the question loses much of its importance when we know that a deferment of menstruation is possible, and indeed more conveniently effected, by the administration of medicaments (even on the basis of estro-progestational elements) during the second phase of the cycle or even just before menstruation is expected to start, when ovulation is already completed. Here there is no longer a question of sterilization but only of a much less important interference in the generative function.[5] Nevertheless, the case is still under discussion and must lead to further reflections on the essential concepts underlying the whole question.

Here we must record a negative opinion which considers intervention in such cases as illicit because conducive to sterility. It could be considered licit only in cases where menstruation is accompanied by unusually acute pain or by other pathological symptoms, but then the progestational treatment would be justified by its therapeutic intention (even if this were rendered more urgent by special external circumstances), in spite of the sterility which it may temporarily occasion. Perico and (at least apparently) Guzzetti are of this opinion.

Other writers, instead, do not consider this intervention as a direct sterilization. In fact its purpose is not to impede ovulation but to induce amenorrhoea, that is, to defer the shedding of the

[4] Cf. for example L. JANSSENS, 'Morale conjugale et progestogènes', *Ephemerides Theologicae Lovanienses* 39 (1963), pp. 791–2. We shall speak of this article at some length later on.

[5] As regards women athletes, the problem hardly arises. They are unlikely to use drugs which, even if they postpone menstruation, are feared for other possible effects on their athletic efficiency. Moreover, many medical authorities and sports experts assert that there has never been a case of a woman failing in a competition because of menstruation. It was even said that Wilma Rudolph won one of her Gold Medals at the Olympic Games in Rome in 1960 on the third day of menstruation.

lining of the womb (the *endometrium*) by means of drugs which have this precise purpose although they have also the 'side effect' of preventing ovulation; in other words, temporary sterility and deferred menstruation are two equally immediate (*aeque immediati*) effects of the treatment which therefore must be considered an indirect sterilization.

This is the line taken by O'Callathan, Crotty, O'Donnell, Farraher, McCormick, Snoek, Ford and Kelly, Demmer and Navarro. Nevertheless, it cannot be said that the question is already resolved affirmatively; it would be necessary to find an adequate motive to compensate for the evil effect (prevention of ovulation) caused indirectly: and the capacity for greater athletic prowess would hardly prove acceptable as an adequate motive for some of these above-mentioned moralists, like O'Callaghan and Crotty.

It remains, however, possible to include this external 'interference' with the female cycle within the powers which human beings have over their own bodies. This is indeed the most significant theoretical aspect of the question and it is Zalba who expounds it most effectively, not in the article mentioned above (in which he makes only a brief reference to it) but in another study which we shall soon be examining. As regards the exercise of sexual activity, particularly the ovulatory and fertilizing processes, 'no intervention is forbidden to man'; in fact, observes the eminent Spanish moralist, the sexual organs, although given to man 'primarily for the sake of the species and not for his own personal and individual use' do in fact exist in the individual as a part to be controlled for the good of his own person. And it is this capacity of using a part for the good of the whole person which makes it legitimate to intervene with a procedure which indirectly causes sterilization although this interferes with the social purpose of sexual activity. This theory also justifies other interventions with a deliberate purpose of sterilization when this sterilization is properly understood as a physical evil permitted for an adequate moral motive. This means that those who, for example, defer ovulation 'lest menstruation should occur at an inopportune time when a journey must be made, a guest cared for, etc., exercise a reasonable control over their own organisms for their own good'.[6]

[6] M. ZALBA, S.J., 'Casus de usu artificii contraceptivi', *Periodica de remorali, canonica et liturgica* 51 (1962), pp. 176–7.

This is a most significant conclusion, to be added to others which the discussions of this period, 1959–63, produced, and which perhaps unconsciously prepare the way for the most recent debates. What is understood by the term sterilization? What must be considered, from the ethical point of view, as 'natural' in the bio-physiological processes of generation? What power may a man legitimately exercise over his bodily functions, including his sexual organism? These are all questions of moral theology in which the controversies aroused might well be such as to inspire doubts, suggest distinctions, impose revisions and appeal for explanations. So they were able to prepare the way for a new and more general exposition of the whole problem.

III. *A 'test' case: defence against wrongful aggression*

Before we deal with this new situation we must, however, give an account of the discussion which arose (still in the years 1959–63) concerning a special 'test' case, the solution of which, in our opinion, formed the point of transition to a new manner of considering the whole question of progestational drugs.

This is a situation which is of special interest because it brought out into the open some latent doctrinal trends which became apparent during the course of this controversy.

It is the case of a woman, more precisely of a nun, who, fearing she may be raped, makes use of progestational drugs to induce sterility and prevent any eventual conception. It was De Lahidalga who called this a 'test' case, in his (somewhat incomplete) account of the controversy:

I. Mz. de Lahidalga. 'Balance de una polemica: el uso de pildoras esterilizantes en un "caso limite" ' *Lumen* 13 (1964), pp. 19–39.

We shall try to follow this debate in a logical, and wherever possible, in a chronological order.

The discussion (of topical interest because of the terrible occurrences in the Congo) was initiated by the review *Studi Cattolici* in December 1961 in a note under the title 'A woman asks how she can protect herself from violence'. We have been asked, an editorial note explained, to consider this question: in the imminence of revolutionary movements with consequent violations of personal freedom, may an unmarried woman (especially if consecrated to God) who is afraid of being raped, with the consequence of bearing an undesired preganncy, protect herself from the eventual consequences by taking, for example, pills which have the specific effect of preventing ovulation and therefore pregnancy? It is understood that the woman has no intention of consenting in any way to the action violently imposed upon her. This presentation of the problem was followed in the Review by the publication of the answers given by three eminent Roman moralists interrogated on the subject:

P. Palazzini: 'Si può e si deve proteggere l'equilibrio della persona', *Studi Cattolici* 27 (1961), pp. 63-4.

F. Hürth, S.J., 'Il premunirsi rientra nel diritto della legittima difesa', *ibid.*, pp. 64-7.

F. Lambruschini, 'E legittimo evitare le consequenze dell 'aggressione', *ibid.*, pp. 68-72.

All three moral theologians approve of the use of the pills in this case. As is to be expected, in justifying their use in various ways, they appeal to the principles of legitimate self-protection, but for us this is not the most interesting aspect of their decision. We are interested in their defence of such a means chosen for purposes of *self-protection* (at least to the extent of circumscribing as much as possible the evil feared). It is in defending this means that they necessarily confront the whole question of progestational drugs.

Palazzini's answer refers to the traditional justification of the principles of double effect and total good. After having briefly proved that here is a question of indirect sterilization (in as much as 'the intention of the procedure is not the interruption of ovulation but the prevention of the consequences of an eventual violation of chastity') the eminent Secretary of the Council Congregation considers it to be licit because motivated by an adequate reason. In this case it is for the protection of the woman from the physical and psychical disorder produced by fear, not only of the assault but also of its possible consequences, and which would become even more serious if these consequences were actually realized. In other words, it renders fertilization and pregnancy impossible and, in this particular case, succeeds to a certain extent in calming the woman's anguish. Moreover it protects her in fact from some of the even worse dangers to which she might be subject if the imminent threat became actual. Such a good motive as that of the preservation of the present and future physical and psychical wellbeing of the woman is sufficient to legitimize an intervention which moreover (because of this therapeutic intention) constitutes only indirect sterilization.

The reply given by Hürth is more subtle because, in order to prove that the means adopted by the woman to defend herself is not intrinsically wrong, he has recourse to a distinction which we find new and of great interest—the distinction between 'absolute' and 'relative' sterilization. By the first term is meant 'any act which causes sterility in the subject'. But these words do not in themselves denote a wrongful use: for sterilization to be a sin, this sterilizing act must be associated with a carnal embrace freely desired on the part of the sterilized person: it is this 'relative' sterilization alone which has a precise moral character and as such is contrary to the law of nature and condemned by the teaching office of the Church. Thus, a woman who renders herself temporarily sterile without the intention of associating her sterility with any sexual act, is not, in the moral sense, responsible for her sterilization. She has indeed interfered with one of her biological functions (as she might have temporarily suspended her visual, digestive or respiratory functions) but this is not illicit when it is done 'for the total good of the entire organism and person'. This is true of the woman of whom we are speaking. By taking progestational drugs she is not submitting to any true (relative) sterilization, because her will excludes any sexual intercourse. If this should take place it would be inflicted upon her against her will. Moreover in order to justify this interference with her generative faculty, an interference which, as we have explained, is not to be considered as true sterilization, there are sufficiently valid motives inspired by the need to protect her personal wellbeing which is gravely threatened.

Lambruschini's contribution is also original because of certain principles which he brings into play. The Lateran professor believes we have here a deliberate act of sterilization which aims precisely at the prevention of conception; but not all direct sterilizations are for that very reason illicit. The teaching office of the Church has declared to be illicit a sterilization undertaken for reasons of health, and Lambruschini says the reason for this condemnation is quite simple, inasmuch as the people who have valid reasons for not begetting children 'have at their disposal a more radical method of avoiding generation: they can abstain from copulation'.

'Now it is precisely this condition or fundamental requirement which, being absent in this particular case, makes the deliberate temporary sterilization licit': the nun or, more generally, the helpless woman, who has no other means of avoiding giving birth to a child (which she has valid reasons for wishing to avoid) except by making herself sterile, may have recourse to this means. We have here a sterilization which is deliberate but not illicit. Moreover, there are in the hypothetical case under consideration grave reasons for this procedure, first of all for the sake of her physical wellbeing and then also for even more evident reasons of a spiritual order: these also must be taken into consideration because 'the subordination of the part to the whole justifies deliberate mutilation', and this is valid not only for bodily wellbeing but 'even more so for total spiritual wellbeing'. Therefore we cannot deprive the woman who fears she may be raped and has the right to defend herself from an unwanted pregnancy of the right to effect this anti-ovulatory intervention in her sexual function: 'when a physical and physiological process is in opposition to a pre-existent moral and spiritual right, precedence must be given to the latter'.

The editors of *Studi Cattolici* are in our opinion right to list in the order indicated these three different interventions which indeed indicate a very great advance as regards the novelty and scope of the arguments used. If the case now under consideration can be classified, as Palazzini thinks permissible, as a licit indirect sterilization it simply takes its place among the many other 'therapeutic' interventions based on analogous motives: there is nothing particularly new about this. Instead, Hürth's attempt to discern the ethical justification for sterilization, as it applies to this case, has a more general theoretical significance and may be extended to other cases, such as the case (which he himself records although he refuses to put it in exactly the same category as that of the nun and so to treat it *ex professo*) of the married woman who is obliged by her husband to submit to copulation whereas it is really her duty to abstain from it. And the possible applications of the principles laid down by Lambruschini are still more numerous: in their light what is to be said of a married couple who use

progestational drugs to prevent a pregnancy because they have not
at their disposal that 'more radical' method of abstention from
conjugal intercourse, there being serious reasons for counselling
against abstention? What can be said when the 'total spiritual
wellbeing' of a person is invoked to justify a sterilizing treatment
because this wellbeing demands a more reasonable procreation
and education of children? What are we to say if the conflict
between a physiological process and a spiritual right, in which
'the precedence must be given to the latter', arises with regard
to the right and duty which the husband and wife have to express
their love sexually without running the risk of procreation (the
same right which legitimizes the recourse to periodic continence):
in this case too would it be right to accept an intervention in a
merely 'physical and psychological' process like that of ovulation?
It is easy to see what interest may be aroused by the 'test case'
put forward by the Italian review and answered in this way by
three Roman theologians.

A few weeks later Squillaci replied to the thesis put forward by
Studi Cattolici in a brief article the first part of which is concerned
with the problem of sterilization while the second part deals with
the case we have been considering.

> D. Squillaci, 'Sterilizzazione', *Palestra del clero* 41 (1962), pp.
> 113–16.

Squillaci sees in this procedure merely a deliberate sterilization,
'illicit by its own nature' and forbidden by natural law. Guzzetti
is of the same opinion, as we see in his above-mentioned article on
hormonal contraceptives, written a few months later; logically
true to his own interpretation, he considers this sterilization to be
illicit, because the sterilization is *deliberate*, even if only desired
as a means.[7]

These are very brief answers which do not closely follow the
arguments put forward by Hürth and Lambruschini. On the
other hand two articles which appeared successively, one in the
same year 1962 and one in 1963, dedicated especially to the case
in question, exclude the possibility of a licit intervention:

[7] G. B. GUZZETTI, 'Antifecondativi ormonali e morale', *La Scuola Cattolica*
90 (1962), p. 244.

L. Bender, O.P., 'Usu pilularum evitare conceptionem ex stupro', *Angelicum* 39 (1962), pp. 416–35.

A. Peinador, C.M.F., 'Un problema serio de moral respecto a la esterilización temporal de la mujer', *Illustración del clero* 55 (1962), pp. 119–26, 196–204, 245–54, 284–93, 338–45, 540–8.

S. Navarro, C.M.F., 'Una discusión sobre medios modernísimos esterilizantes', *Revista Espanola de Teologia* 23 (1963), pp. 191–208.

All these authors consider we are dealing with an intrinsically evil action, which cannot therefore be justified by reference to the most honourable motives: in fact the woman has recourse to sterilizing drugs precisely for their specific effect and so she is undergoing a deliberate sterilization (although intended only as a means to an end) which violates her natural duty to preserve and defend the integrity of her body and its functions. Bender observes that from the ethical point of view progestational treatment with a therapeutic intention would be quite a different matter. In this case moralists would see a therapeutic action undertaken with a view to procuring that bodily wellbeing which it is man's natural right to maintain, and the sterility would be only an indirect result. In the case we are considering, however, the *only* and *immediate* effect (considered as the necessary means for the end desired) is the destruction of a natural function of the ovaries, the function of ovulating, and this constitutes, in the stern words of Peinador who in his article examines one by one the various other contributions to this debate, 'a real violation of the natural order established by God'. Nor can he agree to the distinction made by Hürth between absolute and relative sterilization: (according to Hürth that which renders a deliberately sterilizing intervention illicit is not merely the suppression of the generative function which is and must be naturally under man's control). Moreover, all three authors point out that the teaching office of the Church, and in particular the doctrine of Pius XII (of whom Navarro speaks at some length) has condemned as forbidden by natural law all deliberate sterilization, whether permanent or temporary: and it is difficult to see how this procedure can be called anything else but deliberate sterilization, even in the case we are examining.

In the 'Notes' we have already mentioned Farraher expresses some diffidence about this case.[8] He considers the treatment is probably permissible, giving as his reasons more the absence of a sinful purpose in the contraceptive measures used than the alleged therapeutic purpose for which the part may be sacrificed for the good of the whole. A sinful purpose means 'the intention of committing deliberately contradictory acts, that is, conjugal intercourse on the one hand and acts which frustrate its effect on the other', but there is in this hypothetical case no intention of co-operating in conjugal acts (here he follows Hürth's reasoning). The American Jesuit is, however, himself more inclined to adopt the attitude of those who consider this to be an intrinsically evil deliberate sterilization, in as much as the subject desires and effects in her own body, even if not for selfish reasons, 'the interruption of a natural function of the ovaries'.

Other and more numerous authors have declared themselves in favour of the opinion expressed by *Studi Cattolici* and they have been, at least up to a certain point, more logical than the three Roman moralists in suggesting other possible applications, starting from this premise.

We draw the reader's attention to an article by Philippe de la Trinité, which appeared at the beginning of March 1962 (preceding the above-mentioned article by Bender who, in fact, criticizes and rejects Philippe de la Trinité's thesis): he asserts that he has already been concerned privately with a case similar to that put forward by the Roman paper, and he declares his own conclusions to be the same as those of Palazzini, Hürth and Lambruschini, although he admits to having 'some reserves with regard to certain of their expressions and arguments'.

Philippe de la Trinité, O.C.D., 'Un dibattimento morale relativo alle pillole anticoncezionali', *Palestra del clero* 41 (1962), pp. 264–9.

This author does not consider it possible to apply to this case the principle of double effect and the concept of indirect steriliza-

---

[8] J. J. FARRAHER, S.J., 'Notes on Moral Theology, Sterilization and moral principles', *Theological Studies* 24 (1963), pp. 81–5.

tion, as Palazzini, in particular, does when he points out that the evil effect, sterility after copulation, is a necessary means to attain the good effect, the maintenance of physical and psychological wellbeing. Philippe de la Trinité sets out, instead, to demonstrate that the means chosen, that is, sterilization, is not, in this case, intrinsically evil because as the Carmelite theologian explains, the woman co-operates only in a material sense. In fact, the prohibition of rendering sexual activity sterile has as its object a voluntary sexual activity, not one which is reduced to a merely physical experience for the person who suffers it, neither good nor evil in itself—as in the case of the woman we are now considering. The woman incurs no moral responsibility for what has occurred, not even the duty to safeguard a possible fertilization: all the blame and all the responsibility are to be laid on the shoulders of the person who has violated her. The author finds this line of argument so convincing that he seems quite sure that the solution will be a positive permission, and he arrives at the same conclusion, although his motives differ, as that of the three Roman moralists.

Three other articles, however, written in 1962, which concern the same 'test case', seem to adopt the same line of argument as Bender, Peinador and Navarro.

F. Peiró, 'Sobre el uso de progestógenes para impedir una fecundación eventual', *Archivos de la Facultad de Medicina de Madrid* (1962), pp. 129–32.
R. Royo Villanova, 'Puede ser permitido el empleo de sustancias anticonceptivas?', *ibid.* (1962), 409–10.
M. Zalba, S.J., 'Casus de usu artificii contraceptivi', *Periodica de re canonica, et morali liturgica* 51 (1962), pp. 167–92 (cf. particularly pp. 172–83).

Zalba's article is the lengthiest and most original. He also considers it is impossible to apply the principle of double effect, and bases his argument chiefly on that of the total good (i.e., a person's total welfare justifies the sacrifice of a particular physiological function). But he examines more closely the specifically moral character of deliberate sterilization. Rendering infertile an unmarried woman, who has no desire whatever for sexual intercourse and indeed is forbidden by her vows from experiencing it, is not from the moral point of view the same thing as sterilizing

her: the only deliberate sterilization which is in itself illicit and
forbidden by the teaching office of the Church is that 'intended to
prevent procreation in a man or woman who wishes to have
sexual intercourse or whose duty it may be to submit to it'. In
our case, concludes Zalba, the woman 'must not, may not and
will not' perform sexual acts: therefore to prevent ovulation is
merely to sterilize her in a 'purely physiological sense', with no
moral implications. Such a procedure may then be permitted
when there are motives of sufficient validity, such as those here
considered. As we see, the line followed by the Spanish moralist
is still that traced by Hürth; but nevertheless it leaves unsolved a
question which can be read between the lines of Zalba's article
much more clearly than in the article written at an earlier date by
his fellow priest: does the moral concept of 'forbidden deliberate
sterilization' include every sterilization of a woman who has (or
may and should have) a desire for sexual intercourse, or who has
(or may and should have) a desire to procreate? Hürth had been
quite clear about the first clause but Zalba's point of view is not
so clear and sometimes presents as a moral situation capable of
being considered from the point of view of sterilization, the right
and duty not to take part in sexual intercourse and also the right
and duty to abstain from the procreative function. The difference
is very significant because the second hypothesis (the right and
duty to refuse procreation) might occur even within a marriage.
If we read the following passage which concludes Zalba's article
we wonder whether this would not be valid also in the case of
anti-ovulationary treatment of a married woman who had been
advised, or even forbidden, to bear children.

'The prevention of ovulation and the consequent removal of
the danger of procreation, in a person who has neither the duty
nor the permission to procreate, but is instead under a strict
prohibition in this matter, and has merely the physiological capacity of procreating (which is in itself substantially imperfect) is by
no means to be thought of as the same sterilization of which
Pius XII spoke, or which is described in documents approved by
the Holy Office.'[9]

Finally the use of the pill when violence is feared is considered
permissible by Fuchs, Snoek, Ford, Kelly and Demmer in the

[9] M. ZALBA, S.J., op. cit., p. 180.

articles already mentioned,[10] and their opinion seems in the main to be the same as that expressed by Hürth and Zalba. But Snoek and Demmer explicitly declare that the case of the use of sterilizing drugs in legitimate self-defence may occur also within a marriage when the husband makes a selfish use of his sexual faculties, and here too (in opposition to the assertions of Hürth and Zalba) Snoek and Demmer think the use would be justified. They also assert, in more general terms, that the solution offered in this case might raise some doubts concerning the binding character of the moral principles which condemn deliberate sterilization and contraception.

We consider that this may give rise to numerous doubts: whoever reads the above quoted articles in ignorance of the actual moral case considered and studying merely the affirmations of principle which they contain, would at once see the much more widely extended moral problem which may now be raised, as we have already pointed out.

We are faced with a case which the traditional doctrine considers one of deliberate contraceptive sterilization, and indeed that it is so, at least in its material content, is admitted by the supporters of the more permissive thesis (with the exception of Palazzini). But these writers do not recognize this procedure as intrinsically evil. To admit even this one exception to the general rule is very new and surprising, in view of the discussion we have already summarized. The arguments which support the theory that the act is not intrinsically illicit, and especially the subtle alteration of the concept of sterilization, are even more significant. Following the irresistible course of logic, from the nun who fears to suffer violent assault to the wife who cannot resist her husband's unjust will, we find ourselves drawn still further forward (remembering the very general line of argument suggested by Lambruschini

---

[10] J. FUCHS, S.J., 'Moraltheologisches zur Geburtenregelung', *Stimmen der Zeit* 170 (1962), p. 364; J. SNOEK, C.SS.R., 'Problemas de Moral matrimonial', *Revista Ecclesiástica Brasileira* 23 (1963), pp. 740–1; J. C. FORD, S.J. and G. KELLY, S.J., *Contemporary Moral Theology: II. Marriage Questions*, Cork 1963, pp. 365 ff.; K. DEMMER, M.S.C., 'Die moraltheologische Diskussion um die Anwendung sterilisiender Medikamente', *Theologie und Glaube* 53 (1963), pp. 429–33. It must be noted that Snoek does not yet consider legitimate the recourse to progestational drugs for 'legitimate self-defence' within marriage, and awaits the opinion of the Magisterium on this question. Cf. the interesting reply he wrote a few months later in 'Anovulatórios', *Revista Ecclesiástica Brasileira* 24 (1964) p. 164.

and Zalba) until we reach a point when it appears possible to wonder whether, in marriage, the woman who deprives herself of her fertility capacity for the whole of that period when she has neither the right nor the duty to exercise it, may perhaps not be acting against the natural moral order, even if she is interfering with a physiological process. Finally, we must notice the great weight and wide scope assigned throughout this controversy to the principle of the total good ; this total good to which a part may be sacrificed (for example the generative function itself or one of its component elements like ovulation) becomes less and less restricted in its application to the merely physical wellbeing of the organism and tends to identify itself with the total wellbeing of the whole person, including spiritual wellbeing when this cannot be protected by other means. Where are we now to find the new limitations to human control over the procreative faculty, and the duty (within marriage) to exercise it? This is the doctrinal question which will be seen to be of conclusive significance in the most recent phase of the discussion.

III

A NEW ASPECT OF THE PROBLEM OF THE PILL: 1964–1965

CONCLUDING their examination and their reflections upon this problem Ford and Kelly wrote in the summer of 1963 that, although certain matters concerning the contraceptive pills were still theologically obscure, at least one thing was clear and certain as regards their use, according to the authoritative teaching of Pius XII and the unanimous opinion of the theologians: to use the pills as contraceptives is gravely sinful and Catholics who intend to use the pills in this way must be refused absolution and holy communion.[1]

Some months earlier there had appeared the much discussed book by Dr John Rock,[2] in which for the first time a Catholic denied the character of illicit sterilization, contrary to nature, attributed to the anovulant use of the pills when these were used for a necessary control of procreation. In fact, as this collaborator of Pincus argued, although they intervened in the generative function they did not impair it; indeed, they enhanced its value. It is interesting to note that among the arguments brought forward by the eminent gynaecologist were some deduced from the previous discussion about the nuns, in as much as he affirmed that in these exceptional circumstances a temporary sterilization was not intrinsically illicit. In Europe, almost at the same time, the moral theologian, Beemer, in an article already mentioned, suggested an analogous doctrine which met with some criticism:[3] he proposed that only those interventions which totally suppress the generative function should be considered as real and actual sterilizations, not in the biological but in the moral sense, while

---

[1] J. C. FORD, S.J., and G. KELLY, S.J., *op. cit.*, p. 375.

[2] J. ROCK, *The time has come*, London, Longmans, Green & Co., 1963. The book had been preceded by a briefer article of a similar nature, 'We can end the battle over birth control', in *Good Housekeeping*, July 1961.

[3] See quotations from two articles by Beemer and Savalle, p. 13, above.

excluding from this category those measures (like the use of
anovulants) which merely alter the rhythm of the generative
function. But these were merely two sporadic opinions and the
former was not put forward by a theologian: the theologians were
still unanimous in their negative attitude, as Ford and Kelly had
stated.

I. *Articles by Janssens, van der Marck and Reuss*

Towards the end of 1963 there appeared at about the same time,
published in authoritative reviews, three theological studies on
this subject which undertook to demonstrate the permissibility of
the use of anovulant pills for the purpose of regulating births
according to a Christian principle:[4]

> L. Janssens, 'Morale conjugale et progestogènes', *Ephemerides
> Theologicae Lovanienses* 39 (1963), pp. 787–826. The article is
> preceded by a briefer note, of a more technical character, by
> Prof. J. FERIN, 'De l'utilisation des médicaments inhibiteurs
> d'ovulation', *ibid.*, pp. 779–86.
> W. van der Marck, O.P., Vruchtbaarheidsregeling. Poging tot
> antwoord op een nog open vraag', *Tijdschrift voor Theologie* 3
> (1963), pp. 379–413.
> J. M. Reuss, 'Eheliche Hingabe und Zeugung: Ein Diskussions-
> beitrag zu einem differenzierten Problem', *Tubinger Theologische
> Quartalschrift* 143 (1963), pp. 454–76.

Janssens' article begins with a brief exposition of doctrine which
justifies progestational treatment on the grounds of the two
principles of double effect and total good in various exceptional
circumstances. But among these there is at least one, treatment
with progestational drugs during lactation (which, following his
earlier article written in 1958, had found some favour with the
moralists), to which those classical principles do not really apply
and which can therefore only be defended in a new framework of
doctrine. And it is this new orientation, according to this moral

---

[4] Cf. also a brief article by M. DAYEZ, 'Le recours aux pilules stérilisantes
est-il légitime?', *Revue diocésaine de Tournai* 18 (1963) 591–6, where the question
does not receive a definitely negative answer; in fact, the author considers that
to condemn this practice as 'against nature' would imply a 'restricted and merely
biological' view of nature: therefore he considers the problem still unsolved.
As we shall see, the author, in a later article, makes it clear that he has now
adopted the more permissive viewpoint.

theologian, which must now be explained and which will prove
the legitimacy of the pill, generally speaking, as a means for controlling fertility. The doctrine seems to us to be summed up in
two points. The first point concerns the conjugal act in its objective sense (and Janssens prefaces his observations with a long
historical synthesis, from St Augustine to our own day). The
objective meaning of copulation cannot be considered primarily
in its function of a procreative act. Undoubtedly the husband and
wife must bring to their marriage a sincere and generous intention
to beget children but this intention, just as it does not insist that
only specifically procreative conjugal intercourse is permissible,
in the same way does not insist that at all times the physical conditions of copulation should be unalterable, or this is not always
required by their intention, and indeed the physical conditions
may sometimes be ineffective, for they may be present and yet—
as happens during periods of deliberate continence—the procreative function may be systematically avoided. If therefore the
objective reality of the sexual act must be left entire, as the Church
has very clearly stated, this is not really in order to preserve the
procreative intention, for if this were so, as Janssens points out,
even copulation deliberately effected during a sterile period would
be sinful, as this also, in the intention of the married pair and in
its actual conditions, is a procedure which positively excludes
procreation:

'The practice of periodic continence positively excludes procreation: it creates an obstacle of a *temporal* order because sexual
intercourse is restricted to the 'safe period', just as the use of
mechanical contraceptives constitutes an obstacle of a *spatial*
order, by interposing a protective screen between the sexual
organs of the husband and wife (the "copulation with withdrawal"
also interposes a spatial barrier, for, as the moralists point out:
"the man's seed is not deposited in the right place").'[5]

The intrinsic intention of the act of copulation between husband
and wife is 'the expression and incarnation of conjugal love' and,
more precisely, 'the intention of expressing this total mutual
self-giving (which love requires) without reserves or restrictions'.
Therefore it is sinful to subject it to a perverted or unnatural
intention because this would introduce into the action 'reserves

[5] L. JANSSENS, *op. cit.*, p. 817.

and restrictions' which make total mutual self-giving objectively impossible. Nevertheless, when the structure of the act is respected and it takes place during a 'safe period' the act itself is still objectively good.

This leads to the conclusion that if the anovulant pills are illicit, it is not because their use entails a positive exclusion from conjugal intercourse of the possibility of procreation: it is not their contraceptive effect (as regards a single copulation) which makes their use immoral. From this point of view, since it does not interfere with the exercise of sexual acts in their intrinsic intention (for the sake of total mutual self-giving) the administration of these drugs is justified neither more nor less than the choice of an infertile period. What, however, may be present in the use of these drugs and absent in the choice of the infertile period, is the apparent 'mutilation' of the ovulatory function of the ovaries, but Janssens points out, as the second point of his argument, that this does not actually occur.

In fact, according to the bio-physiological observations which he gathers from Rock and Ferin, the progestational treatment merely 'arrests' the ovulatory function for a period of repose, preserving for future use some ovules which otherwise would mature and, in the case of periodic continence, inevitably perish: therefore we have here, instead of a 'mutilation', an intervention which preserves the ovulatory power of the woman (and even enhances it, through the well-known effects of hormonic 'rebound') 'for that moment when the husband and wife will decide that it is time to fulfil their obligation of generous procreation'. 'If it is thought that no follicle should be lost', the Belgian moralist shrewdly observes—'the remedy is not periodic continence but the administration of progestogens during the phase of ovarian repose following the birth of a child'. At this point we may well ask (and the theologian is here influenced by the findings of the gynaecologist, Professor Ferin) whether the monthly repetition of the ovulatory process, entailing the sacrifice of ovules which will never be used, may perhaps represent not the norm but an anomaly. If we have followed the author's reasoning correctly, would it not be more 'natural' to make use of a treatment which would bring to maturity only those ovules which were to be fertilized, and so prevent any useless waste? This is what would happen in natural demographic conditions, when pregnancies occur with every new ovulation and so in theory prevent the waste of any ovule. And this is what man may re-obtain by means of opportune external measures in conditions like our own today, in which fertility cannot be left to chance but must be regulated by some responsible control.

In conclusion, if we have rightly understood the author: the use of anovulant drugs, with reference to single sexual acts which they thus deprive of procreative power without however altering their structure, is no more contraceptive than the use of the infertile period, which intends and obtains the same result in the same conditions and, with regard to the ovulatory function, it is even less 'mutilating' than periodic continence because, unlike this, it preserves the object (all the ovules) and enhances the capacity.

In what the sub-title of the article describes as an 'attempt to answer a question which is still open', van der Marck follows a line different from that of Janssens. After a historical synthesis of the discussion, with special attention given to Dutch literature on the subject, the theologian from Nijmegen observes that, despite all the lengthy argumentation and the significant signs of unrest which might lead to a still further extension of the debate, this is still caught in a dilemma which would apparently exclude any third solution: the therapeutic use of hormone preparations is called licit and their use as sterilizers illicit. Is it not however 'possible to justify their use in order to regulate fertility'? This is quite impossible unless the discussion is disentangled from the dilemma we have quoted. The Dominican points out that something similar had occurred in the case of the transplantation of organs: in accordance with the traditional principles regarding mutilation, which justify it only if effected 'for curing or punishing', the immediate conclusion had been that the transplantation of organs was illicit because it did not correspond to these purposes But later on the doctrine was put forward, and afterwards almost generally accepted, that transplantation conceived of as 'service to one's neighbour in a form hitherto unforeseen' was a new case, different from those already considered hypothetically, and might be legitimized for other reasons. This doctrine, the author does not hesitate to say, was receiving ever wider approval 'even during the years when Pius XII was very earnestly re-expounding the traditional teaching on transplantation which had already led to an initial pronouncement against its permissibility'. What then was the reason for this change of judgment about transplantation which could also be used to extricate the argument about the pills from its narrow limitations?

Van der Marck says that one must consider more attentively the 'human act' before judging its moral nature. In fact, 'the analysis of the voluntary nature of the act, that which makes it properly human, must necessarily precede any discussion of its good or evil content'. It is typical of the human act, which is deliberately willed, that it contains 'certain physically distinct elements which are capable of becoming *one* in intention and in view of the desired end'. Let us think, for example, of transplantation. It consists of a first physical state which, considered by itself, might seem a mutilation but it would be mistaken to consider this first element by itself without seeing it as part of that integral intention without which it would not be a human act, for ethics concern only human acts. Thus the donor's intervention, considered as a human act, is already not a mutilation but a transplantation. This does not necessarily mean that as a transplantation it is licit, but merely that it must be judged as such, not in the light of the principles concerning mutilation but in the light of those (already ascertained or still be to ascertained) concerning transplantation. The same thing is true of progestational treatment intended to regulate fertility: it may include an action which, seen in itself and from the material point of view, might seem a mutilation (like the removal of a donor's tissue or organ, considered by itself), but in the total intention which makes it a *human act* it is quite another thing: it is already an act undertaken to regulate fertility, and it must be judged as such ethically. And as such it must be licit, since the control of fertility is the right and duty of every married pair.

Naturally this must not be allowed to interfere with other duties of the conjugal life: although in itself licit, it would become incidentally illicit if it were to compromise the health of the mother or of future children, or if it were used as the excuse for incontinent self-indulgence to the detriment of mutual love, etc. This is the reason—if we have understood rightly the author's argument, not always very clearly expressed—why husband and wife may not adopt, for purposes of birth control, onanistic and neo-Malthusian techniques: it is true that, if adopted with this intention, they are permissible as 'human acts' regulating fertility, but they interfere with another duty of the married state (which is not neglected in the case of progestational treatment or periodic continence) that of preserving the integrity of the sexual act, which must remain intact in every case because of its anthropological and sacramental significance.

This seems to be the kernel of van der Marck's argument in favour of the use of anovulants for the purpose of the responsible control of procreation, but we must not omit to introduce here a marginal note which might throw a new light on the solution already suggested. We mean that whereas in the past we have frequently and too readily identified what is 'natural' with what is 'decreed by God', in the belief that what is 'natural' is opposed to all that is 'technical'; today instead we understand more clearly to what an extent the 'technical' is 'natural' for man. This observation, however, has not yet been sufficiently studied or tested. The Dutch theologian's conclusive argumentation explained above is thus summarized: 'If the two fundamental affirmations provided by ecclesiastical tradition are truly these: (1) the radical willingness of the subject to accept the duty of rendering love fertile and of achieving this result in a rational and human manner; (2) the respect of the person of the other party shown in the preservation of the integrity of the conjugal act as a human gesture and symbol which has a superior sacramental meaning—then it is impossible to refuse approval to the control of fertility and of births by means of hormonal preparations, and to consider this as morally good and acceptable within the above-mentioned context of total intention, and the respect of other moral conditions.'[6]

The Auxiliary Bishop of Mainz, Reuss, also attempts to solve this problem by following a line of his own, with considerations of the general characteristics of human sexuality and marriage which are far wider in scope than those already quoted concerning the use of the pill. And the common starting point is very clear: the declared insufficiency of any theoretical and general concept of sexuality and of its exercise which may be formed exclusively, or even only mainly, on the basis of its bio-physiological nature; on the contrary, he points out, it is only by forming a complete

[6] W. VAN DER MARCK, O.P., *op. cit.*, p. 410.

concept of the human person that we can lay down the principles which regulate the sexual union of men and women.

Reuss points out that in this conception human sexuality has for its object that of enabling the man and woman to effect a total communion of life in body and soul, and this communion becomes at the same time a capacity for procreation. If in this bi-sexual condition mankind is still formed in the image of God (cf. Gen 1: 26–7) and if moreover 'God is love' (1 John 4: 8–16), then the man and woman are morally bound to exercise their sexual faculties (for the sake of integration and propagation) in love, without which their sexuality cannot express itself in a manner conformable with their nature, that is, in a manner worthy of mankind. Therefore marriage also, in which sexuality pursues its two-fold and immediate end, must 'rest on the mutual love of the two persons': it is this love which enables them to grow in that mutual communion by which it is continually fostered, and which in this love enables them to fulfil their task of procreation and education, thereby offering their love daily occasions for more profound expansion.

The same thing is true of every single sexual union, permitted and desired in marriage: it must be a 'meeting in love': 'it must be rooted in love even if this love is at the time not fully grown, and will develop only at a later stage'. We must however note that this two-fold orientation of sexual desire does not in the same measure characterize every individual sexual union: in actual fact this union, as an integrating act on the part of the husband and wife, is more frequently inspired by their mutual love than by their desire to procreate. The love which must inspire the fulfilment of their sexual capacities requires of them that they should exercise these powers for the purpose of generation only as often as is in accordance with their shared intention of generous procreation: to exceed in this would be an action contrary to their love. But these occasions do not suffice for the integrating function which love also attributes to sexual activity in marriage: in order to be fully integrated it is necessary, in the husband and wife's interests, that copulation, as a source of mutual harmony (so necessary for the children's sake!) should be an adequately habitual action of their married life, and to deny this would be contrary to love. So there arises a situation of disharmony in which, the duty of mutal integration conflicting with the necessity of preventing procreation, the love of husband and wife which inspires these two principles of conduct, can find only one solution: copulation rendered sterile. This is the essential point: the prevention of procreation, in the situation of conflicting purposes we have described, is a morally good thing: it is what the married couple in this case can and must wish for each other.

Here we see the authentically positive value of the choice of infertile periods whenever possible, and, for cases in which this is not posssible, the Auxiliary Bishop of Mainz introduces the question of progestational drugs. In reality, he observes, 'no absolute and valid unalterability is possessed in all circumstances by biological and physiological factors and processes in themselves: on the contrary, intervention in these processes, when motivated by a proportionately good result, is always permissible': it remains nevertheless true that the highest values cannot be determined by bio-physiological considerations. Now, if interventions with regard to these factors and processes are permitted, or even commended in view of other good ends, for oneself or for others (this latter case concerns transplantations), one cannot understand why they may not be permitted or even commanded when, the above-mentioned conflict having no other solution and a good end like the mutual love of husband and wife being gravely threatened, it seems logical to think that some physiological aspect of the female process may be sacrificed. And Reuss does not think it necessary to be precise about which contraceptive means are to be used in such cases (for example, medicaments or an operation); he considers this to be beyond the competence of a theologian who 'can merely stipulate that the intervention be effected in such a way as to safeguard the personal dignity of the married couple for the sake of increasing their mutual love'.

From this point of view the author judges not only interferences with the integrity of the bio-physiological processes 'with a view to copulation' but also the use of progestational steroids. As regards those procedures which 'affect integrity of copulation' (such as *coitus interruptus* or the use of the condom), he declares he has not wished to include them in the scope of his reflections.

II. *The first response*

These original contributions immediately aroused enormous

c

interest (January-June 1964) among theologians.[7] Some articles merely summarized the new arguments: we refer to the very careful notes published in the Belgian Review *Sacerdos*, which examines all three articles, by Janssens, van der Marck and Reuss. Quartier's fine review dealt with the whole history of contraceptive methods, without restricting itself to the problem of progestational drugs. Snoek surveyed the problem for his Brazilian review:

'Het verantwoordgebruik van de progestogenen volgens (Prof. L. Janssens); Nieuwe visie of de vruchtbaarheidsregeling (Prof. van der Marck, O.P.); Het conflict tussen liefde en vruchtbaarheid oplossen (Mgr Reuss)', *Sacerdos* 31 (1963–1964), pp. 584– 90, 591–4, 594–8.

D. Quartier, 'Het moreel problem van de geboortenregeling" *Collationes Brugenses et Gandavenses* 10 (1964), pp. 145-204 (cf. particularly pp. 155–62, 180–98.)

J. Snoek, C.SS.R., 'Problemas de Moral matrimonial (II)', *Revista Ecclesiástica Brasileira* 24 (1964), pp. 429–35.

Of especial significance is the review by Snoek, in the course of which he observes that we are now faced with a new idea regarding sterilization, an idea which 'no longer assigns such an absolute value to bio-physiological integrity'. This consideration, says the Redemptorist very frankly, is now presented to fellow

[7] It is neither possible nor convenient here to describe the numerous replies, not all based on theological grounds, which appeared in the daily press, or in reviews and magazines. A selection of these replies, for the year 1964, may be found in the volume *The pill and birth regulation. Documentation of the Catholic debate*, ed. and introd. by L. PYLE, London (Darton, Longman and Todd), 1964. We here quote from only one very short contribution, important because of the authority of the review in which it appeared: a letter from J. O'REILLY, 'Oral contraceptives', published in the *Clergy Review* 49 (1964) p. 250, in which the author, like Janssens but without any reference to him, asserts that progestational drugs which are restricted in their use to prolonging the infertile period, cannot be judged as morally equivalent to the other means of sterilization. He also asks whether a woman is under any moral obligation to ovulate every month or whether she should not exercise her right, as it is now possible for her to do, to control ovulation with a view to responsible parenthood.

Another American book, which recounts the history of the pill and the reactions it aroused in other people besides professional theologians, is written by an American doctor who afterwards became a member of the Pontifical Commission for the family and for births, J. R. CAVANAGH, *The Popes, The pill and the people. A documentary study*, Milwaukee, The Bruce Publishing Company, 1965, 128 pp.; in spite of the date of publication, however, the documentation stops at 1963 and so does not yet record the new trend initiated by the three European moralists.

theologians for a discussion which must not be conducted in an emotional manner but with a profoundly scientific understanding equal to that of the theologian who initiated it.

There followed the first replies, which seemed on the whole favourable (although with certain reserves) to the new line of argument, which was indeed carried still further by some writers. In chronological order we record:

> F. J. Heggen, 'Enige studies over de moraliteit van de geboorte-regeling', *Analecta van het bisdom Roermond* 45 (1964), pp. 40–66; 'Huwelijksliefde en huwelijksvruchtbaarheid', *Te Elfder Ure* II (1964), pp. 117–23.
>
> L. M. WEBER, 'Zur innerkirchlichen Diskussion über die Geburtenregelung', *Schweizerische Kirchenzeitung* 132 (1964), 98–101. The article was re-published in *Theologie der Gegenwart* 7 (1964), pp. 125–33.
>
> N. Seelhammer, 'Zur Diskussion um die Frage der Geburtenbeschränkung', *Trierer Theologische Zeitschrift* 73 (1964), pp. 92–107.
>
> V. Heylen, 'Moralistas y progestagenas', *Mensaje* 128 (1964), 143–51.
>
> A. Auer, 'Eheliche Hingabe und Zeugung: zu einem Diskussionsbeitrag des Mainzer Weihbischof D-J. M. Reuss', *Theologische-praktische Quartalschrift* 112 (1964), pp. 121–32.

Heggen (Holland) and Weber (Switzerland) agree to the new orientation of the argument these two authors had already written on this subject (February–March 1964). The others are new contributors.

Seelhammer refers only incidentally to the new doctrinal standpoint, but does not oppose it. His reply (March–April), which despite the more or less generic title is dedicated very largely to the problem of progestational drugs, deals with the whole question as it had been presented and variously resolved before these three original contributions: he seems generally to adopt the more advanced theses. He quotes, nevertheless, also from the 'thoughtful' article by Janssens (the only one he shows any knowledge of) and considers 'interesting', without hazarding any critical appraisal, the comparison therein defended 'between periodic continence and the use of hormonal preparations'.

The article by Heylen (Director of the Institut des Sciences Familiales et Sociologiques of Louvain, who played a very important role in the debate on these problems) was published in May; it is a careful analysis of the points of view of Janssens and van der

Marck. Although he expresses no personal judgment the author clearly shows himself to be receptive to the new trend of ideas. He leans towards the opinion that 'progestational drugs reproduce, in an intelligent manner, a fact of nature, whereas nature produces the same effect blindly, in order to protect a woman too young to have children, or already pregnant, a nursing mother, or a woman of too advanced an age to bear the burden of fertility'. Moreover, in the Chilean review which publishes it, Heylen's article is preceded by an even more significant editorial, presumably written by the director of the periodical (H. Larraín Acuña, S.J.) in which the author stresses even more clearly the by no means unnatural character of the treatment with progestational anovulant drugs. He points out that if the natural progesterone, in delaying the return to ovulatory activity after childbirth, has a providential eugenic purpose (that of protecting the mother and, even more, the child), then it will not be forbidden to pursue the same purpose with the aid of progestational drugs. This would be a human intervention, it is true, but one with the same profound purpose as the physiological process: that is, by its means man would merely be better preserving, with the intelligent control of the reproductive faculty, its fundamental intention (regular fertility), which seems already divinely ordered in its biological processes.

Auer, however, examines the attitude of Reuss with which he declares he is substantially in agreement. Nevertheless he has some points to make about certain of Reuss's *obiter dicta:* for example, he considers it is not entirely a matter of indifference, from the ethical point of view, what kind of contraceptive measures are taken 'before coitus' (progestational drugs, ligature of the Fallopian tubes, hysterectomy, etc.) and points out that not all these interventions are equally acceptable morally.[8]

[8] We have not yet been able to study an article by MICHAEL O'LEARY, Professor of Ethics at the Sacred Heart Seminary of Detroit, published in *Jubilee*, March 1964, in which the author, after having pointed out some illogicalities in the usual unfavourable attitude to the pill, asserts that there is no moral difference between using the pill and using the method of periodic continence. We must mention also an article by E. TESSON, S.J., 'Discussion morale (ligature des trompes)', *Cahiers Laennec*, June 1964, pp. 64–73, in which the author seems so convinced of the legitimacy of the use of anovulants that he even concludes that 'the question of the moral legitimacy of the closure of the Fallopian tubes has now been raised by the new reflections on the use of anovulants'; the same author, however, seems much more cautious in his later article, 'La régulation des naissances. Nouvelles orientaions?', *Etudes* 322 (1965), pp. 724–30.

Finally, we now come to the contributions which were unfavourable to the new theses: Kelly's article reproduces two lectures given 22 and 23 April at St Mary's College (St Mary's, Kansas); the other two articles were published very soon afterwards. It is interesting to note that three of these come from the United States of America, and that almost all the moralists in this group are already known for their previous contributions to this discussion.

G. Kelly, S.J., 'Confusion: contraception and "the pill",' *Theology Digest* 12 (1964), pp. 123–30.

J. J. Lynch, S.J., 'Notes on moral theology. The oral contraceptives', *Theological Studies* 25 (1964), pp. 237–49.

M. Zalba, S.J., 'De regulatione prolis generandae et de usu compositorum progestationalium', *Periodica de re morali, canonica et liturgica* 53 (1964), pp. 186–259.

F. J. Connell, C.SS.R., 'Is contraception intrinsically wrong?', *The American Ecclesiastical Review* 150 (1964), pp. 434–9.

A. Fz. Diaz-Nava, S.J., 'Castidad conyugal', *Sal Terrae* (1964), pp. 356–407 (only pp. 394 ff. concern our subject).

The least interesting of these articles as regards our present theme is that by Connell. It is mainly devoted to Dr Rock's book and rejects his conclusions, declaring, in particular, that every deliberately contraceptive use of the pill is intrinsically illicit; even their legitimization as self-defence (as in the case of the nuns in the Congo) does not enable him to admit that they may be intrinsically licit when they are administered for a contraceptive purpose, except in those particular circumstances already mentioned. It is indeed true, he concludes, that 'recently there have been alarming attacks, even by Catholics, on the teaching of the Church', and he quotes the attack launched by Janssens, but the eminent American moralist concludes that, 'because of the infallibility of the Church', it is not possible to accept 'any of these alterations in traditional doctrine'. Diaz-Nava also is very summary in his criticism of the new trend. He shows some actual knowledge only of the article by Janssens (whom he does not mention by name but from whom he quotes some passages) and in arguing against him the Professor of Comillas denies that it is possible to compare progestational treatment with periodic continence, since in the latter case (unlike the former) 'the human intervention does not affect the bio-physiological processes and all the functions remain intact'. Therefore the new presentation does not seem to him sufficiently well founded.

Kelly, in his very clear exposition (the last before his death) first of all recalls the teaching of Pius XI and Pius XII and then proceeds to examine the three European contributions. He opposes Janssens' assertion of ethical parity between periodic continence and the use of the pill: the former prevents conception by abstinence whereas the latter represents 'a suppression of the generative faculty and a positive intervention in the vital processes connected with the conjugal act'; he rebukes van der Marck for giving the impression that the question of transplantation has already been approved of by moral theologians whereas instead it is still very controversial, and he considers that in any case 'his verbal rejection of the false principle that the end justifies the means does not prove that he makes no use of it'. Finally, with regard to Reuss, whose article covers a more general field, the American Jesuit re-asserts the foundations of the Christian doctrine: the clarity and immutability of pontifical teaching about contraception, which the theologian has only to explain and illustrate, and the procreational character which by natural law must always be inviolably respected both in the act and in its sexual function (just as the Bishop of Mainz wishes the intention of integration and love to be respected). Moreover, concludes Kelly, Pius XII firmly but with profound understanding, denied the possibility of a dilemma between the conjugal duty to express love and the equally binding duty to avoid procreation. He admitted that in certain circumstances God's law may require prolonged abstention from conjugal intercourse, but he re-affirmed the Christian tradition that in this case God gives abundant graces for the preservation of mutual love. At the same time, he expressed his confidence in man's capacity to co-operate, even to a heroic degree, with this grace.

In his carefully thought out article Lynch rejects most decisively the positions taken up by van der Marck and Janssens (he may not have read Reuss's article) which he at once declares to be 'from the theological point of view quite amazing', and deserving of a 'severe reply'. To the arguments of van der Marck, which we have already put forward, according to which the total intention would determine the character of the intervention in question, qualifying it as a human act, not of deliberate sterilization (always illicit) but of the control of fertility (licit or illicit according to circumstances), Lynch objects that certain acts have a moral significance in themselves and are evil *objectively*, without referring to the subjective intention of the agent, so that when they are chosen there is necessarily implied also an evil end, and that deliberate sterilization is of this sort (being suppression of the generative function simply because it is generative). This is evil in itself and such as may not be intended (implicitly) even by one who declares his final intention is merely to regulate fertility by this means. There is therefore, says the Jesuit, no possibility of justifying in this way the anti-ovulatory use of the pills, which indeed means illicit deliberate sterilization. He also denounces as contraceptive and therefore immoral the intercourse which follows such treatment. His rebuke to Janssens is equally decisive. Leaving aside other aspects of his thought, Lynch rejects his essential argument, the identification, from the moral point of view, of the use of the pills with the choice of infertile periods: in the former case, he objects, the liberation of the ovules is prevented and so there takes place, even if only temporarily, a deliberate sterilization which no euphemism (such as that of giving the ovaries a 'period of repose') will ever be able to conceal; instead, in periodic continence 'nothing is done to interfere with the organic function and to deprive the ovule of that potential life which it may in itself possess'. He concludes that to refrain from conjugal intercourse and so refrain from fertilizing an ovule is merely to exercise a moral right, and therefore, theologically speaking, it is not in any way comparable with the sterilization effected by oral contraceptives. Finally, no new arguments can take the place of the teaching of Pius XII, and the American moralist severely condemns Janssens' absolute silence concerning his 1958 speech (van der Marck, however, puts forward his own opinion as an alternative solution to that of the Pope). Lynch finds it very difficult to understand Janssens' failure to treat this 'extremely important' aspect.

Zalba's long article does not deal at length explicitly with the question under consideration. The Spanish moralist expounds the general doctrine of the Church on birth control and examines the various licit or illicit methods employed for this purpose. As regards the anovulants and the new teaching about them (he quotes only from Janssens but is obviously aware of all the arguments put forward by the other writers) his reply is brief, negative and to the point: 'The sexual act may never rightly be undertaken for a reason which in itself, in intention or in act, frustrates its primary purpose; this happens always whether the sterilization is temporary, before sexual union, or whether it is permanent.'

Nor is it possible to establish a moral parity between the conjugal act deliberately undertaken during a naturally sterile period and the same act after sterility has been deliberately effected by the married pair themselves: 'in the former case the human act is not definitively sterile and is not primarily intended as such, whereas in the latter case it is deliberately made sterile by human intervention and is undertaken only because this sterilizations has been effected'.

Only the use of progestational drugs for a therapeutic purpose is considered licit (Zalba does not, however, admit of their use in cases of cyesophobia, 'fear of pregnancy'), just as it is also licit to administer them for a purpose which nature herself desires, such as the regularity of the cycles or the absence of ovulation during the period after childbirth, provided that this 'natural requirement' is confirmed by medical opinion, concerning which confirmation Zalba expresses some reserves.

At this point of the controversy one conclusion is inevitable. The theoretical position of Janssens, van der Marck and Reuss, accepted and appreciated by the other writers, does not find in its opponents critical arguments of equal worth; one has rather the impression that these opponents merely reiterate the earlier thesis, without a thorough analysis of the new thought and without an objective judgment. On the other hand, another moral consideration is now more explicitly added, by some of the more favourable theologians, to those already put forward by the three authors. This is that the anovulant use of progestational drugs, for the purpose of regularizing fertility, may be in harmony with the profoundly rational nature of the generative faculty, as this is shown (on a purely physical plane) in its own physiological processes.

In any case the question is now left open and we can at least see that the new position cannot so easily be superseded. This is the conclusion reached, at the end of this first series of reactions, in an article by Häring, published as the result of an interview reported in *The Guardian*, which, according to the famous moralist, had misinterpreted his position: the article appeared at the same time, in London, in the *Catholic Herald* of 29 May and in Rome in *Orizzonti* of 21 May. After expounding the Christian principles relating to responsible and generous parenthood, Häring refers to the Catholic doctrine about the methods to be used, which forcefully rejects all those which 'violate the dignity and natural form of the conjugal union' and recommends periodic continence. By choosing infertile days for their intercourse, he says, the husband and wife intend to foster their mutual love, that love which at the same time binds them together and prepares them for the service of new lives to come. As for the pill, Häring first of all refers to the general agreement among 'almost all' moral theologians about their permissible use for the regularization of cycles; in the controversial question of their licit use during lactation he comes out in favour of approving this use, which he considers legitimate and practicable. Finally, with regard to their use at other times (with the aim of preserving the full expression of conjugal love in those difficult cases when, with a sense of full responsibility before God and their fellows, they feel it is impossible to assume the burden of another life), Häring refers not only to the negative judgment but also the the recent affirmative judgment 'of Janssens, Reuss, Weber and others', and considers that 'for the moment it is still not possible to form a final opinion on this problem'. One must be patient and wait until it is possible to weigh the pros and cons, while always remaining willing, theologians and faithful alike, to accept the verdict of the Church's teaching authority.

Indeed the Magisterium was not indifferent to the importance of the discussion, as was proved a few weeks later by the pronouncement by Paul VI, although this was still of a somewhat provisional character.

III. *Paul VI's intervention*

In fact the new turn given to the discussion had not only inspired useful critical reflections among theologians but (as we have pointed out) had also let loose a whole flood of more or less hasty and ill-informed interventions which appeared in various newspapers and reviews, Catholic or otherwise. It was necessary, however, to contain the debate within its proper limits of serious theological discussion, and this was essential in order to prevent the new theories being divulged and approved of and even put into practice. This is what Paul VI had in mind when he delivered his forthright speech to the College of Cardinals, 23 June 1964.[9] 'The problem of which everyone is speaking is that of so-called birth control, that is the problem of the population increase on the one hand and of the moral law of the family on the other. This is an extremely grave question which touches the very springs of human life and the feelings and interests most profoundly experienced by a man and a woman. It is an extremely complex and delicate problem. The Church recognizes its manysidedness, that is to say, the many and various responsibilities involved, the most important of all these being that which concerns the married pair themselves, their liberty, their conscience, their love and their duty. But the Church must also affirm her own responsibility in this matter, that which concerns the law of God, which she interprets, teaches, maintains and defends; and the Church must

---

[9] Meanwhile some Dutch and English bishops had intervened in the discussion. In Holland (where Mgr W. Bekhers, Bishop of s'Hertogenbosch, had in April 1963 expressed some doubt about the inclusion of the pill among traditional contraceptive measures, cf. *Herder Correspondence*, Oct. 1963, pp. 28–30) all seven Bishops, in a brief note, 10 August 1963, on the problems of marriage, declared that although the pill might be considered 'no more acceptable a method, as a solution for general use in matrimonial problems, than the contraceptive techniques used heretofore, Catholic moralists are considering the question as to whether it may be justified in certain circumstances' (*Katholiek Archief* 18 (1963), p. 938). It is possible they were thinking only of those cases (regularization, lactation, cyesophobia, self-defence, etc.) which were then being discussed (and this was the interpretation accepted by, for example, L. L. McREAVY, 'The Dutch Hierarchy on Marriage Problems', *The Clergy Review* 49 (1964), pp. 113–15, and F. J. CONNELL, C.SS.R., 'The pill as a contraceptive', *The American Ecclesiastical Review* 150 (1964), pp. 291–2); but they may have meant something more than this, perhaps even the merely anovulatory and contraceptive use of progestational drugs (this is what *Herder Correspondence*, Oct. 1963, p. 30 had explicitly attributed to the bishops, but the report had been incorrect. J. J. LYNCH, S.J., *art. cit.*, *Theological Studies* 25 (1964) 246–9, thinking that they had this extended use in mind, rejected their supposed doctrine.)

The note published 7 May 1964 by Abp J. C. HEENAN, Archbishop (now Cardinal) of Westminster, in the name of the bishops of England and Wales, answers the attacks made on the traditional Christian teaching about contraceptive methods. One of the most eloquent expressions of this hostility had been written by Abp Th. ROBERTS, S.J., ex-Archbishop of Bombay, in the Catholic review *Search*. Abp Heenan's snote condemns the use of the pill, quoting in this connection from the declaration of the Dutch bishops, but only from the

proclaim this law of God in the light of the scientific, social and psychological truths which in recent times have been the subject of new and vast studies and documentations. This new theoretical and practical extension of the question must be very closely examined and this is what the Church is now doing. The problem is being studied as widely and profoundly as possible, with the gravity and sincerity which such an important subject requires. With the help of many eminent scholars, we hope to be able shortly to conclude this examination. We shall therefore soon publish the conclusions in the form which will be deemed most suitable for the subject matter and for the purpose to be achieved. But let us say now quite frankly that we have not yet sufficient reason for considering as superseded and therefore no longer binding the principles laid down by Pope Pius XII in relation to this question; they must therefore be considered as valid, at least until we find ourselves obliged in conscience to alter them. In all that concerns a problem of such gravity it seems well that Catholics should follow one single rule which the Church authoritatively prescribes,

first part of this where they declare that 'the pill is no more acceptable a method . . . . than the contraceptive techniques used heretofore', and without any reference to their legitimate use 'in certain circumstances' to which the Dutch bishops had alluded; this incompleteness, which however seems to leave no doubt about the negative position adopted by Archbishop Heenan as regards the contraceptive use of progestational steroids, may have been due to the hasty translation of the Dutch document which appeared in the *Universe* of 2 May and which he used. An exact translation which appeared in *The Tablet* of 30 May, cleared up the misunderstanding. The integral text of the English document was published in *The Universe* on 7 May. It had yet another repercussion in the interview granted by Cardinal Ottaviani to the Italian weekly *Vita*, published therein on 3 June 1964. The eminent Cardinal regrets that 'some local authorities are expressing doctrinal opinions on questions under discussion' (the journalist responsible for the interview had mentioned, besides Abp Heenan, also Cardinal Suenens, to whom, however, a declaration favourable to the pill, uttered on 7 May in New York, had been attributed: cf. *The Tablet*, 16 May 1964), and for his own part categorically rejects the moral equivalence of periodic continence and anovulant pills: in fact, the latter 'act directly to prevent the natural outcome of the conjugal act' and are therefore illicit.

Another letter from CARDINAL OTTAVIANI to Abp HEENAN, published 18 June, explained that in his interview with *Vita* he had not intended to deny the competence of the English episcopate to pronounce judgment but had merely wished to defend the traditional doctrine of the Church and warn 'those who launch new theories on questions concerning which the directions of the supreme Magisterium must still be awaited'. Both these interventions by Cardinal Ottaviani may be seen also in *Documentation catholique* 61 (1964), pp. 895–7, and in 'La Pillola e la regolazione delle nascite', *loc. cit.*, pp. 185–8.

and so it seems advisable to recommend that nobody should in the meantime presume to give judgment in terms differing from the principles which are still binding.[10]

This pronouncement, of an obviously disciplinary character, served to remove the discussion from circles which had no competence to deal with it and attempted to restrict it to the purely doctrinal sphere. It did not explicitly reject the new opinion but it excluded its practical applicability. In the meantime the Pope's speech initiated the work of a special Commission which he set up for the purpose of studying the problems of population, family life and birth control.

IV. *The debate which followed*

The Pope's speech did not put an end to discussion in competent circles, that is, among theologians, but it made it more thoughtful and circumspect and crushed certain facile enthusiastic responses which had appeared even among these authorities.[11] At the same time it enlarged in theological circles the scope of the controversy about the permissibility of other contraceptive methods (of which we shall speak in later chapters), and therefore interest in the pill itself became less intense and almost disappeared towards the end of 1965. For the moment, we shall deal only with the arguments about the oestro-progestational drugs.

[10] Paul VI, 'Ad Em.mos Patres Purpuratos . . . .', speech of 23 June 1964: *A.A.S.* 56 (1964), pp. 588–9.

[11] Two new elements of a medical nature now suggested a greater caution. First of all, it was observed by several writers and with increasing insistence, that it would be wrong to under-estimate the harm which a prolonged use of progestational drugs might cause to the woman or to her future progeny. In fact, in the summary of 1964, and not without a glint of irony, de Lestapis enquired in one of his very well informed articles whether perhaps the pill should now be considered a 'museum piece', considering, among other things, the many and various counter-indications concerning its use. (S. DE LESTAPIS, S.J., 'De "pillula contraceptiva": an eius usus florere iam desierit', *Periodica de re morali, canonica et liturgica* 53 (1964), pp. 444–9; the next year, for example, there appeared in theological reviews three more articles written by doctors (the first of this group was a member of the Pontifical Commission for the family and for births) all equally opposed to the use of the pill because of the numerous physical, psychological and doctrinal difficulties of which it was the cause: CH. RENDU, 'La régulation des naissances dans le cadre familial et chrétien', *Nouvelle Revue Theologique* 87 (1965), pp. 606–31; W. UMBRICHT, 'Medizinische und moralische Bedenken gegenüber der hormonalen Geburtenregelung', *Anima* 20 (1965), pp. 388–92; E. DELORENZI, 'Recenti interventi in tema di vita coniugale e di regolazione delle nascite', *Medicina e morale* 15

First we must refer to the position taken up by some Roman theologians: Fuchs and Zalba, both professors of the Gregorian University who had already contributed to the discussion; others, new to the discussion: Günthör, professor of Moral Theology at St Anselm's, Brunec, professor of Holy Scripture at the Ateneo Salesiano, and García Vicente, professor of Pastoral Medicine at the Accademia Alfonsiana.[12]

J. Fuchs, S. J., 'Zur Diskussion um die "Pill" ', *Stimmen der Zeit* 174 (1964), pp. 401-19, reproduced in English with certain additions: 'The Pill', *Studies* 53 (1964), pp. 352-71.

A. Günthör, O.S.B., 'Kritische Bemerkungen zu neuen theorien uber die Ehe und eheliche Hingabe', *Tübinger Theologische Quartalschrift* 144 (1964), pp. 316-50, a summary to be found in 'Zu den Lösungsversuchen von Weihbischhof J. M. Reuss und Prof. L. Janssens', *Theologie der Gegenwart* 7 (1964), 215-16.

M. Zalba, S.J., 'Circa ordinem rectum in usu matrimonii Pius XI et Pius XII quid tradiderint', *Gregorianum* 45 (1964), pp. 795-815; idem, 'De pastorali ratione agendi cum his qui in matrimonio processum ovulatorium uxoris moderari intendunt', *Periodica de re morali, canonica et liturgica* 54 (1965), pp. 309-36.

(1965), pp. 80-8. There was also serious alarm caused by the publication in July 1964 of a study by the American Dr F. J. Ayd, in which there was suggested—also on the grounds of other testimonies from the gynaecological field—the possibility that the sterilization effected by the pill was due not only to its well-known anovulant action but also to an alteration in the cervical mucus and the lining of the womb, so that the passage of the sperm into the womb, or even the implantation of the fertilized ovum, was prevented. If this were indeed true (but Dr Ayd's mistake seems to have been in announcing as an almost certain conclusion an explanation which the other gynaecologists who had spoken on this subject had suggested merely as a hypothesis) the pill would be no other than a contraceptive of the old type, or even an abortifacient, and the moral judgment about it would have to be revised once more. (F. J. AYD, *The oral contraceptives: their mode of action*, Washington, N.C.W.C., 1964; cf. also G. SBARIGIA, 'La pillola antifecondativa', *Brevia* 17 (1964), pp. 73-96; P. BAILO, *Valutazione medica dei mezzi per realizzare la regolazione delle nascite*, Bergamo, Stamperia Ed. Commerc., 1964).

[12] A Roman theologian, F. LAMBRUSCHINI, had already pronounced a somewhat reserved opinion about this matter. In a brief note which appeared in *L'Osservatore della Domenica*, 31 May 1964, after having quoted the opinion of Pius XII, he wrote that the moralists who believed in the possibility of some change of doctrine could not avoid taking this into consideration, although it was not 'absolutely opposed to any favourable viewpoint': 'I am in fact personally convinced', said the Lateran moralist, 'that the present state of the problem does not admit of categorical and final solutions one way or the other'.

M. Brunec, S.D.B., *De valore argumentorum quibus sustinetur doctrina absolutae illiceitatis sterilizationis praeventivae temporariae*, Rome, 1965, 87 pp. (cyclostyle).

J. García Vicente, C.SS.R., 'La régulation des naissances dans l'Eglise catholique', *Le Vie spirituelle. Supplément* 74 (1965), pp. 315–38).[13]

Fuchs' article, though extremely thoughtful, remains inconclusive. After a brief survey of the problem he, too, asks whether the use of anovulants can resolve the conflict between the conjugal duty to foster mutual love (a love which is consciously aided in its normal development by mutual tenderness and corporal union) and the duty of responsible parenthood; but after examining analytically the various arguments brought forward in defence of the pill, he does not consider them adequate to prove its objective legitimacy. Nevertheless, he considers that the pronouncements of the teaching authority of the Church may not be absolutely final and may not exclude further thought on the part of the ecclesiastical authorities.

On the opposing side are Günthör and Zalba. In his reply to Reuss and Janssens (the two authors he is chiefly concerned with) Günthör criticizes first of all some of their preliminary attitudes: the scanty attention paid by both to the teaching of the Magisterium (with its 'unequivocal declarations' on the question of direct sterilization), the inadequacy of the introductory historical survey provided by Janssens and the insufficient knowledge of biblical anthropology shown by Reuss. Then he discusses the problem on its own merits. He considers Janssens' argument a 'very dangerous simplification' which seeks to prove that the immorality of a conjugal act does not depend on its contraceptive character but on its exclusion of the possibility of total mutual giving: in reality, both these purposes (of love and of procreation) must be capable of objective fulfilment in copulation. The moral parity which both the Louvain theologian and Reuss deduce from this, the parity between progestational treatment and the choice of the 'safe period' is equally unfounded. In the

[13] In fact the article, in Spanish, had already been circulated in typescript since June 1964: its publication in the French review was accompanied by a note saying that 'for personal reasons the author had preferred not to have it published'.

latter case the impossibility of conception is a natural condition merely accepted by the husband and wife (*volitum*) and not a condition brought about artificially (*voluntarium*). Nor can progestationally induced sterilization be justified, as Reuss maintains, by reference to the principle of the total good, as transplantation is justified. In fact, in the latter case the function is not substantially destroyed in the individual, and the social purpose, moreover, is achieved. This social purpose, on the contrary, is in the former case compromised, and its violation is all the graver inasmuch as the genital organs have a definite significance and purpose for the human race.

Zalba reiterates his interpretation of the teaching of Pius XI and Pius XII which absolutely excludes, if not all direct sterilization ('in the biological sense' adds Zalba), certainly every sterilization, even if merely temporary, which aims at rendering infertile a sexual activity which is freely chosen and undertaken (this is 'direct sterilization' in the normal sense). Upon this distinction (which was already present in his earlier writings) he bases, on the one hand the legitimization of the use of anovulants for self-defence (even with relation to a husband who unjustly seeks to impose copulation) and on the other hand their exclusion as a means of birth control: these new theories—Zalba adds in the last article to which we have referred—'although supported by a growing number of authors', have insufficient intrinsic probability and therefore cannot be put into practice.

Brunec, however, is frankly favourable to the new trend, and his long article (which we here summarize) is a spirited defence of sterilization with anovulants when there are serious reasons for avoiding the birth of another child and absolute continence seems extremely burdensome and even harmful. Having extricated the problem from possible vetoes, which he considers unjustifiable, based on biblical sources or issued by the Magisterium, the author rejects very decisively the asserted identification of the natural 'physical' law with the natural 'moral' law of ovulation, which ends by considering the ovule as if it were 'a person endowed with inviolable rights'. On the contrary, he observes, it was not the human person who was created for the purposes of ovulation, but ovulation which was created for the service of the human person. For him ovulation is one of those many physical phenom-

ena which do not present in themselves or by themselves an
imperative moral obligation, and is thus entrusted to the superior
direction of man so that he may, as required, subordinate it ration-
ally to the moral obligation to procreate which he has received from
God. The conjugal act, moreover, is intrinsically good as an act
of joyful mutual integration, apart from its procreative purpose,
from which at times it is even man's duty to abstain, and which
in any case does not constitute an absolute good. In conclusion,
with this new assistance from medical science, it is made easier
for men to do their duty of being 'not only good educators but
also, which is no less important, good progenitors'.

García-Vicente is also favourable to the new trend. Surveying
the course of the debate on the pill (the author is a doctor) and
particularly the articles by Janssens, van der Marcke and Reuss,
he arrives at the conclusion that inhibition of ovulation 'for the
purposes of responsible procreation', is legitimate, provided that
the still unsolved medical questions can be resolved in a permissive
sense. On the other hand, 'external contraceptives' which impair
the integrity of the conjugal act are totally unacceptable.

Now we turn to consider other contributions from Catholics
outside Rome, and we classify these according to their geographical
provenance or their language.

In Belgium and Holland, where the problem had been so much
discussed and had followed the new orientation, we must first of
all mention articles by Dayez, Schelfhout and van der Marck, and
another contribution, although somewhat indirect, offered by the
Nouvelle Revue Théologique of the Jesuits of Louvain.

M. Dayez, 'La pilule anovulatoire', *Revue diocésaine de Tournai* 19
   (1964), pp. 505–17.
O. Schelfhout, *De sterilisende pil en de huwelijksmoraal*, Bruges,
   Bayaert, 1964, p. 48.
W. van der Marck, O.P., 'Katholiek Standpunt inzake het gebruik
   van ovulatieremmende middelen', *Ovulatieremmende middelen*,
   Leiden, Stafleu's Wetenschappelijke, 1965, pp. 103-8.
G. Martelet, S.J., 'Morale conjugale et vie chrétienne', *Nouvelle
   Revue Théologique* 87 (1965), pp. 245–66.

Dayez frankly approves of the new direction given to the
question: he considers that, unlike the contraceptive methods

which interfere with the conjugal act and entail 'the grave risk of impairing its profound and objective natural meaning', the use of progestational drugs offer instead a legitimate 'control of the mechanisms of fertility, considered as a good end for the persons concerned and still desired even while they have recourse to the pill'. It is therefore an interruption of the generative function which does not destroy it (this would constitute an illicit sterilization) but merely controls its exercise in the interests of the person concerned. Schelfhout also is favourable to the new doctrine, and begins with a very careful appraisal of the position assumed by Janssens. Van der Marck reiterates the opinion he had already expressed in his previous article. Meanwhile, as we shall see later on, other articles by this Nymegen moralist appeared, in which the attention of theologians was directed to an even more extended revision of matrimonial morality, within which the various methods of birth control (and the author does not make any explicit distinction among these) find their authentic principle in conjugal love, of which they must be the worthiest possible expression and 'incarnation'.

The Jesuit review takes a directly opposite view. In fact, Martelet, in the course of a much more extended and thoughtful defence of traditional conjugal morality, rejects anti-ovulatory treatment because it does not respect the 'life structure'. This treatment may at some future date show this respect, when it will have no other effect than that of regularizing the menstrual cycle, but today this is not the case because 'it merely obtains or at least purposes, its suspension', 'thus imposing on the life processes a sterility which they would not necessarily have produced if they had been left alone'.

In Germany only Demmer expressed an opinion contrary to the new movement, and even then not categorically. The others (Ermecke, Egenter, Böckle) approved. In the meantime other articles by Reuss appeared, which we shall examine later. In these, as in the articles by van der Marck, the problem is made to include even those technical contraceptive measures which interfere with the bio-physiological process of the conjugal act.[14]

[14] From the strictly medical point of view were written also the articles by Dr J. ROTZER, 'Ueber die Wirkungsweise der Pille,', *Orientierung* 28 (1964), pp. 159-62, 172-7, and 'Pille und Geburtenregelung', *Der Grosse Entschluss* 19

K. Demmer, M.S.C., 'Eheliche hingabe und Zeugung', *Scholastik* 39 (1964), pp. 528–57.

G. Ermecke, 'Die Frage der Geburtenregelung. Zur Diskussion uber eine Erweiterung des Bereiches erlaubter inderekter Geburtenregelung nach kircklicher und moraltheologischer Lehre', *Katholische Nachrichten-Agentur. Dokumentation* 33 (12 Dec. 1964), pp. 1–7.

R. Egenter, 'Die Verfugüng des Menschen uber seinen Leib im Licht des Totalitätsprinzips', *Munchener Theologische Zeitschrift* 16 (1965), pp. 167–78.

F. Böckle, 'Die Sittliche Bewertung der operativen Sterilisierung', *Fragen der Geburtenregelung (Schweizer Rundschau. Monatsschrift für Geistesleben und Kultur*, March-April 1965), pp. 220–5. By the same author, previously, 'Veranwortete Elternschaft. Zur innerkirchlichen Diskussion um die Geburtenregelung', *Wort und Wahrheit* 19 (1964), pp. 577–86, and his own re-exposition of his point of view in the review for *Concilium*, of which we shall speak later.

Demmer's criticism, which is directed at Janssens and even more specially at Reuss, begins with a broad ethical survey of the nature of marriage, with particular attention to the relation between the personal and biological nature of sexuality. Certainly the biological intention does not constitute an entirely adequate sexual norm for the human person, who 'transcends his own biological formation'. Nevertheless, 'the personal integration of his own sexuality must be effected while safeguarding, as far as possible, the ontological-biological order, since this belongs essentially to his total person: it is precisely the respect of this biological structure of copulation which objectively guarantees its personal significance as an 'expression of love within a possibility of procreation'. Thus he sees the essential difference between the choice of the sterile period and the artificial procurement of sterility: in the former case copulation remains 'metaphysically capable of procreation' besides being a gesture of love; in the latter case 'since in copulation or with a view to this a biological function is inhibited', even when the subjective harmony of the husband and wife is perfectly achieved, the total objective value is impaired. It is therefore clear,

(1964), pp. 519–23. The author is well known also for his articles on the cycle method: in 1965 he published his fine little book *Kinderzahl und Liebesehe. Ein Leitfaden zur Regelung der Empfängnis*, Vienna, Herder, 1965, 99 pp. Cf. also the above mentioned article (p. 56) by Umbricht.

admits Demmer, that 'the apparent conflict between personal and biological values, which can find no solution by sacrificing the latter, may instead look for it in some sort of controlling direction'. With this in view the author finds it possible to justify anti-ovulatory treatment when it consists of an 'extension of the infertile period which thus subordinates the female cycle to personal needs'.[15]

The other authors, however, argue much more decidedly in favour of the new way of thought, although the reasons they give are different. Ermecke and Egenter have recourse to the principle of the total good, in order to justify anti-ovulationary treatment, and they extend this principle beyond the purpose of the good of the individual within which it was traditionally maintained, to the wider sphere of the good of the community (which might, for example, legitimize this treatment in order to prevent social evils like overpopulation or the procreation of defective children). For Böckle the prospect is even vaster: he makes some criticisms of the new position, especially when he agrees with Günthör that one cannot consider equivalent two differing situations, one of them being the impossibility of conception during an infertile period (which is merely an object (*volitum*) of the human will), and the other being the impossibility caused by anovulants (or, if necessary, by a surgical operation) which is instead an artificially produced effect (*voluntarium*), but he adds that, considering what is the most important factor from the ethical point of view, that is, the 'act of choice', there is no morally important difference

[15] K. DEMMER also published in the same year an explicit and exhaustive treatise on the question of progestational treatment for cases of cyesophobia: 'Die hormonale Behandlung der Schwangerschaftsphobie', *Scholastik* 39 (1964), pp. 197–219. After rejecting as inapplicable in these cases the 'therapeutic' justification of progestational treatment (this being no remedy for the phobia but only a means of procuring the sterility of coitus) the author puts forward what he considers to be the most valid argument in its favour. This is that, as the 'whole personality' of the cyesophobic woman desires sterility and the avoidance of conception it would not appear contrary to 'nature' to render her temporarily sterile. But such an argument presupposes a revised concept of 'nature', which 'needs to be stripped of its merely physiological nature in order to become an integral part of the whole human person', and finds its place in a 'morality of development' which presupposes a human nature in continual evolution and does not project into the present moment, as an unconditional norm, an ideal nature which may belong only to the eschatological moment. Demmer devotes the last and most thoughtful pages of his study to this problem, pointing out very shrewdly the grave restrictions and limitations of that concept of 'natural' morality.

between the deliberate choice which avoids ovulation and the act which suppresses it. Indeed, and here he extends the field still further, he would like the new permissibility to be carried to the logical conclusions reached by those theologians who consider that the whole problem of contraceptive practices should be reviewed, beginning with an ethical conception 'understood in a new way', that is, in its fundamental attitude to nature.

Some Italian authors contributed to the discussion and on the whole their judgments seem to be in line, at least potentially, with the new theses:

A. Nalesso: 'Valutazione morale di alcuni trattamenti ormonici e chirurgici in campo sessuologico', *Sessuologia* 5 (1964), pp. 128–45; the article is prefaced by some medico-moral considerations by N. Pasetto, 'Progestinici: sterilizzazione temporanea della donna?', *ibid.*, pp. 118–27.

G. Ceriani, 'Sulla regolazione delle nascite', *Orientamenti pastorali* 12 (1964), No. 3, pp. 3–22.

G. Perico, 'Nuovi orientamenti nel controllo delle nascite?', *Monitore ostetrico ginecologico di endocrinologia e del metabolismo* 35 (1964), p. 19. Cf. idem, 'Problemi procreativi', *Enciclopedia del Matrimonio*, Brescia, Queriniana, 1965, pp. 326 ff.

A. Valsecchi, 'Valutazione morale dei mezzi per realizzare la regolazione delle nascite', *Convegno di studio sullo stato attuale del problema della regolazione delle nascite*, Gazzada, Ist. Sup. di Scienze Religiose, 1964, pp. 80–93.

T. Goffi, 'Orientamenti teologici odierni sulla regolazione delle nascite', *La Scuola Cattolica* 92 (1964), 537–46.

E. Chiavacci, 'Procreazione e vita coniugale', *Studium* 61 (1965), pp. 191–201.

Pasetto and Nalesso, the former a gynaecologist and the latter a moral theologian, are clearly in favour of the more permissive opinion. They do not consider treatment with progestational drugs to be the equivalent of a real and actual sterilization, as it is restricted to a merely temporary suspension of ovulation. And it is not even a contraceptive action: here, in fact, the integrity of the conjugal act is respected and this seems to be ('in its anthropological intention and in its human and sacramental significance') the fundamental criterion for the Church's moral judgment of birth control methods; therefore 'the term contraceptive, when applied to progestational drugs, contradicts the biological truth and the human significance of their use'.

Ceriani, Perico, Valsecchi, Goffi and Chiavacci are not decided in favour of the new orientation, but are still open to conviction. Ceriani refers explicitly to Häring's article, which we have already reviewed, and to Lambruschini's brief contribution, and concludes that in his opinion the use of these drugs 'would constitute a medical intervention to regulate the natural process of fertility. This process, although temporarily interrupted, is not positively destroyed. Indeed it may be said to be enhanced when its activity is restored and when the parental duty of father and mother can and must be desired and welcomed, with a Christian sense of responsibility.' Perico, having affirmed the permissibility of therapeutic uses (including the treatment for cyesophobia) and for purposes of self-defence, refers to the present medical uncertainty about the action of the pill, which leaves the moralist perplexed, but considers nevertheless that the question must not be considered as finally decided in a negative sense. 'The slight possibility of a moral justification may perhaps become enlarged.'

In our own article we showed we were inclined to think that, without confirming our attention merely to the medico-physiological aspects of the problem, the treatment with progestational drugs may constitute 'a new kind of regulation of the ovulatory process', that is, a deliberate control of this process which would not impair its innermost intention of procreation but would regulate it according to new formulae (no longer spontaneous but determined by man) in favour of a rationalized fertility such as is necessary today for the human species. Goffi considers it may still be possible morally to justify anovulant drugs, used with the intention of effecting a more controlled fertility, when these are used curing lactation to prolong 'the resting period' of the ovulatory process, even beyond the normal period, until the duty of procreation is once more impellent. In this case, in fact (unlike the case of using this treatment at other periods), there would be no destruction of follicles, for none of these would yet have ripened. Nor would the intervention appear contrary to nature, for our duty to human nature 'does not consist merely in conservation, but also in enhancement'. Chiavacci also considers the question 'still open from the theoretical point of view', and for his own part believes that the condemnation of contraceptive methods does not necessarily include 'the Pincus-Rock pill' since, unlike other methods, 'it does not directly interfere with the conjugal act'.

There were other articles in Spanish and Portugese. Apart from one of the regular reviews by Snoek, written in Brazil, there were some original contributions: in Spain (Gonzales, de Lahidalga, Apocada and Mondria) and in Portugal (Silva Soares). There were also two pamphlets dedicated entirely to this theme (Peinador and Charbonneau).

J. A. DA Silva Soares: 'Progestogénios e regulação da natalidade', *Itinerarium* 10 (1964), pp. 156—89.

J. Snoek, C.SS.R., 'Problemas de Moral matrimonial (III)', *Revista Ecclesiástica Brasileira* 24 (1964), pp. 715–19.

N. Gonzáles, S.J., 'Población, familia, natalidad', *Razón y Fe* 171 (1965), 519–24.

J. Mz. DE Lahidalga, 'La regulación de la natalidad y la Iglesia catolica, hoy', *Lumen* 14 (1965), pp. 24–49 (cf. particularly pp. 40–9).

A. Mondria, S.J., 'Normas de moral para el uso de los anovulatorios', *Sal Terrae* 53 (1965), pp. 378–81.

H. Apocada, C.M.F., 'El problema pastoral numero uno: limitación de natalidad', *Illustración del Clero* 58 (1965), pp. 408–52.

A. Peinador, C.M.F., *El problema moral del matrimonio*, Madrid, CoCulSa, 1965, pp. XV–205.

P. E. Charbonneau, 'Carta aberta aos teólogos sóbre um problema do mundo moderno', *Limitação dos nacimentos*, São Paulo, Livraria Duas Cidades, 1965, pp. 13–97. The second part of the pamphlet (pp. 98–127) contains a treatise on progestational drugs written from the medical point of view by Dr J. R. DE Freitas AZEVEDO. The 'open letter' of Charbonneau appeared in a French translation in the Canadian review, *Perspectives sociales*, and was reprinted in the little volume, *Lettre ouverte aux théologiens* . . . , Paris, Les Editions Ouvrières, 1966.

Silva Soares writes immediately after Pope Paul's speech and, after having expounded the traditional doctrine and the new possibilities suggested by Janssens, he declares he cannot find that the asserted moral equivalence between the use of the pills and the choice of the 'safe period' has been fully demonstrated, but he refuses to consider the former as a contraceptive means in the traditional sense: with it, in fact, the 'structure and the intention' of the conjugal act are respected, for this act must be 'the incarnation and expression of the total and mutual self-giving of the husband and wife'. As regards the accusation of mutilation, the author seems to think that this is not direct sterilization, at least in the case of treatment with progestational drugs, which, administered during a period of ovarian repose, serve to prolong this period rather than to suppress the recurrent ovulations.

The other articles are of a more general character and show that their authors have not yet made up their minds: Snoek considers the question still open and considers that Paul VI left it open, although he did not sanction the application in practice of the new theories. Gonzales, after a brief and clear account of the reasons for and against (especially of the reasons in favour of some modification of the traditional teaching) concludes that 'the problem is indeed most intricate' and it is not surprising that it finds no rapid solution in spite of the labours and the competence of the group of theologians who are studying it. For de Lahidalga it is a case of a 'working hypothesis, still in a period of preparation', put forward by a 'very respectable minority'. Mondria, after summarizing the (certainly or probably) licit uses of the pill, does not consider the 'new tendencies' reliable or capable of being put into practice, but he does not condemn them; he rather expresses the hope that they will be further elucidated. Apocada, although the most unwilling to express approval, also leaves the question open.

A contrary attitude is shown by the authors of two brief monographs. The eminent Spanish moralist Peinador dedicates most of his little volume to the confutation of the theses of Reuss and Janssens, whom he is not afraid to accuse of causing confusion and of being ignorant of the most elementary notions of natural law, of the traditional doctrine and of the decisions of the Magisterium. This is not surprising if we consider the premise he puts forward as indisputable, that is, that man has no power over his own body but is simply its custodian, according to God's providential plan as seen in the general framework of bio-physiological laws.

Profoundly moved by the present tragic urgency of the problem, the *Open Letter* of Charbonneau (a Canadian missionary priest in Brazil) begins by explicitly accusing traditional morality of ignorance of the actual facts underlying the problem, but in spite of the somewhat iconoclastic nature of the first pages the author then restricts himself to indicating the reasons he considers to justify the use of the pill and the ligature of the Fallopian tubes: and his arguments are largely based on the writings of Janssens, Reuss, Weber and van der Marck.[16]

We now come to the contributions in the English language. It is difficult to define the position assumed by *The Clergy Review*, which published some very brief views for and against.[17] In Ireland O'Callaghan expresses a clearly permissive opinion, and believes that, although it seems unthinkable that the Church should alter its teaching on contraception in general, nevertheless, after the new studies about this subject, the doctrine of Pius XII on the pill might be modified:

> D. O'Callaghan, 'Changes in Catholic teaching', *The Irish Ecclesiastical Record* 102 (1964), pp. 398–403. 'Pius XII's norms on birth control', *ibid.*, 103 (1965), pp. 178–81.

[16] We have not included in this list of Spanish and Portuguese literature, the article by E. RUIZ AMEZCUA, S.J., 'Las substancias antigametogénicas ante la regulación de la natalidad', *Christus* (Mexico) 29 (1964), pp. 666–78; in fact, although it was written in August that year, the aricle shows no sign of any knowledge of the new trend. Therefore the author (relying on pontifical doctrine) stoutly asserts that every contraceptive use of the pill is illicit direct sterilization; he approves only of those interventions, which he is inclined to think indirect, already discussed in previous years (those intended to regularize the cycles, to correct a functional sterility, during lactation and in the premenopause period, etc.).

[17] In fact here we can see, first of all, the usual moral standpoint of L. L. McREAVY, always decidedly against the new trend, not only as regards the general problem of direct sterilization ('Sterilization as a preventative against dangerous pregnancy', *ibid.* 49 (1964), pp. 633–6; 'Termination of fecundity by removal of womb', *ibid.* 59 (1965), pp. 59–61), but also as regards any possible justification of the pill (cf. 'Significance of doctor's note for supply of contraceptive pills', *ibid.* 50 [1965], pp. 225–6) which he excludes even in the case of cyesophobia ('A misconception about direct sterilization', *ibid.* 50 [1965], pp. 56–9), but not so categorically during lactation ('Hormonal deficiency in lactation and the pill', *ibid.* 50 [1965], pp. 385–7). The review also published some unanswered letters sent to the Editor, like that quoted in Note 7, which suggest a possible revision of verdict at least on the question of progestational pills (cf. 49 [1964], p. 775; 50 [1965] pp. 68–9, 648); and, which is more important, it publishes, as we shall see, two articles which accept the hypothesis of a legitimization not only of progestational treatment (anti-ovulatory in purpose) but also of other contraceptive measures: F. H. DRINKWATER, 'Ordinary and universal', *ibid.* 50 (1965), pp. 2–22; M. DUMMETT, 'The question of contraception', *ibid.* 50 (1965), pp. 412–27.

The American group, however, is decisively against the new trend. Both Connell and Lynch, now supported by two new contributors, De Pauw (in an American review) and Guindon (in a Canadian review) deny any intrinsic probability to the new opinions. The arguments they put forward are not new and are restricted to asserting that the anovulant use of the pills is a deliberately sterilizing and contraceptive act, condemned by Pius XII.

> F. J. Connell, C.SS.R., 'Delaying ovulation', *The American Ecclesiastical Review* 151 (1964), 408–9; 'The confessor and the pill', *ibid.*, 152 (1965), pp. 141–2.
> G. A. De Pauw, J.C.D., 'The pill controversy. What is the position of Fr Janssens?', *Homiletic and Pastoral Review* 64 (1964), pp. 747–54.
> R. Guindon, O.M.I., 'Réflexions d'un moraliste sur la fécondité humaine', *Revue de l'Université d'Ottawa* 34 (1964), pp. 137–63 (of special interest pp. 155*–8*).[18]
> J. J. Lynch, S.J., 'Notes on Moral Theology: The Oral Contraceptives', *Theological Studies* 26 (1965), pp. 254–67.

A discordant note is however struck in Cardegna's long article, in support of Janssens' theme:

> F. Cardegna, S.J., 'Contraception, the pill and responsible parenthood', *Theological Studies* 25 (1964), pp. 611–36.

This Jesuit considers that it is obvious that the doctrine of Pius XI and Pius XII 'concerning contraceptives which destroy the essential structure of the conjugal act' is 'so profoundly rooted in the teaching of the Church as to render improbable, if not impossible, any alteration'. Nevertheless he does not

[18] This article also, like the above mentioned articles by Dayez, Martelet and Rendu, was written in French, but not in France. Two other French articles, which we have not yet seen, must be mentioned: S. Pierre, O.P., 'Le philosophe et la pilule', *Maintenant* 35 (1964), pp. 333–4; C. De Koninck, 'La régulation des naissances', *Perspectives sociales* 19 (1964), pp. 92 ff. The latter author, a doctor member of the Pontifical Commission for the family and births, was co-author with M. Dionne of a cyclostyled pamphlet, *Le problème de l'infecondité*, which was circulated privately in 1965. De Koninck supported the new thesis, basing his opinion on a study of the 'natural' processes of infertility which are present as well as those intended to cause fertility in due time: there is, therefore, an 'intelligent' rhythm which man may assist, with more calculated consequences, by means of oestroprogestational treatment.

appear convinced that the use of anovulants must be included in
this condemnation, and considers it possible that there may be
some revision in this respect; indeed he considers that Paul VI
left the question open. Certainly, from the moral point of view it
is hard to distinguish between the pill and other methods: he
himself recognizes this, and frankly tries to prove and establish
a distinction. Nevertheless he still hopes that 'the use of the
pill as proposed by Janssens may be permitted by the Church at
least as a probable theological opinion which may be put into
practice'.

We now reach the end of this third chapter, which had to deal
with the rise and gradual affirmation of a totally new trend of
thought concerning the problem of the pill and, more generally,
man's power of controlling his generative function for the sake of
responsible parenthood.[19]
The theologians still defending the traditional positions are
few: Lynch, Connell, De Pauw, McReavy, Zalba, Günthör,
Peinador, Martelet and Guindon. Other authors (some of whom
enjoy great prestige) still preserve an open mind about the question
or are definitely in favour of the new tendency. One must also

[19] Finally, we must add that in the course of the discussion on progestational
drugs which we have documented (for the years 1964–65) certain new appraisals
were apparent with regard to some of the arguments previously debated. We
refer particularly to the problem of the treatment of women with progestational
drugs as a legitimate self-defence when they have reason to fear a violent
assault or the imposition of an unwanted and unreasonable sexual activity.
There are some articles devoted *ex professo* to this problem. We list them in
chronological order. A. Fz. DIAZ-NAVA, S.J., ('Anticonceptivos: un caso de
licitud?', *Sal Terrae* 52 (1964), pp. 92–5) approves of legitimization in this
case, as he sees therein merely 'a new application of the principle of the total
good'. E. BOISSARD, O.S.B., writes at more length ('Valeur morale d'un certain
cas de stérilization temporaire', *Angelicum* 41 [1964], pp. 167–209). He is
replying to Bender's article, which we have already discussed and which has
appeared in the same review. For Boissard an intervention in such a case would
be an 'indirect' sterilization, since 'this is not desired in itself or for itself, and
the two results (sterility and immunity from danger) are immediate results
of the drug'. It is moreover indisputable (and here the author relies chiefly
on the teaching of St Thomas) that 'one may will an act which, *materially*
speaking, may be described as mutilation, sterilization, suicide, etc., on condition
that this act be undertaken for a healing, liberating or preserving purpose, etc.
and that it is this good purpose only which is the object of the will'. In reply
to Boissard, P. LUMBRERAS, O.P., ('Controversa sterilisatio, directa aut indirecta?',
ibid., pp. 370–9) considers that the Benedictine, basing his argument only on
the intention of the act, has not sufficiently demonstrated the indirect nature

point out that in the course of the debate the arguments put forward by the traditionalists have been no more thoughtful and profound than previous arguments on this matter and have rarely replied directly to the innovators.

It must also, however, be pointed out that almost all the 'permissive' theologians, whether still undecided or definitely favourable to the new positions, affirm an essential moral distinction between anti-ovulatory treatment and those contraceptive measures which violate the integrity of the conjugal act, and they deny, sometimes very energetically, any possible justification of these latter. But will this opposition last much longer? Or will the logic of the arguments lead to a re-examination of all the methods used? In fact, as we have already indicated, two of the innovators, Reuss and van der Marck, have already begun to set out the terms of such a revision. This is not surprising when one remembers that, during these recent years which we have been considering, there has developed, alongside the new tendency with regard to the pill, an even more radically new and revisionistic outlook with regard to the problem of other methods.

This is what we must now try to document, and it will be necessary temporarily to retrace our steps.

of this sterilization; nevertheless, referring to Hürth's distinction between absolute and relative sterilization, he leaves the question still open as to whether all direct sterilization, or merely indirect sterilization, must be considered illicit.

Finally, a decided opinion in favour of the new theses is offered, in an article written chiefly to contradict Navarro's theory on the same subject, by M. BRUNEC, S.D.B., *De liceitate usus mediorum anticonceptivorum in casu praevisae violationis*, Rome, P.A.S., 1964, 84 pp. (cyclostyled).

Some articles which we have already reviewed devote a few pages to this subject although it does not constitute their main theme. Cf. the brief article by L. L. McREAVY, 'The Dutch hierarchy on marriage problems', *The Clergy Review* 40 (1964), pp. 113–15, in which the English moralist expresses the same opinion as Hürth and Zalba (see note 9). An interesting position is taken up by R. GUINDON, O.M.L., in the article we have already referred to, in which he rejects the theses of the new theological trend on progestational drugs ('Réflexions d'un moraliste sur la fécondité humaine,' *loc. cit.* pp. 158*–162*): he considers, however, that a woman may legitimately defend herself against the consequences of a sexual assault by rendering herself sterile by the use of progestational drugs ('the female organism', he writes, 'is not a laboratory which anyone may make use of to initiate the biological process of fertility . . . . and a woman has the duty to see that her organism may serve this purpose only within the context of the conjugal act') and he recognizes this right also in the case of a married woman whose husband wishes to impose 'clearly unreasonable conjugal intercourse' upon her.

IV

THE DISCUSSION ABOUT
OTHER CONTRACEPTIVE METHODS

WHILE the debate on the pill was being so heatedly conducted theologians were also discussing, with less public clamour, a much more radical question regarding the permissibility of contraceptive measures which interfere with the conjugal act itself (for example, the various mechanical or chemical forms of prevention). In fact, some theologians were asking whether the well-known affirmations of the Encyclical *Casti connubii* of Pius XI, confirmed by Pius XII's *Speech to the Italian Midwives* on October 29, 1961, were to be considered as absolutely irrevocable,[1] or whether perhaps there might be some re-examination and modification of this official doctrine of the Catholic Church.

[1] We quote the famous words of Pius XI: 'Turning now, Venerable Brethren, to treat in detail the vices which are contrary to each of the blessings of matrimony, We must begin with the consideration of offspring, which many nowadays have the effrontery to call a troublesome burden of wedlock—a burden which they urge married folk carefully to avoid, not by means of a virtuous continence (which is permissible even in marriage with the consent of both parties) but by vitiating the act of nature. This criminal abuse is claimed as a right by some on the ground that they cannot endure children, but want to satisfy their carnal desire without incurring any responsibility. Others plead that they can neither observe continence nor, for personal reasons or for reasons affecting the mother, or on account of economic difficulties, can they consent to have children.

'But no reason whatever, even the gravest, can make what is intrinsically against nature become conformable with nature and morally good. The conjugal act is of its very nature designed for the procreation of offspring; and therefore those who in performing it deliberately deprive it of its natural power and efficacy, act against nature and do something which is shameful and intrinsically immoral.

'We cannot wonder, then, if we find evidence in the Sacred Scriptures that the Divine Majesty detests this unspeakable crime with the deepest hatred and has sometimes punished it with death, as St Augustine observes: "Sexual intercourse even with a lawful wife is unlawful and shameful if the conception of offspring is prevented. This is what Onan, the son of Juda did, and on that account God put him to death" (St. August., *De conjug. adult.*, lib. ii, n.12. Cf. Gen. xxxviii, 8–10, S. Poenitent., 3 April, 3 June, 1916).

72

The first doubts arose in the years 1961–63, but they came to the fore for the first time in a lecture given by Fr Schillebeeckx and published towards the end of 1963. In the two following years general discussion began, chiefly among Dutch, German and Anglo-American authors, while at the same time, as we shall see in the next chapter, its repercussions and effects were noticeable even in the Council.

I. *The first doubts* (1961–63)

Certain theological doubts about the Catholic position with regard to the traditional contraceptive technique appeared first of all in some articles which sought to establish a new theoretical basis, no longer starting from the standpoint of the intrinsic procreative purpose of sexuality but showing that contraceptive practices frustrate that full mutual integration of which every coitus should be the sign and substance. This is the line followed, with some references to suggestions from other sources, in a very authoritative article by de Contenson which appeared at the beginning of 1962:

A Renewed condemnation

'Wherefore, since there are some who, openly departing from the Christian teaching which has been handed down uninterruptedly from the beginning, have in recent times thought fit solemnly to preach another doctrine concerning this practice, the Catholic Church, to whom God has committed the task of teaching and preserving morals and right conduct in their integrity, standing erect amidst this moral devastation, raises her voice in sign of her divine mission to keep the chastity of the marriage contract unsullied by this ugly stain, and through Our mouth proclaims anew: that any use of matrimony whatsoever in the exercise of which the act is deprived, by human interference, of its natural power to procreate life, is an offence against the law of God and of nature, and that those who commit it are guilty of a grave sin' (Pius XI, *Casti Connubii*, nos. 53–56, C.T.S.).

In his turn Pius XII affirmed in his speech of 29 October 1961: 'Our predecessor Pius XI, in his Encyclical *Casti Connubii* of 31 Dec. 1930 once more solemnly proclaimed the fundamental law of conjugal acts and intercourse: that every interference, on the part of the married couple, with the conjugal act itself or the development of its natural consequences, an interference intended to deprive this intercourse of its own inherent procreative capacity and so to prevent the generation of a new life, is immoral; no "excuse" or necessity can change an intrinsically immoral action into one that is moral and legitimate. This directive is as binding today as it was formerly, and as it will be tomorrow and for ever, because it is not a precept of human law but the expression of a natural and divine law' (Pius XII, *Speech to the Catholic Union of Italian Midwives*, 29 October 1951: *A.A.S.* 43 (1951) 843).

P.-M. DE Contenson, O.P., 'Fécondité, bonheur et morale', *Revue des Sciences Philosophiques et Théologiques* 46 (1962), pp. 3-44.[2]

While recognizing the grave difficulties encountered by Catholics who seek to justify the condemnation of all artificial means of birth control the author points out that their trustful obedience to the teaching of the Church is prompted by reasons 'of a nature which suffices to give this obedience a certain intrinsic rational value'. This reason is not the necessity of 'paying a purely superstitious respect' to a biological process (the biological order does not by any means have absolute value in Catholic moral teaching, even in other sectors than that of sexuality) but the necessity of preserving in conjugal intercourse its ability to express in the highest possible degree the mutual love of husband and wife. Now, 'although capable of arousing, nourishing and expressing a certain kind of human love, which is not to be despised, these maimed and sterilized acts nevertheless irremediably restrict the human capacities of those who resign themselves to their use', and 'because of the very fact that they are deprived of one of their purposes, and the most profound of these, they cannot even fully accomplish that other purpose (of expressing mutual love) which it was thought could be achieved in this way and which seemed to justify these acts'. That is why 'the

[2] The previous studies referred to by the author are particularly those by P.-M. QUAY, 'Contraception and conjugal love', *Theological Studies* 22 (1961), pp. 18–40 and by B. SIMONET, 'Réflexions sur l'enseignement de l'Eglise', *Cahiers Laennec* 21 (June 1961), pp. 18–28. (The April and June numbers of this review deal with birth control, and were republished in a book, *La régulation des naissances*, Paris, Lethielleux, 1961, which includes the above-mentioned article, pp. 153–71). But DE COTENSON refers particularly to the reflections put forward by PAUL RICOEUR in his comments on the replies concerning contraception sent in by various authors (the most important of whom was S. DE LESTAPIS, S.J.) in the course of an enquiry into sexuality initiated and published by *Esprit* 28 (1960), pp. 1904–19. In fact the French philosopher here suggests the hypothesis that the condemnation of means of birth control is justified by the necessity of safeguarding sexual activity in its full significance as a mutual integration between two persons (this condemnation, he says, is 'the only objective safeguard capable of preserving the nobility of the sexual act'), but he draws the conclusion that one must not get involved with over-subtle distinctions and the 'frequently sordid arguments about means' and considers that the 'teaching of the Catholic Church may possibly be susceptible of revision'. As far as we know, this is the first time this possibility was voiced (not, however, by a theologian) in a Catholic publication.

Church believes she cannot include contraceptive acts among the measures she proposes to her faithful for the regulation of their lives'.

The principles then are unchanged but are supported by a presentation of doctrine different from that seen in *Casti Connubii;* and obviously this new presentation of doctrine makes it difficult to draw a precise and peremptory demarcation line between the licit and the illicit. [3]

These initial uncertainties about the rational validity of Catholic doctrine on contraception were followed by others concerning the possibility of basing the doctrine upon biblical and patristic writings. Dubarle wrote two articles on this theme:

A.-M. Dubarle, O.P., 'La Bible et les Péres ont-ils parlé de la contraception?', *La Vie Spirituelle. Supplément* 63 (1962), pp. 573–610; 'La contraception chez Saint Césaire d'Arles', *ibid.*, 67 (1963), pp. 515–19.

With regard to scriptural doctrine the French Dominican examines the story of Onan (Gen 38 : 9–10), the only biblical text which mentions a contraceptive act. Dubarle asserts, however, that it contains no condemnation of contraceptive measures in

---

[3] A confirmation of this trend could be seen shortly afterwards, even in the brief articles on the problem of the 'regulation' of births, published in *Recherches et Débats* (June 1963), pp. 13–44, two of them written by the Jesuits S. DE LESTAPIS and L. BEIRNAERT. DE LESTAPIS offers an interesting justification of the use of periodic continence, dwelling on its effectiveness in 'gradually transforming itself into a control of love and into an almost spontaneous appreciation of the true character of conjugal love' (p. 39); BEIRNAERT, who asserts that condemnation of contraceptive measures must be accompanied by an encouragement given to married couples to seek a more profound understanding of their marriage and to safeguard 'the quality of their sexual union' (p. 42), goes on to suggest that 'the present opposition between family planning by means of contraceptives and the doctrine of the Church may be overcome'. He says that the Church's final intention is, by teaching a mature control of the sexual instinct, to safeguard 'the value of sexual intercourse apart from procreation' (pp. 43–4). We get the same impression of the difficulty of tracing a clear line of demarcation between licit and illicit means, based on the significance of the conjugal act as personal mutual integration, when we read the treatise by D. VANDENBERGHE, *Verantwoorde vruchtbaarheid, Voor een dialoog met de niet-Katholieken*, Brussels, Scheut-edities, 1963, pp. 115, although it accepts (pp. 83 ff) this new way of proving the illegitimacy of contraceptive measures.

themselves.[4] Certainly, he concedes, it was not merely his failure
to fulfil his levirate obligations which deserved the death sentence:
in fact, for this failure the law prescribed a much less severe
penalty (cf. Deut 25 : 7–10); but neither was it merely his contraceptive deed for which, in fact, the bible specifies no punishment.
Onan was punished by God for his 'perfidious fraud': in fact
he could not legitimately consent, according to the levirate
custom, to marry his sister-in-law (who moreover was not at
liberty to marry anyone she wished) and then to refuse to fulfil
that procreative obligation which alone legitimized the union. It
is therefore not contraception in itself which is condemned, but
contraception deliberately effected in the case of a levirate union,
which imposed upon the man the duty of procreation:[5] the fact
that the law contained no prohibition of this kind 'leads us to
suppose that the wickedness of Onan, in the eyes of the biblical
narrator, consisted in the sterilization of conjugal intercourse in
what was no ordinary union'. More generally, the biblical doctrine
on marriage, which Dubarle summarizes in his conclusion,
assigns to the husband and wife the twofold duty of mutual love
(also through physical union) and of generating and rearing
children; but it links these two factors together without being
concerned with their co-ordination in case of tension or conflict.[6]

In examining the teaching of the Fathers of the Church the
Dominican scholar divides it into three categories. The first

[4] The condemnation is supported, however, in the two monographs on the
story of Onan which Debarle had read: J. B. SCHAUMBERGER, 'Propter quale
peccatum morte punitus sit Onan?', Biblica 8 (1927), pp. 209–12, and C. F.
DE VINE, 'The Sin of Onan, Gen 38: 8–10, Catholic Bibl. Quart. 4 (1962),
323–340; the latter writer considers that Onan's sin was, at least secondarily,
his failure to accomplish his duty in a levirate marriage. Dubarle mentions
also the interpretations of the various biblical commentaries on Genesis, none
of which, however, is based upon a special study of this subject.

[5] In the same way—Dubarle explains—David's census displeased God who
therefore punished Israel (cf. I Chron 21:7, which resembles Gen. 38:10),
not because in itself and by itself his sin deserved this punishment (in fact,
the bible mentions several occasions when a census was not condemned:
Num. 1–3; Esra 2; Neh. 7) but because of the particular circumstances in
which the king had ordered it, that is, for a non-religious organization of the
army and a secularization of the holy war.

[6] These more general considerations on the themes of love and fertility in
the bible were reiterated and more closely studied by the author in an article
which appeared between the two we are examining: 'Amour et fécondité dans
la Bible', Recherches et Débats 43 (June 1963), pp. 105–21.

category includes the patristic writings which, contrary to expectation, make no mention of this subject: certain texts condemn the various forms of self-indulgence or speak of the procreative duty without ever mentioning contraceptive measures (the Didache, the Letter of Barnabas, Clement of Alexandria) or make some comments on the story of Onan but without referring to his contraceptive act (St Ambrose, St Cassian, Theodoret of Cyrrhus). Then come those texts which contain doubtful testimony: some concern Onan, but the judgment they express is merely generic or too involved (Origen, Zeno of Verona, Ephraem); sometimes condemnation is clearly expressed, but it is not equally clear whether this is of contraception or of abortion (texts of Hippolytus, Chrysostom, Isidore of Pelusium); finally, some formulate principles whose application to contraceptive devices is not explicitly referred to (this is especially true of St Jerome). The third group consists of St Augustine and St Cyril of Alexandria, the only writers who express 'downright condemnation' of contraceptive practices. Augustine expresses it in two passages in which he is speaking of *coitus interruptus*, with an explicit reference to Onan, and of sterilizing drugs, which he seems to distinguish from drugs which procure abortion. His condemnation is pronounced in the name of a doctrine which sees in procreation the only fully legitimate purpose of conjugal intercourse (and this doctrine leads him also to reject, in other passages, a procedure which corresponds to the present day method of periodic abstention); Cyril expresses his condemnation more briefly in a passage in which, with reference to Onan, he asserts that he 'violated the law of coitus': his general views on marriage and sexuality are equally pessimistic.[7]

The conclusion, therefore, which Dubarle reaches in his first article, is that in biblical and, even more, in patristic teaching there is no clearly elaborated doctrine on contraception intended as the solution of a moral and pastoral problem which had been explicitly stated with regard to married people: the texts which might be quoted as referring to this are very few and moreover

---

[7] The two passages from St Augustine are: *De coniugiis adulterinis*, II, 12: P.L., 40, 479, C.S.E.L. 41, 396 (the text quoted also in *Casti Connubii*), and *De nuptiis et concupiscentia*, I, 15, 17: P.L., 44, 423–24, C.S.E.L., 42, 230. The passage from St Cyril of Alexandria is in *Glaphira in Genesim*, bk. 6: P.G., 69, 309A.

D

inspired by concepts of sexuality and marriage which have for long been superseded. The first Father who expresses himself openly and explicitly on the subject is St Caesarius of Arles (to whom Dubarle dedicates his second brief note): in four passages in his Sermons he severely condemns contraceptive practices, but he is referring only to the use of potions which were considered capable of preventing pregnancy. It is, however, important to notice the reasons for his condemnation, which is not motivated by an objective consideration of sexuality and marriage (concerning which Caesarius shows the same pessimistic attitude as St Augustine) but justified by the assertion that those sterilizing practices constitute a real attempt at homicide which suppresses the possibilities of a life desired by God, and also a form of magic denoting an idolatrous or superstitious attitude. Caesarius also shows an excessively conservative concept of the fixed order of the created world, which he thinks man must respect as it stands. The good bishop, in the same context, even condemns the use of potions intended to procure for a barren woman the fertility she desires.

Challenged both in its speculative justification and in its biblical and patristic sources, the Catholic doctrine on contraceptive measures associated with the conjugal act was finally attacked also in the support it received from the Magisterium, and this attack came in an article by Schillebeeckx.

> E. Schillebeeckx, O.P., 'De Natuurwet in verband met de katholieke huvelijksopvatting', *Werkgenootschap van katholieke theologen in Nederland Jaarboek* 1961, *Voordrachten en discussie*, Hilversum, 1963, pp. 5–51 (pp. 51–61 contain an account of the discussion which followed Schillebeeckx's lecture).[8]

In fact, the article surveys a much wider field. First it examines the general problem of the variability of moral principles, pointing out that although 'truth itself' (which in the last analysis is God)

---

[8] It is clear that this article, although not published until 1963, had been the subject of a lecture to the Congress of Dutch theologians in 1961: in fact it is dated September 1960. The last part, dealing with the natural law (pp. 36–51), was republished by the author in the second volume of his *Theologische Peilingen* (transl. into French: *Approches théologiques:* II *Dieu et l'homme*, Brussels, Ed. du Cep, 1965, pp. 228–47).

is immutable, yet the avenues by which we approach truth may vary. These variations, which are the inevitable consequence of the relative and approximate character of the knowledge at our disposal, do not produce an unacceptable moral relativity. This would be unavoidable if we considered truth from one single point of view, but it can and must be avoided by trying to approach truth as closely as we can from various angles. This must be done also in the case of the doctrine on marriage: the various points of view from which it was considered, in the history of Christian thought, do not exhaust the possibilites of interpretation; above all, it would be a partisan and 'conceptualist' attitude which led to one of these standpoints being taken as absolute. It is particularly necessary to understand the present-day anthropological standpoint where marriage is concerned, for from this standpoint, instead of considering it in its individual moments, man tries to grasp it in all its complexity as a 'full union of personal life' with its two dimensions of 'mutual responsibility for the personal existence of the two partners and a shared responsibility for the personal existence of the children'.

This very personal point of view makes it even more difficult to accept what is called a 'physical' concept, by which we mean that traditional concept which endows the biological structures of an action with a moral sanction—and this is the point in which we are most keenly interested, and which the Dutch theologian develops in the second half of his article. Biological nature as such cannot constitute an ethical norm: biology merely offers us the biological possibilities of sexuality, 'in which, however, the spirit must be incarnated in a human way, and this means ordered according to a moral principle'. And it is this 'humanization' of biological possibilities which must be at the basis of a moral judgment: we must ask ourselves whether and to what extent these may be expressed in copulation considered as a human action, which must draw its guiding principle from a consideration of all the anthropological elements present.

This is precisely the problem which the teaching authority of the Church tried to solve with an affirmation which, although not an *ex cathedra* declaration, must have been considered by Schillebeeckx as binding, for he asserted that copulation may not be frustrated in its biological purpose of procreation. But what is meant by copulation? Is it the individual physical action, considered in itself, or is it copulation considered as part of human sexual activity in the light of a total anthropological concept? There is no doubt that the particular conjugal act is the object of the moral judgment, even of that of the Magisterium, only in the latter sense. Therefore may we not understand the ecclesiastical condemnation of contraceptives not as referring to every copulation but only to the fundamental purpose of procreation of which every individual copulation is simply a moment? Naturally the Church may extend its condemnation also to the 'individual participatory act', but so far it cannot be said that she has done this, because her condemnation 'did not yet recognize the distinction between the life purpose and the individual act'. That extension might yet be made by theologians, but in that case it is valid only in so far as it is proved, and the responsibility for it is theirs alone, not that of the Church as a whole.

These preliminary studies had the effect of arousing discussion of the Catholic doctrine of contraception and its various theological bases: the rational basis, the biblical and patristic sources and the teaching of the Church. The question which the three Dominicans were putting to moral theologians was quite clear: was that teaching to be considered definitive, or was it, because of some flaw in its theological foundation, to be subjected to a more careful scrutiny, and possibly to a revision? The problem had now been stated and more numerous and decided interventions were soon to appear.

II. *The Flemish-Dutch group*

An article which appeared at the beginning of 1964 in the review *De Maand*, written by the Belgian couple, Herman and Lena Buelens, but edited in collaboration with other 'Catholic intellectuals' and theologians, constituted the first important step towards a 'new outlook'. These new considerations—according to an editorial note in the review—'have now reached a high degree of maturity, reasonableness and diffusion, so that now they can and must find expression'.[9]

[9] Other contemporary interventions by Belgian and Dutch authors express the same or analogous considerations and demonstrate the present state of diffusion of the new theses: A. MARKS, 'Gedachten over de bron van het menselijk leven', *K. Cathol. Artsenblad* 43 (1964), pp. 60–76; J. J. G. ALBERT,

H. and L. Buelens-Gijsen, 'Verkelijkeid en formulering in de huwelijksleer, *De Maand* 7 (1964), pp. 129–40. The article appeared also in *R. Kathol. Artsenblad* 44 (1965), pp. 39–46 and an edition in various languages was prepared in 1964 by DO-C.

According to these authors, in order to judge methods of birth control it is not enough to appeal to 'centuries old definitions about the purposes of marriage'; one must incorporate into the Christian doctrine the elements which emerge from 'the reality which is itself new, that is, the need for some regulation'. Otherwise one would arrive at the paradoxical conclusion that 'the method which seeks to avoid the procreative effect of an act may not be considered to be morally licit unless it respects the procreative character of the act in question'. There are four main elements now available for the formation of a doctrinal judgment on these practices. First of all there is the 'active role' which man now sees he must play in the natural world, a role which consists not so much in respectful conservation as in enhancement and promotion. This is particularly true because 'the present-day demographic problems are only a direct consequence of the creative and controlling work of man in the natural world (hygiene, social organization, etc.)', and so it would seem that one cannot condemn as unnatural the successive human interventions undertaken to correct the 'population overflow' which has now been produced; moreover the 'immutability of nature' is no longer accepted by moral theologians in other spheres, in which they now recognize man's much more active control over his own bodily existence and that of others. Another element is the concept of fertility, which now automatically implies the notion

'Huwelijksontwerp en anticonceptionalia', *Te Elfde Ure* II (1964), pp. 89–116. As an example of the co-operation between theologians and lay people we mention a 'report' published in 1963, shortly before the Buelens' article and showing some points of resemblance: *Huwelijk en Gezin*, Amersfoort, 1963, edited by E. SCHILLEBEECKX, O.P. with the collaboration of TH. BEEMER, J. A. HUYGEN and C. J. STRAVEN; we have not yet been able to see the essay by TH. BEEMER, *Huwelijksmoraal en geboorteregeling*, Adelbert, 1964, 68 pp. Finally, also from Belgium, comes the interesting and very forward-looking article by Dr A. KRIEKEMANS, 'Note sur la famille comme phénomène complet de la sexualité', *Saint Luc médical* 36 (1964), no. 4, pp. 1–10. References to these various works may be found in a book written by another Dutch doctor: A. C. M. LIPS, *Mens zijn in het Huwelijk*, Roermond, Romen and Zonen, 1965, 320 pp. (recently transl. into French: *Mariage épanouissement humain*, Mulhouse, Edit. Salvator, 1967, 325 pp.).

of control, and also that of a resultant educational need. A positive
value is now assigned to 'controlled procreation' for which full
responsibility is assumed'—and 'there is no longer any reason to
feel a contradiction of principle between birth control obtained
by suitable means and the duty of procreation'. In the third
place, there are now new physiological data at our disposal from
which we may learn that most conjugal intercourse is without
any 'natural' relation with procreation. Man no longer considers
the conjugal act as essentially procreative and may even, when
necessary, deprive it of this capacity which, in fact, it effectively
lacks most of the time. Finally, we cannot deny that modern
man's way of thinking is closer to the actual facts and more
constructive, and therefore must influence his concept of reality:
in particular, with regard to birth control, a more practical
viewpoint tends to minimize the present distinctions between
methods which prevent fecundation, whether temporal or
spatial techniques, hormonal preparations or mechanical barriers
are used. A more constructive attitude towards the ethics of
procreation diverts the attention from individual conjugal acts to
conjugal intercourse in general: hence the extreme difficulty of
admitting the culpability of those married people who use
contraceptives but whose lives have shown a generous capacity
for parenthood.

Taking these new elements into consideration, 'modern man
naturally sees fecundity as the general purpose of marriage; in
all conscience and reasoning quite objectively, he does not see
that it must be the purpose of every single conjugal act of union'.
Consequently, the various methods of birth control cease to have
that primary importance which they must inevitably assume
when the duty of procreation is imposed upon every individual act.
This does not mean that there is no longer a moral problem:
there is the question of procreation in general, which obliges the
husband and wife to exercise deliberate self-control for the sake
of their mutual and unselfish love; there is also the question of
the techniques employed which, even if no longer judged by their
conformity with a 'natural order', must still be judged by the
light of the many human interests involved: 'physical and spiritual
health, the peaceful relations between husband and wife and the
harmony of their family life'.

On the other hand, the necessity of safeguarding in its 'natural' integrity the conjugal act itself cannot be based upon the need to express their mutual love: 'this would be just as unjustifiable as believing that the natural integrity of the act was sufficient in itself to attest real conjugal love'. As with procreation, so also with love it is the total expression which must be considered. The form assumed by a single conjugal act 'cannot be invested with the dignity of an absolute value in itself'; indeed, in serving to express a relationship of love, sexuality seems to be even more flexible than in its capacity as a means of procreation. The new doctrinal tendency to insist upon this reason for preserving the formal integrity of the act unwarrantably transforms a spontaneous desire into an indispensable ethical requirement, and attempts to codify 'a subject which is least capable of being so treated'.

Buelen's considerations, as we see, do not start from a positive theological standpoint but are based on purely theoretical grounds. Two Dutch articles, however, which appeared shortly afterwards, approached the problem from the standpoint of biblical thought, and analysed the traditional doctrine.

A. Hulsbrosch, O.S.A., 'Norme etiche della vita matrimoniale. Note storiche e suggerimenti teorici', in DO-C, 1964, no. 160. This original article has been published in various languages by DO-C.

R. S. Callewaert, O.P., 'De middeleeuwse biechtboeken anti-conceptionele praktijken', *Tijdschrift voor Theologie* 4 (1964), pp. 254–74; French tr., 'Les Pénitentiels du Moyen Age et les pratiques anticonceptionelles', *La Vie Spirituelle. Supplément* 74 (1965), pp. 339–66. See also A. Valsecchi, 'I libri penitenziali e la morale cristiana. Alcuni studi recenti', *La Scuola Cattolica* 94 (1966), pp. 260*–8*.

Basing his remarks on an anthropological concept much nearer to biblical thought, Hulsbosch puts forward some moral principles concerning marriage. He starts from the concept of man found in holy scripture, which does not try to define his essential elements from the abstract point of view (the soul as the form or acting subject, the body as the matter or object of action) but seeks instead to consider him, in existential terms, as a subject in which body and soul are operating in unity. From this point of view even the sexual act is no longer an object already unalterably fixed in its physical structure, which the person must respect as an indispensable requirement, but is a human gesture of which even the physical structure is formed anew every time according to the needs of that relationship of love which constitutes its supreme law. Moreover, a step is taken in the new direction when, as has happened with regard to periodic continence, it has been judged possible to admit the value, for the sake of the personal welfare of the married pair, of a sexual act which is incomplete as regards its 'natural' process of procreation. The consequences of this new attitude 'portend on the one hand an enhancement of the value of human sexuality and on the other hand a more relativist interpretation of the natural law with regard to the law of love'. In particular, whereas it is true that the intercourse of a husband and wife reaches its perfection when it completely expresses their mutual love besides respecting the natural order, it must also be added that this latter has only a relative value in relation to love: 'for the sake of love it may become necessary to violate the natural order of sexuality and therefore the use of contraceptive means, although contrary to the natural law, may be permitted in particular cases'.[10]

A more thoughtful analysis is made by Callewaert in his study of the references to contraceptive practices which occur in the

[10] From the point of view of an exegetic scholar is written the article by P. ANDRIESSEN, O.S.B., 'De Zonde van Onan', *Bijdragen* 25 (1964), pp. 367-77. This author considers Onan's sin to have consisted precisely in his profanation of the conjugal act: even the expression 'displeasing in the sight of the Lord' is more applicable to Onan's act than to his motive; in any case the mere failure to fulfil the levirate obligation does not explain why divine punishment did not strike down Juda, for example, although he also had failed to obey that law. On the other hand, we must record that E. SCHILLEBEECKX, O.P., in his lengthy and careful theological study, *Het Huwelijk: aardse werkelijkheid en heilmysterie*, Bilthonen, H. Nelissen, 1963 (publ. in English by Sheed and Ward, 1965) had asserted that Onan's sin consisted merely in his having acted against the interests of his tribe, and these interests 'are the foundation of all Old Testament conjugal moraility and constitute the supreme law for all sexual behavour'.
We must mention another contemporary work: A. HULSBOSCH, O.S.B., 'Theologische reflectie op de huidige belevingsvorm van seksualiteit en huwelijk, Samenstelling der ondervraagde groep echtparen', in *Veranderd gezinsontwerp. Een bijdrage tot het gesprek over geboorteregeling*, Hilversum, Paul Brand, 1964, pp. 145-95. In this book the author develops some concepts similar to those of the DO-C article, but based in particular on information received from twenty-six Catholic married couples: he observes that there is 'no other theological field in which the layman has as much competence as he has in this field of conjugal morality'.

Penitentials: the author consulted forty of these, from that by Viniano (sixth century) to the Decree of Burchard of Worms (1008–1012), and their attitude is presented as influenced by that of the Fathers of the Church, especially by the doctrine of St Caesarius of Arles, which the Redemptorist once more studies in the articles of Dubarle mentioned above.

Explicit references to contraceptive practices first appear in the European Penitentials of the eighth and ninth centuries: earlier Penitentials had referred only to abortive measures, which were punished according to whether the foetus was considered to be inanimate or already animated, whether the abortion took place within marriage or after adultery or fornication, with the attenuating excuse of the mother's poverty or solely with the intention of concealing her immoral conduct. As for contraceptive measures, on the other hand, only one text (the Penitential of Saint-Hubert) records and punishes the *coitus interruptus* with an explicit reference to Onan's misdeed. The silence of all the other Penitentials, especially if we bear in mind the very minute scrutiny to which they subjected sins against the sixth commandment, is considered by Callewaert to be a sign that the conduct in question (certainly not unknown to those peoples) seemed less immoral then than now. In fact, the particular reasons for condemnation which apply, as we shall see, to other contraceptive practices are not applicable to this procedure.

These other practices seem to have consisted of the use of herbal potions in order to prevent pregnancy, and they are always condemned. However, Callewaert observes, it would be a mistake to accept this condemnation as it stands today, for it is always based upon theological, anthropological, sociological and medical presuppositions which our present-day teaching does not accept. First of all, the condemnation is pronounced as part of the general objection to magical and idolatrous practices and its significance is substantially conditioned by this context. No one today would dream of accusing a Christian husband and wife of idolatrous or magical practices simply because they have recourse to contraceptive measures: on the contrary, it is presumed that they are acting in a spirit of prudence, faith, responsibility and mutual love. In the same way one must now consider as destitute of all natural and theological basis the equivalent treatment which the Penitentials deal out to contraception, abortion, infanticide and homicide, as if all these were equally sinful—and indeed this constitutes the fundamental reason for their condemnation. We must add two other generic differences between their fundamental attitude and our own with regard to this problem: their concept of sexuality implies that its sole function is procreative, so that they condemn all conjugal intercourse between a husband and wife who are permanently (because of old age) or temporarily (because of pregnancy) incapable of procreation. Still more generically, their anthropological concept implies that man, like all the rest of creation, is 'a natural thing given as such' which cannot be tampered with in any way. This is the same reason, obviously unacceptable to us, why the Penitentials condemn with equal severity also the use of potions to remedy a woman's biological sterility.

Finally, towards the end of 1964, a book by van der Marck, which reiterated and expanded the considerations he had already expressed in his article of the year before, offered the first systematic exposition of this subject and, nearly a year later, a lecture delivered in Rome by the Dominican Father Schillebeeckx (which was published soon afterwards) reviewed the problem once more:

W. van der Marck, O.P., *Liefde en vruchtbaarheid. Actuele vragen over geboorteregeling*, Roermond, Romen, 1964, 90 pp. The English translation is *Love and fertility. Contemporary questions about birth regulation*, London, Sheed and Ward, 1965. See also J. Snoek, C.SS.R., 'Para uma revisão da Moral matrimonial', *Revista Ecclesiástica Brasileira* 25 (1965), pp. 89–91.

E. Schillebeeckx, O.P., 'I mutamenti nelle concezioni dei Cristiani sul matrimonio', IDO-C, doss. nos. 66, 4–5, (13 April 1966).

Compared with his earlier article this new study by the moral theologian of Nijmegen contains nothing very new in its first two chapters, which provide the historical and theoretical background for the discussion on 'love and procreation' which is the subject of the third. We find the same historical account of the discussion from 1952 to 1964, with the obvious exception of the latest moves which the 1963 article could not foresee; identical in their substance are also the 'general considerations on the human act' which appear in the second chapter. They set out to prove that the human act is a single phenomenon to be judged morally only by its intention, which is not added to it but actually constitutes it and gives it its significance. It is therefore easy to guess the already well known conclusion which van der Marck, at the beginning of his third chapter, deduces with regard to the various methods of birth control: each of these owes its human significance to its imminent intention, which makes it an 'act regulating births', which therefore must be judged according to its proper criterion (whether or not it corresponds to the requirements of responsible parenthood); but here, departing from the sense of his earlier article, the Dutch Dominican no longer endows the sexual act with that 'anthropological and sacramental significance' which he had previously invoked in order to assert the necessity of preserving its integrity: all the contraceptive methods used by a husband and wife are, without distinction, 'regulatory acts' which are all equally permissible when contained within the limits of a Christian sense of responsible parenthood. Certainly the ideal matrimonial life is that of a fully procreative love, without reserves or restrictions, but this ideal must be capable of realization by individuals whose response can only be 'perfect according to their situation': no method therefore can be presented as the ideal expression of procreative love (not even periodic continence or the pill). It is for every married couple to decide which 'compromise' in any particular case least impairs the integrity of conjugal love, which is always a love expressed carnally. Physiological integrity cannot therefore be exalted as an absolute criterion for the sexual conduct of a married couple.[11]

[11] Another Dutch moralist, a Professor at the Redemptorist Scholasticate of Wittem, reaches the same conclusions, but is less categorical in his judgments, expressed in a more general study of the problem of 'compromise': C. A. J. VAN OUVERKERK, C.SS.R., 'Morale évangelique et compromis humain', *Concilium* 5 (1965), pp. 13–25. After the publication of his treatise van der Marck retraced its fundamental lines in a lecture he gave to a meeting in November 1964 at Nijmegen, which was published later: 'Moraaltheologische aspecten', in *Optimale nataliteit. Problemen rond geboorteregeling*, Utrecht-Nijmegen, Dekker und van de Vegt, 1965, pp. 122–38: here he affirms even more clearly that 'there is no real reason for asserting that the sexual-genital activity of a married couple may only be a biologically perfect sexual union. Everything which in this respect is really capable of perfecting their communion is by definition good, because good is simply a brief word to express all that creates communion.' See F. J. HEGGEN's review of the whole volume in *De Nieuwe Mens* 17 (1965–1966), pp. 11–35.

Schillebeeckx's lecture, which reiterated some points of his article, already reviewed, reached the same conclusions after producing a daring historical synthesis of Christian conceptions of marriage. This synthesis leads him to suggest that the idea that the biological structure of sexuality, with its intrinsic procreative purpose, is the absolute moral norm 'is unknown to the Fathers of the Church and to St Thomas Aquinas himself: for them it was not formally biological purpose but human dignity which was to be the objective norm or guiding principle of Christian marriage'. This is obvious where the Fathers are concerned: if they condemn non-procreative sexual union it is not because this frustrates the biological purpose, but because such a union is used merely for a pleasure which, being largely instinctive and irrational, is considered (according to their Hellenistic way of thinking) to be unworthy of man. The dignity of man is also the criterion referred to by St Thomas: he considers sexual activity to be good in itself, being a 'gift of nature' (the incidental pleasure having no other moral significance than that of the natural act which produces it), but in order that this 'gift of nature' may be worthy of man it must be preserved in all its generic animal elements, that is in its bodily function. In fact, its generically animal character, according to the apostolic conception and the Porphyrian logic then fashionable, must have precedence over its specifically human character. We still have here therefore the fundamental principle by which sexual conduct is to be judged: the dignity of man. But, this Hellenistic or Aristotelian conception having been superseded, we have now understood that man's dignity consists in his capacity to 'decide for himself' and to include his corporeal functions also in this slow laborious process of control. Looked at in this light, sexual activity too must submit to a similar process of progressive 'humanization', and this is only possible when it is understood as the 'sign and expression of love between husband and wife'. Naturally this includes also the biological possibility of procreation, but man 'cannot find any absolute value in biological structures as such'. They 'condition' his activity—they do not constitute its norm. They present a 'capacity which may be used' according to the manifold needs of the married couple's obligation to work for their own and the common welfare; they are not a necessity to which the man and wife must inevitably submit, for such submission would dehumanize their union. Therefore, the control of the natural biological structures of sexuality, for the sake of the welfare of persons, may be an act of 'humanizing nature', provided that the contraceptive measures used 'are employed within the fundamental purpose of a fertile marriage (a fertility worthy of man) and do not violate the mutual incarnate love of the husband and wife'.

III *The German group*

Shortly after the intervention of the Buelens a new direction was given to the problem of contraceptives, chiefly by the attitudes assumed by the review, *Theologie der Gegenwart*, and by Mgr Reuss; other writings soon followed.

An article by the Jesuit J. David, which appeared in April–June of 1964, sought to find a new point of view for the consideration of the problem of birth control, and initiated a discussion which attracted other contributions in the same review.

> J. David, S.J., 'Zur Frage der Geburtenregelung. Versuch eines neuen Ansatzes', *Theologie der Gegenwart* 7 (1964), pp. 71–9. Idem, 'Zu den neuen Theorien der Ehepraxis', *ibid.*, pp. 217–31 (contributions by G. Ermecke, R. Hofmann, U. Ranke, Heinemann, G. Teichtweier, J. G. Ziegler, and a reply by J. David).[12]

The author reaches two fundamental conclusions, which he expounds more than once. The first is that 'the purpose of procreation belongs to the sexual life considered in its entirety, not necessarily and directly to every individual act': nature herself separates procreation from the act, suggesting in this way to man also that he has the power to obtain the same results by his own interventions; in this case, moreover, the act still remains

[12] The two articles appear, respectively, in the second and fourth numbers of the quarterly review. The third number also published some studies on the subject under discussion, the article by L. M. WEBER, to which we have already referred, and that by J. M. REUSS, which we shall deal with shortly. The review *Theologie der Gegenwart*, edited by the philosophical and theological Scholasticate of the Redemptorists at Gars am Inn, is directed by the Redemptiorists V. SCHURR, B. HÄRING and H. STENGER. The first article, by FR DAVID, editor of the review *Orientierung*, was signed with the intitials J. D., 'in order not to direct the discussion' (according to an editorial note) 'to the person of the author, but exclusively to the thesis and its arguments'. A presentation of the focal points of his thought, in the context of the discussions then taking place, may be seen also in his review: A. SUSTAR, 'Schwerpunkte der Diskussion um die heutige katholische Ehemoral', *Orientierung* 28 (1964), pp. 261–4.

indirectly and directly in the service of procreation, inasmuch as it serves that conjugal mutual love within which the procreative function is fulfilled. This is, in fact, the permanent significance of the individual act of copulation (and this is the second conclusion which David repeats insistently). Unlike copulation among animals, it 'has among men not only the purpose of procreation, but also that of realizing and deepening conjugal love, and it is just as important for the personal welfare of the man and the woman as it is for procreation'.

For this reason, the immediate moral principle governing the single act is not 'its generative capacity' but its 'power to enable husband and wife to acquire a greater knowledge of each other, and to express their union and love', a power which—as may be attested by psychologists, anthropologists and particularly by married couples themselves, much more validly than by theologians—is in no way diminished by the use of contraceptive measures.

These statements, the German Jesuit admits, certainly conflict with those of Pius XI and Pius XII, but he adds that one must recognize that 'in spite of the authoritativeness of papal doctrine, the question has never been considered as definitely resolved or submitted to responsible scientific investigation', and 'very many of the faithful and even many theologians, who were first of all inclined to an obedient attitude, have tried very hard to accept this doctrine but without any inner conviction'. In conclusion, 'when a husband and wife are determined to respect all the essential purposes of marriage, and fulfil these in due time in a responsible manner, and when the individual sexual act is not separated from the matrimonial context, that is, not undertaken as a merely animal act but in the interests of their marriage, of its real harmony and of mutual understanding, of their love and fidelity and their shared aspirations, then its subordination to both natural desire and the purpose of marriage seems quite surely safeguarded: this conduct is worthy of man and responsible, even when the individual act, because of a natural impediment or because of a deliberate and responsible human intervention, is infertile'.

The article was 'open to discussion' as the author said in his concluding words, and this discussion appeared in the same review in the last issue of the year.

Of the various contributors only Ermecke is opposed to David's views, although he declares himself to be convinced that 'the present doctrine of the Church with regard to marriage permits of further developments, but without contradicting the declarations already made which are absolutely clear and binding'. He considers the German Jesuit's primary mistake consists in having 'minimized the matrimonial doctrine of the Church, which is not confined to the Encyclical *Casti connubii*'. More particularly he is to blame for having considered the conjugal act in isolation, as distinct from the totality of the various good purposes which it must serve, thus 'arriving at the impossible conclusion that every copulation, in whatever way it is effected, is morally permissible provided that it fosters conjugal love'. Nor should it be said that man may do in a rational manner what nature does in her own way, for 'nature causes the death of the innocent also . . .'. The need for coitus should not be exaggerated, as it is when considered 'from a prevalently emotional and subjective viewpoint', for even from a personalistic point of view marriage is seen to be also a 'communion of self-denial and sacrifice' and, according to the Christian interpretation, a means of perpetuating Christ's sacrifice on the Cross. Many of our modern difficulties may instead be solved by 'interpreting and enlarging the so-called principle of the total good', which would permit (and not only for therapeutic motives) the procuring of conditions of temporary or definitive sterility in which coitus has no procreative effect, as long as this respects the requirements of the integrity of conjugal intercourse. This is the suggestion favourable to oestro-progestational treatment which we have already seen put forward by the moralist of Paderborn.

The other contributors, however, agree with David: we mention the most important. For Hofman, of the University of Freiburg, the responsibility for procreation may not be unilaterally restricted to the individual conjugal act and to its completion 'according to nature': and even less so when this 'natural way' is erroneously deduced from prevalently biological premises. To generate a human being is much more than merely to repeat a physical process: it is a task which occupies the husband and wife for the whole of their married life, and the part played in it by sexual activity goes far beyond the phenomenon of biological fertility which it may produce. Other principles must be sought to prove the virtue of the coital act, bearing in mind that the individual conjugal act is only a 'single factor' in the husband and wife's experience of procreation and love and therefore it is not necessary that it should always be totally realized in its capacity of serving fertility or love. As for the declarations of *Casti connubii*, 'they must be understood and interpreted in the context of that period': 'they served, perhaps in the only way then available, to ward off the attacks which were threatening to destroy the greatest values of marriage'.

The well-known moralist of Passau, Teichtweier, [13] was also in favour of David's position: in fact it seemed to him the only one capable of fully justifying the approval granted by Catholic teaching to the method of periodic continence. If the same viewpoint (the responsibility for parenthood being assigned not to the single conjugal act but to the marriage as a whole) may be used to justify other contraceptive methods besides that of the sterile period, then this conclusion must be arrived at only 'after profound reflection and discussion by all the scientific bodies concerned with this problem'. Nevertheless, 'even if a positive solution to this question is found', there will have to be 'a long, prudent, discreet training of consciences, to direct them clearly to the irremovable obligation of procreation, in order that the new doctrine may be applied with the hoped-for success in the lives of individual married couples'.

Finally, a revision of the present-day teaching of the Church about marriage is considered necessary by Ziegler, of the University of Mainz, especially because this teaching is based, not so much on revealed truth and on the unanimous conscientious opinion of the Church, 'as on ethical systems and medical knowledge which originated in ancient and pre-Christian times'. Moreover, the 'Copernican revolution' which must initiate this doctrinal re-examination came 'with the distinction introduced in 1951 by Pius XII between regulation of births and birth control'. David also pointed out these new factors, the only ones, according to the moral theologian of Mainz, which are capable of providing a 'justifying principle' for the method of periodic continence.

[13] See also his interesting work: *Eheliches Leben heute* (Veröffentlichungen des Bischöflichen Seelsorgeamtes Passau), Passau, Verlag Passavia, 1963. We shall shortly be speaking of J. G. ZIEGLER's well known historical study: *Die Ehelehre der Pönitentialsummen von* 1200-1350, Regensburg, Pustet, 1956.

Moreover, if procreation may be excluded from the conjugal act in the inner purpose of the husband and wife, it is hard to see why it cannot be excluded from their external conduct by the use of any contraceptive method which is not shown to be 'unequivocably evil in itself'. There is, however, one aspect which, in Ziegler's opinion, makes David's solution provisional and not definitive: this is the subordination, in sexuality and in marriage, of the personal function of mutual integration to the social function of procreation, whereas a more balanced interpretation ought to consider these two functions, and the religious function too (according to which marriage is the image of divine love) as 'three dimensions inseparably joined and integrated'.

These were the replies to David's article, to which he added some final conclusions of his own. While admitting that the reflections offered in the discussion were 'not yet matured', he declared himself once more convinced of the validity of his thesis, and congratulated himself on 'not having received any admonition from his superiors'. His purpose had been, on the one hand, to consider the conjugal act as an 'integrating part of the marriage' and, on the other hand, to recognize that it had 'a value of its own for the development of personality and the perfecting of the conjugal union'. Now he is led to this final conclusion by an examination of Catholic teaching which, having already for some time past asserted the permissibility of conjugal intercourse between sterile partners, has now justified the deliberate choice of infertile days and is moving towards the approval of other contraceptive measures such as the pill. Therefore it is always worth bearing in mind the possibility of 'a new conception of conjugal intercourse as a means of expressing, demonstrating and fostering love between husband and wife'. This does not mean that the exercise of the sexual instinct must not be regulated by objective principles. First of all, its effective purpose in marriage, being procreation according to God's will, must always be safeguarded and then all sexual intercourse must be 'worthy and genuine', with all that this implies of mutual respect, spiritual dominion and sense of responsibility.

The other important German debating point was the position personally assumed by Mgr Reuss, Auxiliary Bishop of Mainz.

We have already referred to his previous statement (December 1963) in favour of treatment with anovulatory drugs for the purpose of a responsible regulation of fecundity. Now two new contributions come from his pen, and they extend the permissive judgment to other contraceptive measures as well.

> J. M. Reuss, 'Hinweise zur pastoralen Behandlung der Fragen um Ehe und Elternschaft', *Theologie der Gegenwart* 7 (1964), 134–9; French tr., 'Suggestions pour une pastorale des problèmes du mariage et de la fécondité,' *La Vie Spirituelle. Supplément* 72 (1965), pp. 5-12. Idem, 'Nochmals zum Thema: "Eheliche Hingabe und Zeugung". Eine Antwort an P. Anselm Gunthör O.S.B.', *Tübinger Theologische Quartalschrift* 144 (1964), pp. 445–76.

The first article (July–September) is devoted mainly to pastoral questions: he does not, therefore, wish to make any particular contribution to the doctrinal problem as to whether 'every intervention in biological and physiological factors and processes is to be considered as illicit and contrary to nature', but only to show 'how it is possible to help married couples in the fulfilment of their conjugal task in conformity with the will of God'.

The two general directives which the spiritual director must always recommend to Christian couples are, first of all, that their married life must be founded on a mutual love inspiring all its manifestation and, secondly, that they must know that they have a duty to procreate which they may not avoid, and which they must carry out with a sense of full responsibility.

In reconciling love and fecundity, when the husband and wife can (temporarily or finally) have no other children, the first authorized solution to suggest is that of the choice of the infertile period. It is not right to recommend as already authorized the various forms of intervention in the biological and physiological processes related to the conjugal act, but nevertheless it is impossible, if questioned, to disguise the fact that there is a difference of opinion in the Church about this subject, also because it would be unwise to imperil the good faith of those who know that these problems are already discussed.

If, finally, the only possible solution is continence, the married couple must be persuaded to accept this in such a way that it does not impair their union of love but may even make it more

profound. In any case, to a husband and wife who do their best
not to fall into sin, but sometimes fail, one must say that 'it is at
least doubtful whether their sin is such as to prevent their being
in a state of grace', and that therefore they may partake of holy
communion even without having received the sacrament of
penance. However, when later on they go to confession they
should be encouraged to admit these failings also, not only in
order to become more resolute and loyal to their obligations but
also in order that they may receive that sacramental grace for the
growth of their union with God which is bestowed upon them
even in a 'devotional confession'.[14]

In the second article, however (October–December), in which
Mgr Reuss replies to the criticism which Fr Günthör, as we have
seen, had directed at his former article, the subject is more
doctrinal and for this reason, too, the viewpoint is further widened.

Reuss is here particularly explicit, also in his reply to Günthör,
in his examination of the teaching of the Magisterium on the
subject of birth control. This teaching, as is the case with some
papal declarations, not pronounced *ex-cathedra*, may not only
be considered as 'neither definitive nor immutable' but—which is
even more significant for the problems under consideration—
may be seen to contain a certain contradiction between the
declared permissibility of periodic continence and the declared
illegitimacy of any other contraceptive measure either before or
during copulation. Now, when we reflect on the former of these
two declarations, we see that it involves a revision of the second. In
fact, in the deliberate choice of infertile days the actual purpose
of the husband and wife is to enjoy copulation precisely because
it is infertile (and this is 'much more than merely accepting and

---

[14] A similar tolerant attitude had been suggested, in the preceding year, by
C. Bouchaud, P.S.S., 'Eléments de théologie morale', in *Sexualité et limitation
des naissances* (Recherches et Débats, no. 43, June 1963), pp. 58–67. Here such
tolerance is seen as a positive, if temporary, step towards the ideal solution;
even more clearly is this permissive attitude shown, during the same year, by
Canon P. de Locht, *La morale conjugale*, Brussels, Centre Nat. de Pastorale
familiale, 1964, fifth Conversation, in which the author explicitly proposes
contraception as a solution which, although in itself faulty, is the best that
can be found now, given the many varied values to be reconciled ('in this case
to assume the attitude which in all conscience, and with all the generosity
required, seems to us the least unsatisfactory, that is, the best possible, may be
a valid and unblameworthy, or even a wise, decision'). As we shall see, this
trend of thought was to have other followers.

making use of the fact that procreation is impossible, as Günthör maintains'). If, therefore, the procreative purpose does not characterize copulation in such a fundamental way as to make its exclusion illicit, it cannot be invoked as the criterion for a judgment on its moral honesty: nor will it be illicit to have recourse to other contraceptive measures, for their intention is just the same as that of periodic continence. Nor is it possible to distinguish between interventions which are preparatory to intercourse and interventions during its course, once the 'question of principle' has been resolved. It is only necessary that 'the method chosen to render the copulation infertile serves also the purpose of expressing the union between man and woman'. The decision as to which methods 'leave intact their mutual self-giving as a manifestation of their love' is a task much more suitable for the psychologist or the sociologist than for the theologian, and above all, bearing in mind their personal qualities, most suitable for the married couple themselves.[15]

[15] These new interventions by Reuss met with a reply from A. GÜNTHÖR, 'Zum derzeitigen Stand moraltheologischer Diskussionen über Ehefragen', *Seminarium* 17 (1965), pp. 347–63. After expounding Reuss's thesis, Günthör warns his readers of the danger that an exclusively pastoral study of a problem may result in less fidelity to moral principles, and that excessive attention to personal values may lead to forgetfulness of the objective needs of human nature. The Roman theologian admits that Reuss's criticism of the traditional teaching would be valid if he had considered the primary end of copulation to be actual procreation. But he considered it to be the 'capacity to procreate', so that it is clear that the choice of infertile days, which he says respects this capacity, *aptitudo* (but in what sense can this be true, if it aims at rendering the coitus infertile?), is licit and that other contraceptive measures which destroy this capacity are illicit.

Shortly before Günthör's reply, Reuss had been answered in another article, written in German by his fellow-citizen J. KRAUS, Professor at the University of Mainz: 'Inkonsequenz der seitherigen kirchlichen Ehemoral? Kritischer Beitrag zur Diskussion um "Eheliche Hingabe und Zeugung" ', *Freiburger Zeitschrift für Philosophie und Theologie* 12 (1965), pp. 96–119. He considers that in the notion of the end or purpose of the conjugal act (*finis operis*) the act refers to the coitus itself and by the 'end' of the act is meant the result of the act when it is faithfully carried out, with respect for the laws of nature. Thus the *finis operis*, the immanent purpose of copulation, when effected according to nature, requires the 'transference of the spermatozoa': to deprive it of this objective end means depriving it of its immanent content, its specific nature, and is therefore an intrinsic moral disorder

GÜNTHÖR and KRAUS are, as far as we know, the only German writers who adopted a decidedly negative attitude to the new trend during the years 1964–65: in fact, the article by DEMMER, mentioned above (pp. 62), dealt only with oestroprogestational treatment, and ERMECKE, also already referred to (pp. 89), is at least inclined towards the acceptance of this last method of birth control.

Thus initiated by the review *Theologie der Gegenwart* and carried on by Mgr Reuss, the debate on contraceptive techniques was continued in more articles, favourable to the new attitude, in the German language towards the end of 1964 and in 1965.

First of all there were articles written by Böckle, Bruch and Schöllgen:

> F. Böckle, 'Verantwortliche Elternschaft: Zur inner-kirchlichen Diskussion um die Geburtenregelung', *Wort und Wahrheit* 10 (1964), 577–86; 'Grundlagen der moraltheologischen Beurteilung', *Fragen der Geburtenregelung (Schweizer Rundschau. Monatsschrift fur Geistesleben und Kultur*, March–April 1965), pp. 176–87.
>
> R. Bruch, 'Die naturgesetzlichen Grundlagen der Lehre vom abusus matrimonii in moraltheologischer Betrachtung', *Theologie und Glaube* 55 (1965). pp. 23–49.
>
> W. Schöllgen, 'Erwägungen zur Geburtenbeschränkung', *Der Seelsorger* 35 (1965), pp. 88–101.

The position of the first of these writers is already partly known to us, since we reviewed it when discussing the question of the pill. But we must admit that the eminent theologian of Bonn tends (as is, moreover, obvious in the bibliographical review in *Concilium*, of which we shall speak shortly) to deny any real difference between interferences with the procreative function in general and contraceptive measures used during the conjugal act itself: in any case he considers these contraceptive measures all equally justifiable when judged from the point of view of a more personalistic conception of marriage and, more generally, of a more human and historically based conception of 'nature' and 'natural law'.

In fact, a brief historical survey of the 'natural' foundation for the doctrine concerning the 'abuse of matrimony' is offered by Bruch, of the University of Graz, who indicates its limitations and the necessity for superseding them. The statement that every contraceptive intervention is against nature is, even in St Thomas' doctrine, derived from the philosophical and scientific notions of his age, which on the one hand consider the intrinsic purpose of the genital organs to be reproduction of the species, and on the other hand consider the man's seed to be 'potential man'. This doctrine, especially as expressed by Tomaso Sanchez (who adds to it his own idea of the illicit 'waste of seed' that would occur in contraceptive practice) is accepted by the moralists of the seventeenth and eighteenth centuries and, in the nineteenth century, reappears even in certain replies given by the Roman Congregations. But Bruch considers that 'natural' foundation for the doctrine to be unacceptable. Sexuality cannot be presented simply as a reproductive function, and even less can one hypostatize the seed which it produces. Indeed in this matter nature appears to proceed according to a 'principle of waste', for she achieves her procreative aim at the cost of innumerable useless acts. Once more it is the definition of copulation as 'an act in itself conducive to the expression of love' which the author insists upon, in order better to understand the 'natural' meaning of sexuality.

Similar observations are put forward by Schöllgen, Professor of Moral Theology at the University of Bonn. Physical nature itself, in human reproduction, is not guided by a principle of maximum economy but by one of maximum extravagance. Moreover, it has its own automatic controls which in particular circumstances suspend or prevent the generative function. Why then, should not man be permitted to control this natural system, by means of his own knowledge and for his own wellbeing? In fact he is not the passive custodian of nature, as Tertullian believed, but, according to the Thomist conception, its promoter and controller. It is true that certain contraceptive practices modify the union between the husband and wife, but the 'one flesh' desired by scriptural doctrine is not to be understood merely in a physical sense.

As we see, the basic arguments for the new position now tend to follow more or less the same lines. So from the pages of the theological reviews they spread to the books concerned with marriage and married life which are now being published or re-edited. In these the new attitude is re-examined and put forward as at least permissible in the framework of a more general Christian doctrine on marriage. We note in particular the books by Scherer and Weber, but we must also quote the most recent work by Doms, which re-elaborates the theory he has already put forward, that the primary purpose of matrimony and of the sexual act is unity between husband and wife, and starting from this theory it is more easy to approve of the new solutions suggested concerning the problem of contraceptive practices:

G. Scherer, *Ehe im Horizont des Seins. Zu einem neuen Verstän dnis der Sexualität*, Essen, Verlag Hans Driewer, 1965, especially the third chapter of the second part (pp. 172–225: 'Liebe und Fruchtbarkeit').

L. M. Weber, *Ehenot-Ehegnade. Handreichung zur priesterlichen Heilssorge an Eheleuten*, Freiburg im Breisgau, Seelsorge-Verlag, 2nd ed., 1965, especially chapters IV–V (pp. 47–116: 'Lösungsversuche zur Geburtenregelung' and 'Sonderfragen'). By the same author, see also the 2nd ed. of his well-known book: *Mysterium magnum. Zur innerkirchlichen Diskussion um Ehe, Geschlecht und Jungfräulichkeit* (Quaestiones disputatae, 19), Freiburg-Basle-Vienna, Herder, 2nd ed., 1965.

H. Doms, *Gatteneinheit und Nachkommenschaft*, Mainz, M. Grünewald, 1965, pp. IX–145. This is not the right place to discuss Doms' classic and weighty volume *Vom Sinn und Zweck der Ehe*, Breslau, Ostdeutsche Verlagsanstalt, 1935 (English translation: *The Meaning of Marriage*, London, Sheed and Ward, 1939).

IV. *The English language group*

The English language group included a number of lay thinkers, even more numerous than those in Belgium and Holland, who added their contributions to those of the professional theologians, but the Anglo-American writers were much more divided in their opinions than the Dutch and Germans, and there was more lively opposition to the new trend.

In America it was a layman, the philosopher L. Dupré of the University of Georgetown, who initiated the discussion with two articles, later published in book form; in the meantime another American layman, C. G. Grisez, of the same university, stoutly defended the traditional doctrine:

L. Dupré, 'Towards a re-examination of the Catholic position on birth control', *Cross Currents* 14 (1964), pp. 63–85; 'From Augustine to Janssens', *Commonweal* 80 (1964), pp. 336–42. The book in which the two articles re-appeared was: *Contraception and Catholics. A new appraisal*, Baltimore-Dublin, Helicon Press, 1964, 94 pp.

C. G. Grisez, *Contraception and the natural law*, Milwaukee,
The Bruce Publishing Company, 1964, 245 pp. The author
expounds his theories again in 'Reflections on the contraception
controversy', *The American Ecclesiastical Review* 152 (1965),
pp. 324–32, and in *Contraception—is it always wrong?*, Hunting-
don, Our Sunday Visitor, 1965.

This second volume, which was greeted with approval by
theologians also,[16] follows a well-trodden route: procreation,
with its essential concomitant of education, is one of the fundamental values of human life which it is not permissible to oppose
directly, especially when the intervention concerns the procreative
act itself. Grisez also disapproves of the new tendency to exalt
and subjectivize copulation as a necessary expression of love;
with an intelligent education and the aid of grace there may be
preserved, within marriage, a chastity which, in a well ordered
mutual self-giving of the husband and wife, in service to their
children and their social obligations, may render them capable
of real sexual control, without the recourse to contraceptive
measures. Dupré instead follows the other line of thought. First
of all he observes that the question cannot be said to have been
irrevocably decided by the teaching authority of the Church,
especially if we consider its insufficient biblical-patristic foundation (here the American philosopher quotes from Dubarle);
moreover, the traditional doctrine contains some ambiguities
(here he quotes from Janssens' article on progestational drugs).
He also points out that once any contraceptive measure has been
declared permissible (as has been done in the case of periodic
continence and as is being done in some cases with the use of the
pill) there is no longer any serious reason for excluding the
others: between one automatic method of preventing conception
and any other, at least when coitus is not interfered with (and this
is true even of methods using the diaphragm, vaginal douche or
a spermicidal substance) there no longer emerges any clear
distinction.

[16] Cf for example: J. G. MILHAVEN, 'Contraception and Natural Law: a recent
study,' *Theological Studies* 26 (1965), pp. 421–27; R. A. McCORMICK,
S.J., in *The American Ecclesiastical Review* 153 (1965), pp. 119–25. An interesting
critical analysis, from the point of view of a philosopher, is that of G. E. M
ANSCOMBE, 'Contraception and natural Law', *New Blackfriars* 46 (1965),
pp. 517–21.

Lay writers mingle with professional theologians also in the book edited and introduced by Archbishop T. D. Roberts, S.J., who puts forward an impressive case for a change in the Church's teaching on contraception: the book came out towards the end of 1964, but was published in several editions and in many translations:

> *Contraception and Holiness: The Catholic Predicament.* A symposium introduced by Archbishop Thomas D. Roberts, New York, Herder and Herder Inc., 1964, 346 pp. Successive editions were published by William Collins and Sons, London.

Besides Abp Roberts, who in the Introduction refers to what he had already written for the review *Search* and insists particularly on the irrationality of the Catholic position and its limited views on sexuality, three other theologians contributed to this book.

Stanley E. Kutz, C.S.B., Professor of Moral Theology at St Michael's College, Toronto, after some shrewd doctrinal observations on marriage as a vocation of love undertaken in the service of life, concludes that 'the bond between love and life is so strong and so spontaneous that any *arbitrary* separation of one from the other would surely seem to be unnatural'. Indeed, 'this indestructibility of the bond between love and life is the unchanging value which the Catholic teaching on the ends of marriage has sought to preserve and affirm, even if the ways in which this teaching was proposed have not always been the most adequate'. The conclusion to be drawn from this is that 'every sexual expression of marital love which is so planned or executed as deliberately to exclude the possibility of procreation will be experienced by the Christian married couple as a gesture of love which is less adequate than, ideally and in the abstract, they would wish it to be'. Nevertheless, man never lives in an ideal world and his actual condition is such that he must often try to find a temporary equilibrium between the many obligations which press upon him at the same time; in marriage, the choice of a contraceptive measure, even if in the abstract this is not an ideal solution, in practice may be accepted humbly and joyfully. It matters little that the coitus may no longer be biologically integral; besides considering the physical integrity of the act we have also to consider its significance in the total human and Christian

context of marriage. Moreover 'the real religious and moral
challenge of procreation in Christian marriage . . . cannot be
identified simply with the question of the licitness of various
means of contraception'. It must not be objected that this is
a conditional and relative ethical code, because here, too, there is
a decisive norm that is valid for all human conduct—the norm
of open and generous love.

A re-examination of the Catholic position (which 'has perhaps
not been catholic enough, in the sense of embracing the whole
reality of sex in marriage') is made by Kieran Conley, O.S.B.,
Professor of Dogmatic Theology at St Meinrad Seminary. The
fundamental basis of his position is the 'personalist' attitude of
Christian morality: even the morality of family life is based upon
the 'selfless response to God who calls us in and through the
persons we confront'. Seen in this light the principle of the total
good becomes much more widely applicable, and moreover
helps us to understand why the maxim 'the end does not justify
the means' is true only for those means which in themselves
destroy a personal good. Still more particularly, it helps us to
understand that the conjugal act has not only a procreational
purpose but also tends to increase mutual love and the development
of the personality. To refuse conjugal intercourse rather than use
a contraceptive device would seem like repelling one person's
approach to another, in which the will of God is much more
clearly seen than it is in the biological fact of periodic fertility:
moreover, it is natural for a man 'to use physical or chemical
means to attain the legitimate aim he sets for himself', provided
he uses them for the total good of the person.

Fr Gregory Baum, O.S.B., the most eminent of the contributors
to this book, the Director of the review *The Ecumenist* and a
Consultant to the Secretariat for Promoting Christian Unity,[17]
expresses the opinion that a change in the present attitude of the
Church is possible and even desirable. He points out, first of all,
that the 'ordinary' teaching of the Popes, which must be accepted

[17] A brief anticipatory summary of G. BAUM's article had already appeared
under the title: 'Is the Church's position on birth control infallible?', in *The
Ecumenist* 2 (1964), pp. 83–5. See also by the same author and expressing the
same ideas: 'Birth control and the Council', *Commonweal* 81 (1964),
pp. 280–87; cf. pp. 515–17, in which the Benedictine takes his cue from the
Council debate of 1964 which had just ended and reiterates his view; 'The
Christian adventure. Risk and renewal', *The Critic* 23 (1965), pp. 41–53.

with what theologians call an 'internal religious assent', has in the moral sphere a binding character 'not because it is necessarily a definitive statement of Christian truth but rather because it is a pastoral measure in proposing the safest solutions for grave and urgent problems'. This is also the case with the Pope's condemnation of contraceptive measures, which was certainly a directive necessary for the safeguarding of certain possibilites of conjugal life which would otherwise have been lost, particularly that of generous procreation freed from its ever recurrent temptation of hedonism. Nevertheless, it cannot be regarded as definitive, particularly because in the meantime the teaching office of the Church has itself admitted certain factors previously unknown: for example, the duty of responsible parenthood and (admitted in the legitimization of the 'safe period') the fact that sexuality has an autonomous value quite apart from its procreative purpose. Therefore, by changing its attitude to contraception, the Catholic Church would not be so faithless to herself as to become unrecognizable. Still less could she be accused of accommodating self-indulgence: sexual activity must always respond to the needs of true conjugal love, needs which are far more difficult to satisfy than the needs of mere 'fidelity to biological structures', and concerning which the choice of one or other contraceptive method is a question more of aesthetics than of ethics.

On the validity of the Church's teaching, in particular that of '*Casti Connubii*', concerning contraception, L. Dewart's article is the most significant contribution from a layman and the longest in the book. According to this author, the condemnation contained in Pius XI's encyclical has definitive validity only in this sense: copulation, as a 'matrimonial act' or 'use of matrimony' (the Pope's own expressions) may not be deprived of its natural generative power, which means that contraception is against nature because it deprives marriage of its essential good, that is, children. But the extension of this condemnation to every single contraceptive act would imply a concept of sexuality as exclusively intended for procreation, and this Pius XI did not teach. It would, moreover, have been out of place in a document written mainly for the purpose of defending the value of conjugal fidelity. This fidelity was understood in a positive sense as the mutual love of man and woman, proper to marriage only, in which it originates, and which in its turn completes and perfects the marriage. Certainly the Pope did not state what part sexual intercourse should play in marriage in view of this doctrine about conjugal fidelity being its own good end, and we may regret this silence. But this very indefiniteness prevents us from considering that the problem of the legitimacy of a single contraceptive act has already been decided in a negative sense. Therefore, as the author concludes, 'a hypothetical reformation of the doctrine should not be construed as a direct contradiction of the teaching of Pius XI in every aspect', but as a different . . . . conclusion drawn in the light of a fuller elaboration and a more thorough development of the same Christian dogma on marriage on the basis of which, and for the sake of the preservation of which, Pius XI issued the condemnation.[18]

The survey of the first American answers to the new presentation of the doctrine may be concluded with a quotation from the

[18] The other collaborators are: R. RUETHER ('Birth control and the ideals of marital sexuality'). J. PLEASANTS ('The Lessons of biology'), E. A. DAUGHERTY ('The lessons of zoology'), W. V. D'ANTONIO ('Responsible parenthood and the population dilemma'), E. R. BALTAZAR ('Contraception and the philosophy of process'), J. G. LAWLER ('On discovering natural law').

We must note that, before the appearance of Abp Roberts' volume, lay people and theologians in collaboration had produced the essays contained in the special number (5 June 1964) of *Commonweal* dedicated to the subject of 'Responsible Parenthood', but these writings present nothing particularly new. At the same time another work had appeared, written in collaboration by fifteen lay Catholics, all married: *What modern Catholics think about Birth Control*, New York, New American Library of World Literature, 1964, 256 pp. This book contains two remarkable articles, one by M. SULLIVAN (pp. 28–73: 'A history of Catholic thinking on contraception') which offers a somewhat incomplete history of Catholic thought on contraceptive methods, arriving at the rather hasty conclusion that a tradition which condemns contraceptive measures is really hard to find before the last thirty years; the other article is by M. NOVAK (pp. 109–28: 'Towards a positive sexual morality'), in which the author asserts that procreation is the purpose not of every individual conjugal act but of conjugal sexual intercourse as a whole, and that the sexual expression of love, when procreation is no longer desirable, may be effected equally well with the help of contraceptive means.

M. NOVAK was also responsible for editing *The experience of marriage*, London, Darton, Longman and Todd, 1965, 173 pp., containing the contributions of thirteen intelligent and experienced Catholic couples, which demonstrate the difficulty of the recourse to absolute or periodic continence; two couples declare themselves conscientiously convinced of the right to adopt other means besides the choice of the infertile period. An interesting review of the German translation, written by Dr. J. RÖTZER: 'Zur periodischen Enthaltsamkeit', *Theologie der Gegenwart* 9 (1966), pp. 224–7, shows, however, that the criticism levelled by these rather ill-informed American couples against the method of periodic continence was without any medical foundation.

Jesuit sociologist, J. L. Thomas, who also favoured the legitimization of contraceptive methods, starting from the consideration
that 'what is procreative is not the single instance of sexual
intercourse but what may be called the whole process of sexual
relations':

> J. L. Thomas, S.J., *Catholic viewpoint on marriage and the family*,
> Garden City, Doubleday and Co., 2nd ed., 1965, 200 pp. (cf.
> especially pp. 101–37); 'The church and responsible parenthood',
> *Theology Digest* 13 (1965), pp. 255–68. The author had already
> indicated his views in his article: 'Marriage and Sexuality:
> the Catholic position', published in the volume already referred
> to (p. 10), *The problem of population. Moral and theological
> considerations*, ed. D. N. Barret, University of Notre Dame
> Press, 1964, pp. 42–57.

Meanwhile the discussion had moved from America to England.
The first important contribution was a brief essay by the Dominican Fr H. McCabe, written in November 1964:

> H. McCabe, O.P., 'Contraceptives and Natural Law', *New Black-
> friars* 46 (1964), pp. 89–96.

In criticizing earlier commentaries, the author observes that
sexual activity requires much more than a single act to achieve
its intrinsic procreational purpose and, so that this purpose may
be pursued and achieved, it may temporarily tolerate some
contraceptive interventions. He explains (with a characteristically
English metaphor) that in football the aim of winning a goal is
present in every single action of the players, and not only in the
final act, and is not contradicted even when it is necessary or
advisable to kick the ball backward. Then, a little later, in
reply to a note by L. L. McReavy in *The Clergy Review*, which
energetically re-stated the traditional doctrine (pointing out that
the attitude of *Casti Connubii* was an 'authoritative doctrinal
declaration infallibly confirmed by the ordinary and universal
Magisterium'), there appeared in the same review two articles,
one by Canon Drinkwater (January 1965) and the other by
M. Dummett (June):

> L. L. McReavy, 'Immutability of the Church's teaching on
> contraception', *The Clergy Review* 49 (1964), pp. 705–8.

F. H. Drinkwater, 'Ordinary and universal', *The Clergy Review* 50 (1965), 2–22. (The article was later re-published in the same author's book, *Birth Control and Natural Law*, London, Burns and Oates, 1965, 93 pp., which also contains other articles he wrote for *The Universe* and *Search*.)

M. Dummett, 'The question of contraception', *The Clergy Review* 50 (1965), pp. 412–27.

Drinkwater's conclusion is that the use of contraceptional methods has not yet been irrevocably condemned. Whereas he himself accepts without reserve the opinion expressed by Fr Baum, he criticizes rather harshly the 'emotional tendency', so common today, to 'exaggerate the infallibility of the Church'. Dummett then reflects on the rational motives which, in the present absence of a definitive pronouncement by the Magisterium, acquire much more authority when used to defend the traditional attitude. But the author considers that these motives also have not yet been formulated in a clear and conclusive manner: in fact, procreation is the only biological end of copulation which also, however, serves other purposes (in certain specific and not incidental ways), and we are not obliged to believe that it is the will of God that the safeguarding of its biological possibilities must always have precedence before the other essential functions which it must fulfil for man.

Some contributors to the debate in English were against the new trend: until now we have mentioned only Grisez and McReavy. In America the opposition came from two moral theologians, directors of the American Jesuit review *Theological Studies*, Lynch and McCormick, in the course of their bibliographical surveys of the subject. But there seems nothing new in the reflections they put forward (the intrinsically procreational nature of the conjugal act and the resultant intangibility of its biological structure) or in their appeal to the teaching of the Magisterium (which had indeed been challenged).

J. J. Lynch, S.J., 'Notes on Moral theology: Contraception in general', *Theological Studies* 26 (1965), pp. 251–4; R. A. McCormick, S.J., 'Notes on moral theology: Contraception', *ibid.*, pp. 633–47.

The response was most clearly heard in Ireland where, apart from the brief notes by O'Callaghan, to which we have already referred, there was a longer reply by Mgr Daly, Reader in Scholastic Philosophy at Queen's University, Belfast:

> C. B. Daly, *Natural Law Morality today*, Dublin, Clonmore and Reynolds, 1965, pp. 41. This small volume contains a lecture originally given in April 1965, which was published in the *Christus Rex Journal of Sociology*, St Patrick's College, Maynooth; it appeared again in *The American Ecclesiastical Review* 153 (1965), pp. 361–98.

After establishing some general premises based on natural law, the author affirms concerning contraceptive practices that their moral condemnation has traditionally received, from St Augustine onwards, a much wider and more unanimous consent (event among non-Catholics) than the innovators would have us believe. He then proceeds to rebut the arguments for the new position: the 'personalist' attitude, for example, which they use as a pretext, must not allow us to forget that man is indissolubly both nature and person, and so their new concept of a generalized procreative obligation does not justify the conclusion that the question of method is a matter to be decided by considerations of efficacy or aesthetic preference rather than by moral principles. Even the traditional doctrine never isolated the act from its total context, because it understood that in every chosen means there is the implicit choice of the desired end. In the same way, the affirmation of the primacy of love in conjugal sexual intercourse does not imply that all its ways of expression are equally ethical, just as the presence of love does not mean that precepts based on the natural law are no longer necessary. The campaign for the approval of contraceptive methods is therefore not well supported by its arguments: in fact, Mgr Daly considers it is a local phenomenon found in certain restricted circles in Holland, England and America, and in unrepresentative and mainly lay Catholic opinion.[19]

---

[19] The Anglo-American discussion on birth control, initiated by lay people and encouraged by their constant contributions (see above, note 18) showed that in 1965 also the lay contributors were among the most competent: cf. two volumes, one by an American authoress and the other by a well known Irish Catholic doctor) which give an account of the problem and its most

V. *Other interventions. Noonan's great work.*

Just about the time this judgment was being formulated, a review written by Böckle and McDonagh (the latter, a new contributor to the debate, is Professor of Moral Theology at Maynooth) in the new international theological review *Concilium* offered an adequate, if incomplete, survey of the extension of the debate on birth control, within the Church itself:

> F. Böckle: 'The internal debate in the Church about birth control. Review of publications in German, French and Dutch', *Concilium* 2 (June 1965), pp. 111–47.
> E. McDonagh, Moral theology of marriage: recent literature in English, *ibid.*, pp. 149–78. In other editions of *Concilium* these two articles were published in no. 5 (May), an issue devoted to moral questions.

The preference which these two authors felt for the new trend became evident in the course of the information which they furnished. It is less evident in the case of the Irish theologian who, in conclusion, expressed a wish that there should be a re-examination of arguments based on revelation, reason, philosophy, scientific research and personal experience, in order to provide the Church with a new and final interpretation. Böckle was clearly more favourable to the innovators. In fact, he approved of the attitude of the 'radical group' who were determined to face the 'central problem', that is, whether the individual person is less important than the pre-determined biological structure of an act, or whether these biological structures should be subordinated to the moral purposes of the individual person. He accepted the conclusions, that is, that married couples should have a conscientious intention to beget children, within the general scheme of their marriage, and that a serious moral reason would be necessary to justify the prevention of fertility in any single act. As regards the means employed, it was generically stated that

recent solutions, in a spirit of general understanding and appreciation of the new attitudes: D. D. BROMLEY, *Catholics and birth control*; forewords by CARDINAL CUSHING and J. L. THOMAS, S.J., New York, The Devin-Adair Company, 1965, pp. XVI–207; J. MARSHALL, *Catholics, marriage and contraception*, Dublin, Helicon, 1965, pp. XVI–212. The latter author was, from the beginning, a member of the Pontifical Commission for the family and for births.

this should correspond as closely as possible to the mutually respectful love of which the act of union must be the expression. 'If this way of respectful love', concluded Böckle, 'and of the noble art of love, is expressed by faithful Catholics, we need not fear a decline in sexual morality.'

These two reviews concerned only the three above-mentioned linguistic groups (of French writings Böckle recorded, among recent studies, only Janssens' article on progestational drugs), and this is quite justifiable, considering their prevalence over all other groups. However, to complete the general survey, one must mention some other articles which appeared before or after the *Concilium* reviews:

J. Mejia, El. Crimen de Onán: *Teologia* 3 (1963), pp. 95–105.

W. Bertrams, S.J., 'Notae aliquae quoad structuram metaphysicam amoris coniugalis', *Periodica de re morali, canonica et liturgica* 54 (1965), pp. 290–300.

H. Caffarel, 'Note sur la régulation des naissances', *Nouvelle Revue Théologique* 87 (1965), pp. 836–48.

P. Chauchard, *Amour et contraception. Pour une sexualité responsable*, Paris, Mame, 1965, 293 pp.

J. Coutelier, 'Réflexions tres provisoires sur la régulation des naissances', *Amour, sexualité, régulation des naissances*, ed. J. M. Ray, Paris, Les Editions ouvrières, 1965, pp. 71–124.

P. Montaigne, 'La régulation des naissances. Le point de vue moral', *Etudes de Sexologie*, Paris, Ploud et Gay, 1965, pp. 415–36.

Mejia continues Durbarle's study of the scriptural text and accepts some of his conclusions, admitting that the story of Onan cannot be unconditionally accepted as a condemnation of contraceptive practices; in fact, and here he parts company with the Dominican, the object of the condemnation 'is not even contraception effected in a levirate marriage'. What is condemned instead, is the simple fact of a 'deliberate and systematic opposition to procreation', which appears in direct contrast with the biblical assertion of the procreative purpose of marriage: the moral judgment therefore does not concern the means chosen: 'if Onan had used the Ogino-Knaus method the judgment expressed by the sacred author would have been the same'. Moreover, observes the eminent Argentinian theologian, it is not even clear what was the exact nature of Onan's action (*coitus interruptus*, masturbation or other practices): a most careful study of the actual words used in the biblical texts, compared with words used in other passages, does not help to solve this problem.

Of the other contributors, the first three develop similar lines of thought, in opposition to the innovators' theses, and base their arguments on the value of the conjugal act as an expression of love. In fact, reasons Bertrams (April–June issue), it must signify a mutual and integral self-giving of husband and wife: therefore every contraceptive expedient (whether adopted before or during copulation) 'modifies the body's part in the conjugal act', with the result that 'the husband and wife do not give themselves completely but reserve some elements prepared by nature, which should form part of the conjugal act in order that this may be the exterior sign of interior spiritual love'. This is why the Magisterium condemns every sort of contraceptive measure as constituting an 'abuse of conjugal love' because 'it injures its very root and destroys its essence'.

Identical conclusions are put forward in Dr Chauchard's book, which appeared at the same time as this brief article by the Professor of the Gregorian University, but here the conclusions are deduced from considerations which are more medico-psychological than metaphysical. 'Contraceptives must be forbidden in the name of love because they are above all else inimical to love.' This is true not only of localized contraceptive measures 'which destroy the fleshly union by unnatural behaviour or artificial devices', it is also, and even more so, true of the use of the pill, which 'violates the very nature of the woman, altering her psycho-physiology' and therefore in the end impairs her capacity for perfect womanly self-giving. The same thesis is warmly supported by Caffarel, in the note he published in the September–October number of the above-mentioned Louvain review (it had been prepared on the eve of the third session of the Council in order to answer questions put by some bishops). It is a thesis, in the opinion of the illustrious founder of the '*Equipes Notre-Dame*', and the review *L'anneau d'or*, which 'may strengthen' the justification traditionally put forward in opposition to contraceptives. In fact, if the conjugal act 'is the expression, the realization and fulfilment in the flesh of the total interior mutual self-giving which the husband and wife seek in marriage', those methods must be condemned because they 'deprive it of its structural capacity of expressing and effecting the mutual self-giving of the two persons': 'the corruption of the biological structure by means of contraceptive interventions does not leave intact the interior structure; indeed, it corrupts it'.

Is there, therefore, no possible justification for a Christian husband and wife who have recourse to contraceptives? Indeed, and here the author differs from the jurist of the Gregorian University and the Catholic medical practitioner of Paris, some loopholes are still left open. Caffarel is fortified by twenty-five years of experience in the spiritual direction of families (in fact, as he declares, his 'note' is based on the examination of thousands of replies received from married couples). First of all, he maintains, because the subjective evaluation of the behaviour of husband and wife must be of a general character, that is, must concern the whole moral life and not merely certain particular acts, and also because in many difficult cases it is impossible to depend upon the choice of infertile days, while total abstention would be harmful, one may then appeal to the principle of the lesser evil. This would then take away the guilt from an onanistic act committed 'in order to save an essential good'. This, observes Caffarel, is the sort of situation which frequently occurs, in which there is a 'conflict of duties'. These cases of conflict had been referred to some months previously by Coutelier, in his 'interim reflections': 'cases, that is, in which it is impossible in practice to obey commands which prescribe, at the same time, contradictory actions'. It is then (when the needs of love, of faithfulness, of procreative responsibility or of the mother's health, etc., are in conflict) that we must affirm also, as a necessary 'law of growth', a 'law of tolerance' which allows persons provisionally to pass through stages which are still imperfect and intermediary, in order to rise above them. This may be also the provisional solution for those married couples who have recourse to contraception in similar cases of conflicting duties. Contraception, reasons Coutelier, may not be defined as good in itself, and the Church, 'whose task is to define the total and perfect good', will never declare it to be intrinsically good; nor may it be accepted or presented as a principle of conduct. Nevertheless, it may not be declared, here

and now, to be evil in itself, when one considers the temporary
predicament (which will be overcome) in which the husband and
wife find themselves. They must indeed understand that 'even
if the confessor may not go further than reminding them of the
absolute law, this reminder is but one element of the problem
which they alone have to solve'.

The most decidedly 'permissive' article is, however, the last-
mentioned, by P. Montaigne, Professor at the Catholic University
of Lille.[20] If marriage is ordained by God 'in order that husband
and wife may learn to live together, and by loving each other may
edify the human community', then sexuality also must be included
in this purpose; it must 'bring about the union of two people in a
loving intercourse which is capable of giving life to a third
person', and therefore needs to be always and increasingly animated
by love. 'To respect nature is therefore very different from
forbidding any intervention in a biological process which has
been labelled "natural"; moreover, this passivity would be a
truly scandalous abdication of responsibility, in opposition to the
will of God who entrusted the earth to man and told him to
subdue it; to respect nature means to respect the purpose of
human sexuality which is, in its fleshly dimension, the teacher
of liberty and love.' Contraceptive measures must then be judged
in this light: while they free a man from the eventuality of an
undesired procreation, they do not exempt him from the obligation to make his sexuality serve a truly human purpose; indeed
they offer him a possibility of fulfilment which he must not
neglect. Consequently, it is not possible to deliver, in the abstract,
a moral judgment about the use of any contraceptive method,
including that of periodic continence; this judgment can only
be made within a historical and personal context. None of the
methods permitted is always good, and none of those forbidden
is always bad: the problem of birth-control is therefore not a
problem of what is forbidden and what is permitted. It is a

[20] The volume which contains this article by Montaigne was prepared in
collaboration by a 'group of priests and lay people', Cardinal Liénart writes
in his Introduction, 'at the Catholic University of Lille, with the purpose of
formulating a doctrine on those sexual, conjugal and family problems which
so gravely concern the world today'. The third part of the volume (pp. 307–452)
is in fact devoted to the problems of birth control and contains, besides a study
of the moral laws involved, other studies on medical, demographical, psychological and pedagogical aspects of the problem.

question of a husband and wife attaining a control of procreation which may also enable their sexuality to express itself adequately: it is in this context and in relation to their own situation that married couples must conscientiously decide their own conduct.

It was agreed, however, that 'a historical study of the moral tradition' with regard to contraception was very urgently required. This was the conclusion reached in the course of his reflections by the author we first mentioned, Coutelier. A powerful reply came in the autumn of 1965 with the publication of the historical monograph by J. T. Noonan, Director of the Institute of Natural Law and Professor in the Faculty of Law of the University of Notre-Dame.

> N. T. Noonan, Jr., *Contraception. A history of its treatment by the Catholic theologians and canonists*, Cambridge (Mass.), Harvard University Press, 1965, pp. 561.[21]

As the sub-title states, this book constitutes a historical survey of the teaching of Catholic theologians and canonists on the theme of contraception, but this particular problem is constantly viewed in the context of general ideas on sexuality and marriage, as these appear. The author is not content to furnish data (taken at first hand from all available sources): he discusses these and tries to discover their underlying reasons and to trace their evolution. He distinguishes four principal periods.

In early times (A.D. 50–450), the account of which is prefaced by Noonan with a brief summary of the concepts of the Greco-Roman world as well as of concepts inherited from Judaic and scriptural sources, he finds that Christianity was faced with this problem on two different fronts: in opposition to Gnosticism and, later on, to Manichaeism. The Christians rebutted the numerous Gnostic doctrines about sexual questions, not by quoting biblical authority (the Old Testament, in particular, could not be drawn upon, because the Gnostics scorned it), but by quoting the Stoic point of view, which still survived in Jewish

---

[21] Among the reviews of Noonan's book we mention those by C. MERTENS, S.J., in *Nouvelle Revue Théologique* 88 (1966), pp. 205–6; A. JANSSENS in *Ephemerides Theologicae Lovaniesnes* 42 (1966), pp. 329–30; E. TURRI, in *Riflessi* 18 (1966), pp. 72–9; G. EGNER in *New Blackfriars* 47 (1966), pp. 304–17.

intellectual circles (cf. Philo of Alexandria). According to this concept, passion must play no part in marriage and is only justified by the necessity of propagating the species. As a consequence of this point of view there was, in general, a climate of opinion unfavourable to contraceptive practices. It is not clear, however, how far their exclusion is due to their being considered as magic practices, or to the fact that sterilizing measures were considered to be abortifacients. Nevertheless, it is clear that their condemnation did not refer to individual contraceptive acts but to habitual conduct. The same Stoic concept of sexuality and marriage gave rise also to the Manichaean doctrines which exalted the sexual act in itself and at the same time scorned procreation. Augustine instead puts forward a pessimistic and ascetic concept of sexuality, in which he finds nothing rational and spiritual (see his observations on concupiscence during his controversy with the Pelagian heretics), and consequently he thinks it is justified only by its procreative intention. On this basis he naturally condemns every contraceptive expedient, including the choice of sterile periods. If one studies the few texts which expound his general doctrine, one has the impression that his condemnation includes all individual contraceptive acts.

The thousand years which followed (450–1450) form the second period distinguished and examined by Noonan: it sees, on the one hand, the consolidation and universal application of the condemnation expressed in the preceding centuries, and on the other hand the appearance of some new considerations about sexuality and marriage. There is no doubt about the condemnation: the Penitentials, the monastic texts, the Scholastic writers are all unanimous in condemning contraception, which is indeed pronounced against in a canon (*Si aliquis*) included in many official collections; nevertheless, the need to justify the condemnation is still felt. The first argument expressed in this very canon, that contraception is a form of homicide, is more often put forward during the first centuries of this period (perhaps it was felt necessary to bring weighty argument to bear upon the early Christians) but is found again in Scholastic writings. Nevertheless the main reason is still one which originates in Stoic-Augustinian thought, made more rigid in the light of the even more pessimistic ideas of St Gregory the Great. This reappears even in the doctrine of St Thomas Aquinas, although he no longer scorns sexual pleasure in itself. He considers contraception to be 'against nature' because copulation is intended 'by nature' for the propagation of the species. However, alongside this universal and reasoned condemnation there began to appear also some new trends of thought, especially in the twelfth to fifteenth centuries: for example, the main emphasis is now placed on the material and spiritual well-being of the offspring instead of on the procreation of many children; there is an admission, although not yet supported by clearly elaborated doctrine, of an obligation to 'render the debt of marriage', consent is granted to marriage between old or sterile persons for the reason that it is also 'a comfort for human dignity'; there are also St Thomas's re-evaluation of pleasure, the legitimization of certain sexual practices such as the *amplexus reservatus*, and of some drugs like anaphrodisiacs which were no longer considered unnatural.

These new trends became more apparent during the third period, 1450–1750, although the principle of the sinfulness of contraception remains substantially unaltered. First of all there is apparent a new line of thought concerning the value of sexuality in marriage: Dionysius the Carthusian, Martinus de Magistris, Giovanni Major and other writers now acknowledge, in general terms, the value of copulation in itself and numerous individual reasons which legitimize it unreservedly quite apart from purposes of procreation: the old Augustinian attitude is therefore gradually softening, and we soon find Thomas Sanchez explicitly admitting that copulation does not need any new 'special intention' to justify it, and that husband and wife, in order to express and foster their mutual love, may even use other forms of sexual contact. Moreover, together with this re-evaluation of sexuality, there also appears a new understanding that conduct intended to limit the number of offspring (particularly for economic reasons) may also be licit: this result may be obtained through continence, or through the *amplexus reservatus*, or through the use of anaphrodisiacs.[22] In this new climate of

[22] An interesting historical study of this subject is offered by E. ORSENIGO: 'Il problema della famiglia numerosa nei moralisti dei secoli XVI-XVII', *La Scuola Cattolica* 94 (1966), pp. 36–50. Apart from economic difficulties, the author records other reasons for a legitimate limitation of births recognized by moralists of that period, as when for example one partner is '*maculati sanguinis*' (a Jewess or a Saracen) or when it is feared that a child may be born abnormal or affected by a grave illness. We can refer here also to another

opinion contraception is still condemned, but certainly with less severity. This is shown by the less emphatic doctrinal arguments used against it (for example, contraception is less and less frequently represented as a form of homicide) and, in practice, by the greater willingness to admit, in many cases, the good faith of the married couple or (in the case of the woman) the permissibility of co-operation with the husband's resort to onanism.

But how long could this condemnation last? We now come to the last and most critical stage of the debate (1750–1965). It is true that in this period, with the pronouncements uttered last century by the Roman Congregations, the declarations made by some national episcopates during the early years of this century, and finally with the encyclical *Casti connubii*, the condemnation acquired more official authority, but it was widely agreed that it did not take into account the new historical phenomena and the doctrinal developments now approaching maturity. This is true of Pius XI's encyclical, irreproachable in its presentation of the 'classical doctrine' but quite indifferent or in opposition to the contemporary historical context. Nevertheless, new historical phenomena are bringing a strong influence to bear upon the question; these are the rapid growth of populations, the changed status of women, who now play a decisive role in the assertion of matrimonial freedom, the new social situation of a family which, forming a self-contained unit, is now more deeply involved in these questions, morally and economically, than was the case in former times, medical research and discoveries with relation to procreation and fertility, the theoretical analysis, effected in competent circles, of sexuality considered as the proper field for the expression of conjugal love, and a newly revised theology of marriage which emphasized its fundamental spiritual values, and in the elaboration of which lay people have played an active part. At the very moment in which the condemnation of contraception, anchored to a tradition which is already being challenged, acquires official strength and authority, there is also taking place, because of these new and impressive factors, a radical re-examination which is apparently already present even in the teaching of

historical monograph which appeared a little earlier than Noonan's and which deals here and there, indirectly, with our problem: J. E. KERNS, S.J., *The theology of marriage. The historical development of Christian attitudes towards sex and sanctity in marriage*, New York, Sheed and Ward, 1964, 302 pp.

the Magisterium. The proofs of this new attitude are seen in the full legitimization of periodic continence, the implicit admission that *amplexus reservatus* is not intrinsically illicit, and the frankly acknowledged perplexity (cf. Paul VI's speech, 23 June 1964) concerning the problem of treatment with progestational drugs. Are we then at a turning-point? That this may be so could be seen even in the Council discussions, when in the course of the first debate on family problems (during the third session, referred to by Noonan) the new trend was clearly apparent. The continuity of Catholic teaching is not thereby destroyed, for in forbidding contraception the Church's main intention was above all to safeguard certain values of conjugal life which could not be protected by any other means, but for which this condemnation now threatens to become a narrow prison and no longer, as had been intended, a protective wall.

So ends the diligent and voluminous record of research by the American historian and jurist, a Professor at Harvard University: a fundamental contribution, made by a layman, to our discussion. His final judgment, which favours a possible change in doctrine, gave powerful support to the same opinion which, during the period we have surveyed in this chapter, had been put forward by other authors and with other arguments.[23]

---

[23] Following Noonan's work, but before the conclusion of the Council and the promulgation of *Gaudium et spes*, there appeared two articles of DO-C: V. HEYLEN, 'Le problème moral et pastoral des moyens de régulation des naissances', DO-C 216; PH. DELHAYE, 'Le marriage et la famille', DO-C 217. The second article has nothing to say about the problems of birth control (beyond expressing the hope, in the words used by Cardinal Alfrink in his speech in the Council, that science and morality may agree on other means besides that of periodic continence and that the Church will not impose moral sanctions except in the presence of a real certainty), and the author of the first article, already known to us, devotes his whole contribution to this question. He does not conceal his preference for that new concept of 'nature' and the 'natural order' which enlarges its content beyond the limits of biological data ('contemporary opinion no longer understands why the fundamental values of the future must be bound to a merely animal evolution that may not be interfered with') and he concedes to man a more extended power over his vital functions. He concludes that grave pastoral problems still remain to be solved in order that the use of contraceptive means no longer declared intrinsically illicit may not result in grave harm to conjugal and family life (a lack of respect for procreation, the mechanization and degradation of coitus, a hedonistic view of marriage, etc.).

We must mention a few other works written in the years surveyed in this

It is the support of one who, having made a careful and detailed
examination of the evolution of this doctrine, was in the best
position to judge it in its synthetic presentation, and to foresee
its future development.

chapter, which we have been unable to consult: TH. S. ACKER, S.J., *Three
dimensions of birth control*, Glen Rock (New Jersey), Paulist Press, 1964, 48 pp.
A. VAN GANSEWINKEL, 'Ueberblick über die moraltheologische Diskussion
bezüglich Geburtenregelung', *Pastoral Blätter* (Cologne) 16 (1964), pp. 258–66;
C. RIETERMAN, 'Birth control and Catholics', *Journal Scient. Study of Relig.*
4 (1965), pp. 213–33; G. W. HEALEY, 'Contraception. On the eve of the
Council's decision', *Philippine Studies* 13 (1965), pp. 670–89. R. A. McCORMICK
S.J., tells us (in his review in *Theological Studies* 26 [1965], pp. 637–8) of a
report presented in June 1965 to the Catholic Theological Society of America
under the title: *Responsible Parenthood: a philosophical view*, by the Jesuit
R. O. JOHANN, who favours the new trend. We have not yet seen this book
published.
   Finally, the reader will not have found mentioned in this chapter some
articles on birth control which belong to this period (1961–65) but which
restrict themselves to reiterating the traditional teaching without apparently
being aware that it had been opposed in Catholic circles, and therefore without
making any special attempt to defend it from recent attacks: we refer, for
example, to an article by M. TISSOT, 'La prévention des naissances', *Itinéraires*
80 (1964), pp. 67–91, in which, to the 'appeal' sent out to the Council by the
'French movement for family planning' in order to ask the Church 'to revise
her attitude to birth control', he replies that 'the Church cannot and will not
go against the laws of nature, and still less can she yield to the materialism, in
whatever form, which is concealed in these arguments'; the same may be said
of the book by J. DE CASTRO REYES, *La regulación de los nacimientos. Reflexiones
teologicomorales para una acción pastoral*, Santiago de Chile, Editorial Universi-
dad Católica, 1965, pp. 101, which makes no reference to the new trend of
thought (except on p. 88 in a note), not even as regards the pill.

V

THE TEACHING OF THE SECOND VATICAN COUNCIL

THE theological discussion we have been considering was bound
to have some repercussions in the Council and to be echoed
in its final document on marriage, in the first chapter of the
second part of the *Pastoral Constitution on the Church in the
Modern World* (*Gaudium et spes*) which was promulgated, at the
conclusion of the Council, 7 December 1965. We will now
endeavour to draw up a brief summary of the Council's work.[1]

[1] The brevity of our survey is due also to the fact that there already exist
several good accounts of the history of these conciliar labours, cf. for example
the exhaustive studies by G. DE ROSA, S.J., 'Dignità del matrimonio e della
famiglia e sua valorizzazione', in *La Chiesa e il mondo contemporaneo nel
Vaticano II*, Turin, Elle Di Ci, 1966, pp. 679–804; PH. DELHAYE, 'Dignité du
marriage et de famille', in *L'Eglise dans le monde de ce temps*, II *Commentaires*,
Paris, Ed. du Cerf, 1967, pp. 387–453; D. TETTAMANZI, 'Matrimonio e famiglia',
in *La Chiesa a colloquio con il mondo*, Milan, Massimo, 1965, pp. 446–78, and
'Dignità del matrimonio e della famiglia e sua valorizzazione', in 'Commento
alla Costituzione pastorale sulla Chiesa nel mondo contemporaneo, *Gaudium
et Spes*', ibid., 1967, pp. 291–340; a close study of the events of the last conciliar
session may be found in J. GROOTAERS, 'De drie lezingen van Schema XIII en
in het bijzonder van het Huwelijkshoofdstuk', *De Maand* 9 (1966), pp. 36–49,
88–111 (re-edited also by IDO-C, nos. 66–5, 7, 8: *'Le tre letture dello Schema
XIII ed in particolare del capitolo sul matrimonio'*, and reproduced in *Questitalia*
9 [1966], pp. 273–95) and also, more sympathetically, in V. HEYLEN, 'La note
14 dans la constitution pastorale *Gaudium et Spes*', *Ephemerides Theologicae
Lovanienses* 42 (1966), pp. 555–66, and in PH. DELHAYE, 'Impressions conciliaires.
Esquisse d'une axiologie chrétienne. Constitution pastorale, II partie, chapitres
1 et 2', *L'Ami du clergé* 76 (1966), pp. 593–607. Finally, regarding the work
of the third (1964) and fourth (1965) sessions, one can refer to the better
known 'chronicles' of the Council, such as A. WENGER, *Vatican II: III Chronique
de la troisième session*, Paris, Ed. du Centurion, 1965, pp. 418–32, IV. *Chronique
de la quatrième session*, ibid., 1966, pp. 174–99; R. LAURENTIN, *L'enjeu du
Concile. Bilan de la troisième session*, Paris, Ed. du Seuil, 1965, pp. 193–209
and *Bilan du Concile. Histoire. textes, commentaires avec une chronique de la
quatrième session*, ibid., 1966, pp. 168–75, *et passim*; R. LA VALLE, *Fedeltà del
Concilio. I dibattiti della terza sessione*, Brescia Morcelliana, 1965, pp. 406–36,
and *Il Concilio nelle nostre mani*, ibid., 1966, pp. 159–68, 565–72, *et passim;*
G. F. SVIDERCOSCHI, *Storia del Concilio*, Milan, Ancora, 1967, pp. 437–43,
609–17; and above all to the very complete 'information' supplied by G.
CAPRILE, S.J., of *La Civiltà Cattolica* (publ. also in the volumes *Il Concilio
Vaticano II*, Rome, Edizioni della Civ. Catt.: the third session is described in
vol. IV; the last volume, about the fourth session, is not out yet); for the particular problem with which we are concerned see R. ROUQUETTE, 'Les derniers
jours de la quatrième session du Concile', *Etudes* 324 (1966), pp. 217–32.

I. *Previous work*

The starting point was indeed very obviously the traditional doctrine, especially that found in the *Casti Connubii* of Pius XI. A schema *De Castitate, virginitate, matrimonio, familia*, edited by the Preparatory Commission and sent to the Council Fathers on 13 July 1962, proposed in the four chapters of its second part a doctrinal synthesis of marriage, in which its primary end was declared to be 'solely' the procreation and education of children, giving as its 'secondary' purposes those of 'mutual conjugal assistance' and 'the remedy for concupiscence'. Contraceptive practices, including 'conjugal onanism', were condemned as intrinsically and gravely sinful, but the document affirmed the right to regulate fertility according to the conditions of individual families and of society as a whole, with a prudent judgement which took God's providential assistance also into account.[2]

In so far as concerns our present purpose, it was then the teaching usually put forward by moral theologians without incurring open opposition: there was evident, however, a certain predominance of the canonical-juridical mentality and an obvious polemical preoccupation with errors and deviations (these four chapters contained twenty-one condemnations).

But this Schema was never discussed. In fact when, at the end of the first Council session, it was decided to reduce the Schemata to be examined to seventeen, it was also decided that the

---

[2] *Schema constitutionis de castitate, virginitate, matrimonio, familia. Pars altera: De matrimonio et familia*, Typis Polyglottis Vaticanis, 1962, 49 pp. The affirmations referred to occur respectively in Chapter I, no. 13 (*Matrimonii fines*): in Chapter II, no. 18 (*Jura et obligationes quoad bonum prolis*); in Chapter IV, no. 29 (*Responsabilitas parentum quoad numerum filiorum*). As regards the second point, most clearly connected with our subject, here is the text of the Schema: 'As regards the procreative act itself, which, inasmuch as it is ordained by God, is in itself good and lawful, it is the right and duty of married couples to make use of such things as are according to nature in all their conduct. Therefore, in a lawful marriage, the desire, so praiseworthy in itself, to have offspring by one's own spouse, while it does not make artificial insemination legitimate, does not prohibit artificial means of assisting the conjugal act. In like manner, all methods or means by which, in the marriage act, the procreation of children is prevented by human action, must be considered gravely and intrinsically sinful. Conjugal onanism and formal co-operation in this are never permitted. As regards *amplexus reservatus*, pastors and faithful must behave in strict accordance with the doctrine and decrees of the Holy See.' In the notes are frequent quotations from *Casti Connubii* and Pius XII's *Speech to the Italian Midwives*.

material prepared on the subjects of marriage and the family should be included, with other subjects (many of which had been suggested by Cardinal Suenens in his famous intervention in the Council debate, 4 December 1962) in a new specially prepared Schema which was to deal with the Church's relations with the modern world. The responsibility for this Schema was entrusted to a 'Mixed Commission', which included some members of the doctrinal Commission and other members of the Commission for the Lay Apostolate. The result was 'Schema 17', which was debated in a plenary session in May 1963, under the title: *De praesentia efficaci Ecclesiae in mundo hodierno*, and the third of its six chapters was dedicated to marriage and the family.[3] The Schema presented a synthesis very different from the one previously drawn up by the Preparatory Commission: it was shorter and more given to general statements, and it started with the assertion that marriage was a vocation tending to an increase of holiness in husband and wife ('communi conatu prosequendam'); it then dedicated a whole section to conjugal love and to marriage as the communion in which it is intended to develop; finally, as regards the problems of fertility, it stated, among other things, that 'the nature and institution of marriage are contradicted by the assertions of those who maintain that the procreation and education of children are of secondary importance and may be subordinated to the other good purposes of marriage, or radically and arbitrarily detached from it. Every deliberate human intervention which impairs the personal conjugal act is contrary to divine law and to the institution of marriage; nor is this procedure conducive to the integrity of conjugal love.'

As we see, new elements were present even with regard to the condemnation of contraceptive practices: the condemnation was still there but was made to derive also from the fact that these were contrary to the integrating purpose of conjugal intercourse; the manner of defining it was also new: 'every deliberate human inter-

[3] These are the six chapter headings: Concerning the human vocation; concerning the human person in society; concerning marriage and the family; concerning the right promotion of progress; concerning the economic order and social justice; concerning the community of the peoples, and peace. This Schema was never printed because, as we shall see, it was rejected by the co-ordinating Commission. We have not been able to see it and we have learnt its contents, as regards the problem we are considering, from G. De Rosa, S.J., *op. cit.*, pp. 682–5.

vention which impairs the *personal* values of the conjugal act'.[4]

Even this new text failed to reach the Council: in fact, it did not find favour with the Co-ordinating Commission (after Cardinal Suenens had read a substantially negative report about it, 4 July 1963), and the Commission ordered that a new text should be prepared. This was to elaborate particularly the doctrinal part contained in the first chapter, whereas the material of the other chapters was to be added to the text in the form of five additional notes (*Adnexa*). But meanwhile the second session of the Council (29 September–4 December 1963) had ended. During this period the Mixed Commission had indeed received a new document prepared in Louvain by Cardinal Suenens (*Adumbratio schematis XVII de activa praesentia Ecclesiae in mundo aedificando*) but as it was not able to choose between this Schema and the one it had already prepared, it preferred to set up a 'Central Sub-Commission' (formed by eight bishops, presided over by Mgr Guano, and some experts, among whom Fr Häring was chosen to act as secretary), charged to prepare a new Schema. Five other Sub-Commissions were set up to edit the five *Adnexa*. Thus began, in December 1963, the work of editing which, after many contributions had been received from various sources and the necessary additions had been made and approved by the Mixed Commission (which met March 4 and 8 and June 4–6), produced the Schema in four chapters *De Ecclesia in mundo huius temporis*,[5] which also contains the five *Adnexa* which expounded the principles set out in the fourth chapter.[6] Section no. 21 (in the fourth chapter) of

---

[4] One might ask, for example, whether this progestational treatment enters this category of contraceptive measures. It must however be added that, at the time this Schema was drawn up, no theologian had yet advanced the hypothesis of a general legitimization of this treatment.

[5] *Schema de Ecclesia in mundo huius temporis*, Typis Polyglottis Vaticanis, 1964, pp. 45. The headings of the four chapters are: *de integra hominis vocatione; Ecclesia Dei hominumque servitio dedita; de ratione Christianorum re gerendi in mundo in quo vivunt; de praecipuis muneribus a christianis nostrae aetatis implendis* (of the whole vocation of man; of the Church in the service of God and man; of the conduct of Christians in the world; of the special duties of Christians in our day). This last chapter, after a brief introduction (no. 19), expounds (20–25) general considerations on the individual arguments treated, in a more searching manner, in the *Adnexa*.

[6] *Schema de Ecclesia in mundo huius temporis. Adnexa*. Typis Polyglottis Vaticanis, 1964, 63 pp. The subjects of the five *Adnexa* are: concerning the human person in society; concerning marriage and the family; concerning the right promotion of progress; concerning economic and social life; concerning the community of peoples and peace.

the Schema and no. 2 of the *Adnexa* are devoted to a consideration of marriage and family life.

The doctrine contained in no. 21 of the Schema (four paragraphs) starts with the affirmation that God willed marriage 'not only for the procreation and education of children and for the mutual assistance of husband and wife in earthly matters, but also for their mutual sanctification and glorification of God, so that by their means not only their children but the whole family circle may find the way to holiness and salvation'.

In this way the whole argument about the proper purpose of marriage (the word 'purpose' is totally absent from the texts, both of the Schema and of the *Adnexa*), is by-passed with a non-juridical statement about the various good things procured by marriage. Of these good things the first mentioned is conjugal love 'which is beneficial not only to the married couple but to the whole family'. Its 'real nature' is thus described: 'Real conjugal love, a true and free mutual self-giving in one spirit and one flesh and a mutual interior formation, tender in affection and agreeable in practice, far surpasses the ephemeral inclination of the sense which, if selfishly followed, soon dies miserably.'

This love should promote fertility, the absence of which does not deprive marriage (which is not a 'mere instrument for procreation') of its fundamental value and indissolubility. Nevertheless, marriage, by the very nature of conjugal love, is 'naturally directed' towards procreation.

'Hence the true observance of conjugal love and the whole significance of the family life which springs therefrom have this purpose: the generous and firm intention of husband and wife to co-operate with the love of their Creator and Saviour who by their means daily enlarges and enriches his family.'

This fertility must, however, be not only generous but effected 'with a full and conscious sense of responsibility, such as befits God's gift and the principle of true love': and this requires prudent judgment on the part of the married couple 'not without prayers and joint effort'. It is precisely this requirement—the Schema adds in the last Section—which may present 'frequent difficulties', as for example when it is a question of deciding 'their responsibility at times when they consider an increase of offspring temporarily inadvisable, and the cessation of the tender practice of their love may often lead to estrangement between them'. Nevertheless, the Church encourages them not to be downhearted, while she invites competent authorities of the various spheres of study to assist the theologians to examine 'the order inscribed by Providence in nature' and to think out practical solutions which 'are already to some extent apparent and to some extent may still be hoped for'.

The Schema said nothing more about methods of birth control, but the *Adnexa* returned to this subject (10 pages) after having in the first five paragraphs closely examined the nature of love and conjugal fidelity. First of all an important observation was made concerning the procreative intention of the individual conjugal act: 'Even though, in accordance with the natural order, not every individual copulation is intended to result in generation, yet the nature and expression of this act, and the intention of husband and wife, should be such as to foster a generous disposition towards the procreation and education of children.'

Then, in the same words which had been used in the 1963 Schema (and quoting in a footnote the well-known text of *Casti Connubii*) it was declared that 'every deliberate human intervention which vitiates the effect proper to the personal conjugal act' is 'contrary to the divine law and the institution of marriage', as well as having a harmful effect on the integrity of the mutual love of husband and wife. Finally, after some words of sympathy and encouragement for married couples 'who do not yet attain that total chastity which is their intention' (these words also are quoted from the earlier Schema) it was recalled that periodic continence had been declared a permissible solution, 'although it is not possible to claim that every difficult and tense situation can at once be resolved by this means alone'. As for 'other practical solutions' the Schema reiterated its appeal for more profound and co-ordinated research (by specialists, theologians and married couples) and reminded the faithful that it was not possible for the Magisterium to find a quick and ready answer to the new and complex problems now awaiting solution.

II. *The first debate in the Council*

Section no. 21 of Schema 13 (as it was to be called) was debated in the Council, 29–30 October 1964, and as this was the first time that the Fathers were discussing the problems concerning family life, the results were eagerly awaited.

Nevertheless there were two facts which, from the very beginning, indicated that the Assembly would not arrive at a solution of the most critical problems such as that of birth control, about which there was an animated discussion, both inside and outside the Council, especially with regard to the 'pill'. First of all, as Mgr Guano had pointed out, 20 October, when he presented the Schema in accordance with the wishes of the Mixed Commission which had drawn it up, the *Adnexa* were not to be put forward for discussion and deliberation by the Council (although the Fathers were invited to send in their observations in writing), but only offered 'as an instrument to assist the study of our Schema'.[7] The intention of withholding from discussion in the Council problems (like those of matrimonial morality) for which it was believed that the Fathers were not, in general, sufficiently prepared, was obvious, and expressed the anxieties of the 'progressive' group, but this decision robbed the discussion, which began on 29 October, of its practical interest. Secondly, as we know, a few days before the Schema was circulated to the Fathers, Paul VI had reserved to himself the solution of some grave problem relating to the family, such as that of the means of birth control, particularly the use of the 'pill', and had set up for further study of these problems a special Pontifical Commission which had not been able to conclude its study before the beginning of the Council session. This was another reason for foreseeing that the

---

[7] *Relatio super Schema de Ecclesia in mundo huius temporis*, Typis Polyglottis Vaticanis, 1964, p. 14. As Mgr Guano observed (see the interview he granted in February to *Orientierung* 28 [1966], pp. 25–7), the mixed Commission had established this in the last Plenary Assembly of 13 October, repeating what had already been decided in the earlier meetings, particularly in that of 4–6 June: in fact, in this meeting (as the 'Report' at the end of the Schema, p.41, relates) the question of the value of the *Adnexa* came up: it was included so that it should be made public like any other official commentary on the Schema.

It may be remembered that on 1 October Mgr Felici, replying to questions asked by some of the Fathers (among whom the *Adnexa* had been distributed the day before) had declared that these should be considered as documents without any official character; but, as the result of an immediate debate about this (in which Mgr Glorieux, Secretary to the Commission for the Lay Apostolate, was prominent), Mgr Felici at the close of the Congregation corrected himself, adding that the *Adnexa* were not merely private documents, as he had earlier announced by mistake.

debate in Council would be inconclusive. In fact Mgr Guano himself, in his declarations of 23 October (which concluded the general discussion of the Schema, before passing on to discuss the individual chapters) reminded the Fathers that, with regard to the problems of birth control, since the Pope had set up an extra-Conciliar Commission, any interim resolution adopted by the Council would be premature.[8] The same opinion was voiced by Abp Dearden, Archbishop of Detroit, when, on 29 October, he presented the text for discussion: he pointed out that it entrusted the responsibility of procreation to the married couples themselves, but left the decision on the means of birth control to the Church; but there was to be no mention of progestational drugs either in the text or in the discussion which followed, since the Pope had reserved this enquiry to himself alone.

In spite of these restrictions, the debate in Council was of great significance, at least for the general lines of doctrine which it presented. Cardinal Ruffini, Archbishop of Palermo, opened the debate with a brisk attack on the spirit and letter of the Schema; as for the problem of the size of a family, he observed, the text is obscure and equivocal: it must therefore be re-written, bearing in mind the condemnations pronounced by the Church ever since Augustine, and above all the teachings (most explicit about this matter and ignored by the Schema) of *Casti Connubii* and of Pius XII's Speech to the Midwives. The same negative attitude was shown, the following day, by the co-ordinated interventions of Cardinals Ottaviani and Browne. Holding fast to general principles, the former (with a moving reference to large families and the suggestion that the whole question of births should be entrusted to the will of Providence) left it to Cardinal Browne to deal more particularly with the problem of the means to be employed. After

[8] It was Abp Heenan who had asked the Council to make a particular study of this problem, and in particular of the problem of the 'pill', in order to find a solution. On 22 October he had intervened in the discussion, with a spirited attack on the Schema and (not without some fairly obvious references to Häring) to the *periti* who had prepared it ('timeo peritos et adnexa ferentes', he had misquoted jestingly). As regards the pill, he had regretted the fact that both the Schema and the *Adnexa* left the impression that it was, at least hypothetically, legitimate, by affirming that some practical solutions had already been found and others might follow, and had added that it was scandalous that the Council, faced with such urgent and important problems, should have restricted itself to generic affirmations. The complete text of Abp Heenan's intervention may be read in *La Documentation Catholique* 61 (1964), pp. 1559–62.

a clear exposition of the traditional doctrine of the 'three good things' (offspring, mutual fidelity and the sacrament) which legitimize marriage and the conjugal act itself, Cardinal Browne noted that in every case (according to the doctrine clearly set forth also in *Casti Connubii* and by Pius XII) the act must be 'according to nature' and that therefore there was no other problem awaiting solution except that concerning the medical confirmation of the utilization of infertile periods. Moreover, as Mgr Hervas (*prelatus nullius* of Ciudad-Real) speaking for a hundred and twenty-six bishops, said in his speech which was greeted with applause, large families must be viewed not with alarm but with respect and admiration. The Council too, mindful of the numerous religious vocations which flourish in large families, must not conceal its admiration for them. In their speeches of 29 October Cardinals Léger and Suenens and the Patriarch Maximos IV spoke in favour of the new Schema, and so did Cardinal Alfrink and Mgr Reuss, 30 October (the latter speaking in the name of a hundred and forty-five other bishops).[9] Cardinal Léger spoke at great length, pointing out that if the theology of marriage needed revision this was not in favour of an accommodating opportunism but in order to make a more thorough examination of the problems involved (like the survey already initiated) and because of the recent results of biological, psychological and sociological research. He therefore asserted, firstly that procreation is a duty incumbent less upon an individual act than upon the state of matrimony as a whole; secondly, that conjugal love is not intended merely for procreation (as the Schema itself still asserted) but is a true end of marriage in itself, with its own laws and requirements, and is a valid reason for the conjugal act itself, rendering it perfectly legitimate even when there is no specific procreative intention. Cardinal Suenens' speech,[10] which was very courageous and listened to with great

[9] The integral text of these speeches, except in the case of Mgr Reuss, may be read in French in *La documentation catholique* 61 (1964), pp. 1603–16; Mgr Reuss's speech may be found in the book (which we shall deal with in our next chapter) by J. DAVID, S.J., *Neue Aspekte der kirchlichen Ehelehre*, pp. 40–2.

[10] 'Lively applause greeted this direct and courageous appeal. His impressive style, the gravity of his theme and the novelty (for some of those present) of his conclusions created a stir in the Council. Rarely have I felt such excitement in the course of a Conciliar debate' (A. WENGER, *op. cit.*, III, p. 427).

attention, paid more attention to practical applications: he considered that a re-examination of the Church's teaching on marriage was necessary, certainly not in order to refute what had already been definitively obtained, but in order to integrate it with elements hitherto overlooked, and particularly the significance of marriage as a 'communion between two persons, ratified and sanctioned by the sacrament'. It might be asked whether perhaps in the past the primary purpose of procreation had not been 'unduly emphasized', to the detriment of an equally imperative purpose, the perfection of the conjugal union. The concept of nature also must be re-examined, in the light of the new scientific research which attributes to man 'new possibilities of power to direct the course of nature', and which may in the end lead to a revision of the former distinctions between what is 'according to or against nature'. Still more explicit about the problem of birth control, which is one of the most 'painful and difficult questions for vast numbers of men and women today', was the Patriarch Maximos IV, who saw 'the authority of the Church challenged over a wide field'. It is easy to see, in the questions he raised, the profound theological perplexity already expressed in discussions outside the Council. 'Should not the official attitude of the Church on this matter be revised in the light of modern scientific research, theological, medical, psychological and sociological? . . . Have we not the right to ask ourselves whether certain official attitudes are not derived from concepts now superseded, and even perhaps from the psychosis present in celibates who are extraneous to this sector of life? Are we not, unconsciously, still burdened with the Manichaean concept of mankind and the world, according to which the work of the flesh, in itself corrupt, is only justified by the expectation of progeny? Is the exterior biological integrity of sexual acts the only moral criterion, without any regard for family life, the moral attitudes of the husband and wife and of their whole family, and the grave demands of prudence, a basic principle of all our human activity? Moreover, does modern exegetical research not compel us to observe a greater caution in the interpretation of two passages in Genesis: the words "increase and multiply", and the story of Onan, both so long quoted as classical Biblical testimony to the radical sinfulness of contraception?'

The Patriarch did not attempt to answer these questions except by asserting the need for wider research to be conducted by theologians, scientists and married couples (among them some non-Catholics and non-Christians), and by affirming that the 'duty of the Church is to train the moral conscience of her children to a sense of personal and common moral responsibility, nurtured in Christ, rather than to involve them in a web of prescriptions and commands which they are merely asked to obey blindly'.

The two speeches of Alfrink and Reuss, delivered 30 October and very similar in character, presented to the consideration of the Fathers the new terms of the problem now engaging our attention. 'It is clear that in order to solve men's difficulties,' said the Dutch Cardinal, 'the Church, custodian of the divine law, can never change this law by adapting it to human weakness', yet the 'moral conflict' in which husband and wife are frequently involved with regard to their intimate relations, 'is too serious for the Church to be able to resolve it in an ingenuous and possibly premature manner'.

'This is the conflict: if in their intercourse the husband and wife decide to safeguard the biological intention, then they do so at the cost of their human duty to bring up the children already born, or who will yet be born to them, in a truly Christian manner. On the contrary, if they wish to safeguard their conjugal fidelity and their duty to educate their children, then the question is whether, apart from the use of periodic continence (which many Christian married couples practise very virtuously but often under great difficulties) or complete continence (which requires of husband and wife, among other things, a moral strength superior to what they are generally presumed to possess), there may not be some other solution besides that of depriving the act of its fruit, at least occasionally. Obviously, if this avoidance of fecundity is obtained through means which are intrinsically evil, the Church can never permit the sacrifice of one particular value in marriage in order to safeguard the total value. But with our new anthropological information, especially the essential distinction, ever more widely accepted, between purely biological sexuality and human sexuality, many married couples feel a legitimate doubt, shared by some scientists and theologians, at least with regard to the arguments put forward to prove that complete or periodic continence is, on moral and Christian grounds, the only fully effective solution for these conflicts which arise in the conjugal life of Catholics in good faith. And the Church cannot and must not bind or loosen the consciences of her faithful before real certainty has been reached in the knowledge of the authentic content of the divine law.'

That 'human sexuality may not be considered on a purely biological plane and is essentially different from all non-human sexuality' was the starting point of Mgr Reuss's speech (as it had been of his articles): he deduced therefrom that 'conjugal love forms the basis of marriage' and that the degree of fertility should be left to the responsible decision of the husband and wife; as for the means used to obtain this, 'the Schema is to be praised for the prudence and moderation with which it is expressed: it says no more than can be said today'.

These were the principal speakers in the debate and no one could fail to note the authority of those who spoke in favour of the new trend. They showed an underlying concept of marriage which, generally speaking, betrayed a more 'personalist' estimation of its values. For example, certain aspects such as 'union between the husband and wife' are more highly valued. In particular we note a new attitude towards the problem of responsible parenthood and of the means to attain it, and the keen awareness that on this last question the traditional teaching cannot be considered as final. The theological debate was not without repercussions beyond the Council. Moreover, various new and practical questions were raised in the theses examined by the Council, such as, for example, the distinction between biological and human sexuality, the attribution of the procreative purpose to the whole state of matrimony rather than to every individual conjugal act, the necessity of studying more closely the meaning of 'nature' and the 'natural', the uncertainty of biblical references to this question and the acknowledgement of the situations of actual conflict caused by the traditional presentation of the doctrine.

Moreover, outside the Council there was not only a theological discussion still continuing, but also a public opinion which was becoming vocal: it had shown itself, for example, in a message sent 19 October to the Council Fathers and signed by one hundred and eighty-two lay Catholics of twelve nations 'engaged in various fields of secular activity'.[11] This message put forward the familiar arguments: the moral permissibility, already conceded, of human interventions in other realms of physical life (transplantation of organs, the sacrifice of one's own life, etc.), the necessity of some control to compensate for the imbalances caused by earlier human interventions which aimed at eliminating factors hostile to life, the incongruity of accepting, as an absolute norm, respect for the conservation of biological processes, the attribution of the procreative purpose to the whole series of conjugal acts (of which the greater number are now found to be sterile by physiologists themselves), the profound human implications of the sexual bond and the importance of its expressions for the well-being of the children. The conclusions were quite logical: 'These facts indicate that certain elements in the present doctrine of the Church, particularly a certain concept of the natural law, of man's rights over his body, and of the intention attributed to the sexual act, have become at least debatable. We would ask therefore that the teaching of the Church should lay less emphasis on certain formulations of her doctrine which are largely influenced by their historical context. We would further ask that a way be opened for the new scientific and philosophical discoveries in this field to be incorporated into the theology and living thought of the Church. We are convinced that a place must be found for a concept of the natural law which does not exclude man's effective assumption of responsibility with regard to procreation. It would also seem essential not to exclude the permissibility of a view of sexual morality in which the objective morality of the sexual act, within the context of married love, would depend, not on a certain intention of deliberate procreation in each individual act, but on the orientation of the whole of married life towards a generous fecundity.'

As we have already pointed out, these considerations also had

[11] *Address to the Second Vatican Council on the subject of the problems of the family*, originating with an international group of lay Catholics, *pro manuscripto*, October 1964, 15 pp. The pamphlet contains also a French version of the document. Among those who signed it we mention only the writers already known to us, or whom we shall soon be dealing with: the Buelens, De Guchteneere, Dupré, Férin, Grootaers, Kriekemans, Leemans, Novak, John Rock, Schockaert, and Trimbos. Only one Italian added his signature: Prof. Giovanni Caletti of the University of Padua, Head of the Dermatological Section of the Civil Hospital 'Umberto I' of Mestre.

found authoritative expression in the Council speeches of the second group.

III. *Between the third and the fourth Council Session*

On the basis of suggestions offered in the Council, work began at once on a new edition of Schema 13: the most striking result was the incorporation of the *Adnexa* in the new text of the Constitution, but it was necessary also to take into account the great mass of specific proposals concerning the content (eight hundred and thirty pages of *animadversiones* (observations) concerning the whole Schema) which the debate had produced. The work, as is well known, was started in a meeting at Ariccia, 1–6 February 1965, of a hundred experts (29 Fathers, 38 specialist scholars and a score of other lay consultants). A 'working commission', presided over by Mgr Heuschen, Auxiliary Bishop of Liège, and including among its experts and collaborators Schillebeeckx, Delhaye, and Heylen, who edited the text, concentrated on the chapter on marriage and the family. From Ariccia the project was passed on to Rome, where the Sub-Commission (now increased to fourteen bishops and experts, still presided over by Mgr Guano) examined it carefully and set up special sub-committees to revise it. The Committee for the chapter on marriage was still presided over by Mgr Dearden, assisted by Mgr Heuschen, with Mgr Heylen as secretary. From 29 March to 16 April the text, thus revised, was examined, in a series of plenary sessions, by the Mixed Commission (now consisting of sixty bishops). It is known that there were very lively debates on the problem of conjugal morality. However, also because the conclusions of the Pontifical Commission had not yet been published,[12] the bishops still hesitated to include in

[12] A few days previously, 27 March, when receiving the members of the Pontifical Commission who were meeting in Rome for the fourth time, the Pope himself tried to accelerate their work. Although he admitted that a 'lively sense of the need to allow certain problems to mature may impose some reasonable delay', yet 'he begged them insistently not to lose sight of the urgency of a situation which required from the Church and her supreme Authority some extremely clear directives' (*A.A.S.* 57 [1965], pp. 388–9).

The same appeal was made in his speech of 24 June 1965, to the College of Cardinals, a year after his first intervention: after recalling the history of the question, Paul VI affirmed: 'the Commission has worked wonderfully well, but has not yet concluded its investigations. We do not wish to cut them short but we beg the Commission to be as speedy as possible, so that we may hope before long to be able to pronounce judgment, assisted by the light of human learning, and we beg the Lord to grant us also the light of his wisdom, to help us to decide on a theme of such vital importance' (*A.A.S.* 57 [1965], pp. 639–40).

the project (as more than one member had suggested) any clear directions about the birth control measures which were considered licit or illicit. So, after the incorporation of the various amendments suggested by the bishops of the Mixed Commission, the project received, 11 May, the approval of the Co-ordinating Commission and the official title of *Pastoral Constitution on the Church in the Modern World*. The text was sent to the bishops on 28 May and on 26 June they received a French version (prepared for reference purposes in the modern language most frequently used during the preparation of the Schema) with the promise that other translations would be ready by the beginning of the fourth Council Session.[13]

Of the new Constitution, the first chapter of the second part (nos. 60–64) sets out the doctrine 'de dignitate matrimonii et familiae fovenda': it is the product of the combination of no. 21 of the earlier Schema with the second *Adnexa*, in the same order previously followed, but with the inclusion of numerous 'amendments' proposed by the Fathers. Starting (no. 61) with the consideration of certain 'signs of the times' (and here were mentioned, in order to content some of the Fathers, some actual dangers such as eroticism and hedonism) the Schema then deals (no. 61) with the 'sacred character of marriage and family life', representing Christian marriage as a source of happiness and holiness for husband and wife, of education and sanctification for the children, of the expansion of civil society and of the Church. It develops (no. 62) the already familiar themes about conjugal love, seeking to follow a 'middle line' between the various opinions expressed by the Fathers, and to expound (as a 'large majority' had requested) the value and nature of love in conjugal life. Here was inserted a description (which must also be taken as a norm) of conjugal acts, a new addition to the earlier texts: 'This joy is particularly expressed and perfected in the conjugal act.

---

[13] *Constitutio pastoralis de Ecclesia in mundo huius temporis*, Typis Polyglottis Vaticanis, 1965, 122 pp. The title does not make it clear that this is really still only a 'schema' for a Constitution, as is evident in the French translation: *Schema de la Constitution Pastorale: L'Eglise dans le monde de ce temps, ibid.*, 1965, 102 pp. Only the Latin edition, to which the Fathers had to refer during discussion in the Council, includes at the end (pp. 84–118) the two *Relationes*, or Reports, one being a general Report and the others dealing with individual chapters, and we shall refer to these later on in so far as they are concerned with our subject.

Accordingly those acts through which married couples are intimately and honestly united are honourable. Expressed in a truly human way, they signify and foster total mutual selfgiving.'

Nos. 63–64 are concerned with the problems of fertility, and it is not hard to perceive, when we peruse the 'special report' on these points, that these pages were among those most modified by the 'observations' presented by the Fathers. This section tries to set fertility in marriage in its proper place, in a passage which, although the order of words is different and it contains some slight modifications, is copied from the earlier Schema: 'Such is the nature of marriage and conjugal love that they are ordained for both the procreation and the education of children. True conjugal love, therefore, and the whole meaning of family life which springs from this, have this aim: the generous and firm intention of the husband and wife to co-operate with the love of their Creator and Saviour, who by their means daily enlarges and enriches his family. Marriage, moreover, is not instituted solely for procreation. Rather, its very nature as an indissoluble contract between persons, and the well-being of their children, both demand that the mutual love of the husband and wife also be expressed in a fitting manner, so that it may grow and mature.'

The duty of the married couple to undertake responsible parenthood is still clearly affirmed: this was the opinion, says the 'special report', of the great majority of the Fathers, although some of them had insisted on the need for trustful abandonment to Providence, without any human calculations; nevertheless, as also had been requested, there was added a word of praise for large families and an important passage, of which only the final words were present in the earlier Schema, which (according to the declared intention of the editors) 'clearly affirms that the conscience of the married couple is directed in this matter by objective laws, and reaffirms that dishonest means are forbidden'.

'Married couples are aware that, in founding and rearing a family, they may not act as they please but must be ruled by a conscience properly submissive to God's law, and determine the size of their family according to the gifts of God and the intention of true love.'

Which these 'dishonest means' are is a problem which ought to receive a solution in no. 64, *God, the Master of Life*, but the editors at once affirm that they have proposed 'only the general principles and not the practical solutions, so that the Council may not have to descend to the consideration of particular cases, and in order to leave the matter entirely in the hands of the Pontifical Commission, to which it has been entrusted'. So, after having explicitly acknowledged the frequent and grave difficulties which married couples experience, especially in their attempts to reconcile the expression of their love with the needs of responsible parenthood, the Schema restricts itself to excluding the 'easier solution', that is, abortion and infanticide, both of these being 'grave sins'; otherwise, the document keeps to generalizations: 'The human power of procreation, wonderfully superior to that of lower forms of life, and the conjugal acts themselves, when effected in accordance with true human dignity, are to be honoured with great respect. Thus married couples, closely adhering to the divine law, firm in faith and strengthened by the grace of Christ, will constantly fulfil all their duties in mutual harmony.'

This was all. It is true that, as the editors assert, the text did not include the proposal put forward by a few Fathers 'not to exclude the use of contraceptive measures in the gravest cases'. Nevertheless no explicit condemnation of these was formulated and the condemnations of *Casti Connubii* and of Pius XII were not quoted. The principles which inspired the committee which produced the final text are well summed up at the end of the report: 'The method used in the discussion was chosen, after much debate, in order to satisfy the wishes of the Fathers who ask (a) that the question must be dealt with; (b) that the so-called 'methods of birth control' must therefore be discussed; (c) the question must not be expounded in terms that are too technical; (d) the Fathers particularly ask that the more general principles may be set forth, so that the way may be prepared for theological examination; (e) and that those principles may be drawn not only from biological or animal life but also from a consideration of the human order and the dignity of the human person.[14]

IV. *The second debate in Council. The final text*

When, on 23 September 1965, Schema 13 was presented to the

---

[14] This passage occurs in the 'relationes particulares', *ed. cit.*, p. 108. The reference to the Fathers who did not condemn contraceptive measures in very grave necessity is on p. 105.

Council by Mgr Garrone (who had taken the place of Mgr Guano, prevented by illness from attending) it was in fact a new document which had to go through the same process as the others: more discussion, the modification of the text, the first voting and the presentation of new suggestions, the final revision of the text and final vote. The same fate awaited the chapter on marriage, which was discussed 29 and 30 September.

The contributions to the discussion were not as original and abundant as they had been in the previous session, but nevertheless they showed that the Fathers were still divided into two opposing groups.[15] The traditional attitude was represented by, among others: Cardinal Ruffini who again asserted the primacy of the procreative purpose and demanded explicit condemnation of methods of birth control which impaired the integrity of the conjugal act, and of the 'pill', wrongly called by some writers the 'Catholic method'; Cardinal Browne, who also dwelt on the problem of the relative importance of the ends of marital inter-course and the alleged primacy of the procreational end; Mgr Nicodemo, who, among other things, complained of the Schema's silence about contraceptive drugs, undoubtedly illicit. The newer trend was defended by Cardinal Léger who described marriage as, first of all, 'an intimate communion of life and love', 'not closed within itself but incorporated within the great purpose of the creative providence of God'; Cardinal Suenens put forward a proposal to encourage scientific research in the field of sexuality, especially of conjugal sexuality, adding: 'We would point out that this proposal does not imply any theological or philosophical option in favour of one or other method of birth control: it does not deal with questions which are still controversial among mora-lists and it is useful in all hypotheses, whatever may be the final doctrinal judgment on this matter.' Mgr De Roo gave a masterly exposition of conjugal spirituality founded on love, which possesses great possibilities for human happiness and may reach sublime heights with the aid of grace. He said that the intimate expressions of conjugal love 'may provide consolation in moments in which the husband and wife are feeling discouraged, or are encountering grave difficulties, or at times when the home has lost the serenity which is so necessary for the well-being of the children'. And both

[15] The speeches, in adequate résumés or even in their complete text, may be read in *La documentation catholique* 62 (1965), pp. 1889–902.

tendencies were apparent also among those Fathers who explicitly requested that, while awaiting the Pope's pronouncements, the Council should avoid expressing an opinion on any problem connected with birth control: Cardinal Heenan, a member of the former group, was of this opinion and so was Mgr Reuss, of the second group.

Cardinal Giovanni Colombo, Archbishop of Milan, followed a middle course in his speech. He first of all praised the document's 'fully human and personalist' concept of the values and purposes of marriage, in which conjugal love is presented 'as an intrinsic end of marriage, just as essential as the procreative end'. He even affirmed an 'intimate correlation between conjugal love and the transmission of life, so that the very fecundity of the marriage, and a generous fecundity, springs from the nature of the love between husband and wife; it is born of love and belongs wholly to love'. This fecundity must become responsible, not through a 'concession to human weakness, but in order that the parents, interpreters and instruments of God's love to his creatures, may see that procreation takes place in the best possible conditions'. 'This principle of responsible parenthood', he said, 'which includes the procreative faculty within the sphere of reason enlightened by love, implicitly also includes the possibility of seeking and the permissibility of using all honourable means which may attain this end.' In fact, the Cardinal added, the Schema should say, even more clearly, that conjugal love and generous and responsible parenthood must be the supreme guiding principles of conjugal intercourse: 'Conjugal morality would then be a more complete whole. From now onwards, it must be very clear that every sexual act must necessarily, in order to be virtuous, take place in a context of truly Christian matrimonial love and in view of a generous but prudent fecundity. Unfortunately, however, in the manner in which the moral doctrine on marriage is presented, emphasis seems almost to be laid on the physical integrity of the conjugal acts alone.' Nevertheless, concluded the Archbishop of Milan, this physical integrity of coitus also, 'although it is not the only or supreme rule for married couples, must also be affirmed by the Council as a moral consideration which must not be ignored': the Council's silence on this matter might be interpreted as an indication of some change in doctrine. In reality, however, 'the physiological integrity of the act, which does not in itself constitute a moral value, is nevertheless an intrinsic element of that complete mutual love and sincere procreative intention which, as we have said, are the supreme laws of married life. In fact, the very greatness and dignity of conjugal love demand that the husband and wife shall be fully united in those acts without reserves or limitations; in the same way, only if it is perfect can the act be the sign and symbol of that profound and constant procreative purpose which must always be present in husband and wife even where "here and now" it cannot or must not be realized in fact. Just as love and the procreative purpose cannot be separated from each other in the sublimity of the spirit, so they must not be separated in the humility of the flesh.'

This is an assertion which, in line with the earlier teaching of the Magisterium, needs to be reaffirmed, although, from other points of view (here the Cardinal was probably thinking, for example, of the treatment with oestro-progestational drugs, which in itself respects the integrity of intercourse) 'the continuing progress made in knowledge of the moral law, apparent in the field of matrimonial morality, may lead to a greater understanding and a more profound analysis of many details'.

To conclude: on the problem of methods of birth control, the Council debate brought into the light two different attitudes. There were some who asked for a reaffirmation of the traditional condemnations, and there were others instead who wished the problem to be passed over in silence, or at least to be restricted to some general assertions, in order to leave the way clear for the theological discussion which was meanwhile continuing with fervour on both sides. The rigidity of the two opposing groups made it clear that neither would win the day and that a solution would be found in some compromise—and this is exactly what happened.

The whole of October was taken up with revising the text, in order to incorporate the Fathers' observations. The chapter on marriage was first of all entrusted to the special Sub-Commission[16] to which were added—at the request of Mgr Carlo Colombo and

[16] This Sub-Commission consisted of the following members: the Bishops Dearden, Carlo Colombo, van Dodewaard, Petit, Morris, Castellano, Scherer; the experts Heylen, Lambruschini, Géraud, Delhaye, Prignon, Schillebeeckx, van Leeuwen; the lay auditors Minoli, Work, Adjakpley and the married couple, Alvarez.

Mgr Castellano—four members of the Pontifical Commission: Zalba, Fuchs, Wisser and Ford.[17] Then, in the context of the whole Schema, it was discussed by the Mixed Commission, at the end of October. When the new text was completed it was presented to the Council for voting on 16 November:[18] in his report of the second part of the Schema Mgr Hengsbach informed the Fathers that 'in the chapter on the dignity of marriage and the family they were not to develop the teaching of the Church on those points which are the subject of the special Pontifical Commission; the questions under discussion were still open; in the doctrine of conjugal love, with regard to its nature and purpose, the text follows the teaching of Pius XI and Pius XII; in all that it says about the honour due to the conjugal act and responsible parenthood emphasis is placed on objective moral principles and the teaching of the Magisterium; more space is given in the new text to conjugal spirituality and moral teaching on this theme'.[19]

An examination of the new text immediately shows that the most significant additions concern the problem of fecundity (to which are devoted nos. 47-52, taking the place of the previous nos. 63-64), and express the intention to lay down objective rules ('in order to avoid any form of subjectivism', says the report) to guide married couples in their decision about the number of their offspring, and the various means of birth control. With regard to the former question a new passage was inserted in no. 50: 'The parents themselves, and no one else, should ultimately form this judgement in the sight of God. In all they do, let Christian husbands and wives remember that they may not act arbitrarily but must always be guided by a conscience enlightened by the divine law itself, and they must always submit to the Church's teaching office which authentically interprets that law in the light

[17] In fact, Ford seems to have been added to the Commission by Cardinal Ottaviani himself. In any case, he was unable to leave the United States and so took no part in the debate. Of the four, Wisser, Zalba and Ford certainly belonged to the 'traditionalist' party. It must be noted that, among the experts of the Sub-Commission, Lambruschini and Delhaye were also members of the Pontifical Commission.

[18] *Schema Constitutionis pastoralis de Ecclesia in mundo huius temporis. Textus recognitus et relationes*, Typis Polyglottis Vaticanis, 1965, part I,61 pp.; part II, 91 pp.

[19] *Relationes super Schema Constitutionis pastoralis de Ecclesia in mundo huius temporis*, Typis Polyglottis Vaticanis, 1965, p. 13.

of the gospel. That divine law safeguards the full meaning of conjugal love and guides it to its true human fulfilment'.

As for means of birth control, after a more understanding account of the difficulties in which married couples may find themselves, the text rejects all 'solutions unworthy of man', pointing out immediately that there can be no contradiction between the divine laws which govern the transmission of life and the fostering of true conjugal love; after having proposed once more the already mentioned consideration about the 'respect' to be shown to conjugal acts ('according to the true dignity of human order') it adds this new explanatory passage: 'Therefore the moral aspect of the reason for conjugal acts, when it is a question of harmonizing conjugal love with responsible parenthood, does not depend solely upon sincere intention and an evaluation of motives but must be decided according to objective standards. These, based on the dignity of the human person in itself, safeguard the full significance of mutual self-giving and human procreation in the context of true love. The children of the Church must be imbued with these principles in order that they may not adopt methods of birth control which are forbidden by the Magisterium.'

The Council's intention was—as is explained in the Report—to 'exclude all subjectivism and assert the insufficiency of personal intention and of the evaluation of individual motives as a basis for moral judgment; instead the faithful must be offered objective criteria by which there may be safeguarded, in the procreative act, the intrinsic significance of mutual self-giving, in a context of true love, so that this true love may express itself rightly'. In order to emphasize the objectivity of these criteria, reference was made to the teaching of the Magisterium, but without explicitly quoting the condemnations pronounced by Pius XI and Pius XII. In any case there always remained 'human dignity as an objective moral criterion', as the Report says, and it is not difficult to understand—in the light of the theological discussion still continuing—that this criterion was far more authoritative than that other, proposed by the earlier teaching of the Magisterium, based on the 'nature of the act'.

On 16 November a vote was taken on the first chapter of the second part: it was approved with 1596 *'placet'* against 72 *'non placet'* and 484 *'placet juxta modum'*; the more detailed vote on paragraphs 54–65, including also the passages on birth control, had, shortly before this, resulted in 2163 'placet' against 140 'non placet' (in this case the vote 'juxta modum' was not allowed). After approval, therefore, the text could no longer be subjected to any substantial modifications, although it was still necessary to proceed to the examination and adoption of the emendations suggested by the Fathers. The new and definitive text was to be presented for the final vote on 4 December.

Meanwhile the work on the emendations began. The Sub-Commission for the chapter on marriage, presided over by Bp Dearden, began the revision on 17 November; again the Sub-Commission was strengthened by the presence of members of the Pontifical Commission, this time in greater number.[20] The very numerous emendations (modi) were sifted and carefully examined. A score of these (proposed by about sixty bishops) concerned the paragraphs we have already quoted about the question of sexual conduct when it is necessary to reconcile conjugal love with responsible parenthood, and some amendments, which suggested different versions with regard to the 'objective' moral criteria therein invoked, said to be derived from the 'dignity of the human person', were expressed in the new formulation of the objective criteria deduced from 'natural personal acts', in which it was intended (as the expensio modorum points out) to emphasize that 'these acts also are not to be judged from the purely biological point of view, but inasmuch as they are proper to the human person according to an integral and adequate conception'. On the contrary, an amendment proposed by two Fathers, requesting that there should be an explicit reference to the condemnation of onanism contained in Casti Connubii, was not accepted because it was considered to be too unilateral in relation to the general doctrine of the Magisterium.[21] Generally speaking also, various

[20] Besides the four members already mentioned (Ford, Fuchs, Visser, Zalba—Ford also was sometimes present) there were also the Bishops Binz and Reuss and the theologians De Riedmatten (Secretary of the Pontifical Commission), Auer, de Locht, de Lestapis and Perico. It has been written that 'some of those who advised this procedure may have intended in this way, with the addition of representatives of the "traditionalist" party, to dominate the more progressive group which had formed the majority of the Conciliar Sub-Commission', but in fact only the Bishops had the right to vote in Commission and it must be remembered that even the members of the Pontifical Commission are divided in their opinions.

[21] 'Correct procedure requires that more than one passage should be quoted and this is not possible here' (from the unpublished relatio subcommissionis de

requests for more detailed references to methods of birth control were also rejected, because they trespassed on ground reserved for the Pontifical Commission.

However, there was little general agreement, and this was evident in the course of an extra-Conciliar meeting, held at the request of Mgr Carlo Colombo on 21 November (Sunday), attended by members of the Sub-Commission and bishops and theologians of the Pontifical Commission. During this meeting ten of the members present proposed that the chapter on marriage should be withdrawn because 'it dangerously added to the confusion, both by its silences and by its manner of referring to new viewpoints which permitted conclusions opposed to traditional doctrine',[22] but the contrary view of the great majority of those present prevailed. It was pointed out that this chapter, which had been long awaited, although not yet complete, contained a very rich contribution of doctrine on marriage and the family. The evening of 24 November (the day before the new text was to go before the Mixed Commission) the Cardinal Secretary of State notified the President of this Commission that the Pope personally proposed four amendments.

All these, in various ways, concerned the problem of fertility in marriage. In the first amendment the Pope asked that among the erroneous modern manifestations which impaired the dignity of marriage (polygamy, divorce, free love) mentioned in the first section (no. 51) of the chapter, there should be mentioned also 'contraceptive devices'. The second proposed the suppression of the word *etiam* (also) which had been introduced into the 'revised text' in no. 54 where it was said that '*verus amoris coniugalis cultus totaque vitae familiaris ratio inde oriens etiam eo tendunt . . .*'[23] ('The growth of conjugal love and the whole character of family life deriving from it *also* tend to this . . .'.) and the addition of the following clause: '*filii sunt praestantissimum matrimonii donum et ad ipsorum parentum bonum maxime conferunt*' ('children are the supreme gift of matrimony and bring the greatest benefit to

---

Matrimonio Commissioni generali mixtae ad expensionem modorum, quoted by V. HEYLEN, *op. cit.*, p. 559.

[22] *Rapport de la session commune de la sous-commission conciliaire 'de Matrimonio' et des théologiens de la Commission pontificale*, also unpublished, p. 560.

[23] Cf. the actual text, which we have quoted above in full (p. 134), as it was before the introduction of '*etiam*'.

their parents'). Then came the third amendment, the most significant of all: in it the Pope asked that the conclusion of the passage on birth control, which we have quoted above, should be materially altered to include the words: 'Fortified by these principles (we teach) the children of the Church that in matters concerning birth control they are not to resort to methods which have been forbidden or are now forbidden by the teaching authority of the Church', and that explicit reference should be made to the two most important documents which deal with this question, *Casti Connubii* (in particular the passage which condemned onanism) and Pius XII's Speech to the Midwives (of which, however, the emendation mentioned no one passage in particular). Finally, the fourth amendment proposed that, after the account of the difficulties in which married couples may find themselves (no. 55), the document should affirm the need for husband and wife 'to make a sincere effort to cultivate conjugal chastity' in order to overcome these difficulties.

These four amendments, and an accompanying letter from Cardinal Cicognani, were read by Cardinal Ottaviani on the morning of 25 November to the Mixed Commission, which had met to examine the suggested amendments to Schema 13. He gave this accompanying letter 'a somewhat restrictive interpretation of the Commission's competence with regard to the amendments put forward. On the other hand, the text of the letter insisted on the importance of the pronouncements by Pius XI and Pius XII, and on the necessity of preventing a fatal confusion spreading among the public. The papal initiative, in the form in which it was presented, seemed to surpass the bounds of prudence hoped for by the Fathers. The consternation felt by all present was soon followed by doubts about the Pope's real intentions: did he wish to prevent abuses by appealing to the principles he had already laid down, or did he wish to reaffirm the old doctrines?[24] Moreover it could not be denied that 'a minority, to some extent "integralist", had wished to seize this chance of playing their cards for the last time';[25] it seemed improbable that the Pope could suddenly require from the Council the solution of a problem which had been withdrawn from its sphere of competence and

[24] V. HEYLEN, *op. cit.*, pp. 560-1.

[25] *Ibid.*, p. 561.

entrusted to a special Pontifical Commission. Therefore, seeing the impossibility of obtaining any valid results in such a confusion, the Commission contented itself on that day with the examination of other amendments proposed for the chapter on marriage. T next day a new letter from Cardinal Cicognani, referring to his previous letter, informed the Fathers that the Holy Father merely intended to offer some suggestions and that he was willing to examine, for eventual approval, any counter proposals which the Mixed Commission might send him: this approval was in fact granted, 29 November, after the Commission had, two days earlier, sent him the new text and the relative report.[26]

The first amendment, which is in the name of sixteen Fathers (two of whom, however, speak of 'onanism') was accepted by the Commission, but with a notable change of wording: the expression *artes anticonceptionales* (contraceptive devices) was dismissed as too technical and ambiguous, and the more generic expression *'illiciti usus contra generationem'*[27] (illicit methods of birth control) was substituted for it. As for the second amendment, which corresponded to the requests of several other Fathers, the adverb *etiam* (also) which (as explained in the *expensio modorum*) 'had been introduced not to circumvent the problem of the relative values of the purposes of matrimony, but to emphasize the fact that procreation is not its only purpose', was replaced with the formula 'without neglecting the other ends of marriage'. There was then added 'in order to teach the importance of progeny', the clause suggested by the Pope: 'children are the supreme gift of

[26] Among the various approaches made to the Pope during those days was a letter sent to him by the lay members of the Mixed Commission and by the auditors who had been present at the discussions. G. DE ROSA, S.J., *op. cit.*, p. 736, quotes from it the following passage: 'The *Modi* (reflections) deal with questions to which public opinion is extremely sensible . . . . It seems to us of supreme importance that the solution given for these problems shall be as comprehensive as possible and shall be offered in conditions which will enable it to be trustfully received by the faithful and with respectful understanding by the world which is observing us. We consider that such a reception would be gravely compromised by a partial reply, which would be unwelcome, consisting merely in a series of last minute corrections added to a text which is already familiar and well known to the public. It will be better understood if the Council, while awaiting Your Holiness's decision on these extremely delicate matters, will restrict itself to a declaration of the essential principles, which in no way prejudice the results of the research now being carried on.'

[27] We quote the explanatory references to the new papal amendments from the report contained in the volume of which we shall speak in note 29.

matrimony and bring the greatest benefit to their parents'. As regards the reference to the cultivation of conjugal chastity (fourth amendment), this was in fact inserted, but not in the place which had been suggested 'lest it might be thought that the Council proposes conjugal chastity as the only means of resolving these difficulties'.

The study of the third amendment was more complex. First of all, the Commission retained the earlier version *'quae a Magisterio improbantur'* ('which are forbidden by the Magisterium'), rejecting the words 'which have been forbidden or are now forbidden'. It seemed impossible to defend these words, explains Heylen, 'when we consider the history of the Ordinary Magisterium which, at a certain moment in the past, condemned even periodic continence, now declared permissible'.[28] It accepted, however, the more rigid formula *'non licet'* instead of the earlier *'ne ineant'* and added, in line with suggestions put forward by some Fathers, *'in lege divina explicanda'*, in order to indicate better the Magisterium's proper sphere of competence and lest it should be thought that its function was merely disciplinary. So the final text was as follows: 'The children of the Church, fortified by these principles, may not use methods forbidden by the Magisterium in the course of its exposition of divine law.'

As regards quoting the condemnations pronounced in *Casti Connubii* and in Pius XII's Speech to the Midwives, this was done in Note no. 14, but with the immediate addition of a quotation from Pope Paul's speech of 23 June 1964, in order to prove that the Council did not intend merely to reaffirm teachings which Paul VI had said were to be subjected to a thorough re-examination. Moreover, to avoid any misunderstanding, this was explicitly stated in the concluding paragraph of the same note: 'Other problems which require further and more thorough investigations have, by command of the Supreme Pontiff, been handed over to the Commission for the study of population, the family and births, in order that, when this task has been completed, the Pope himself may give judgment. This being the present state of the teaching of the Church, the Sacred Synod does not propose to put forward practical solutions at this juncture.'

It is, however, clear that the attitude constantly adopted by the Sub-Commission, the Mixed Commission and the Council (all

[28] V. HEYLEN, *op. cit.*, p. 562.

resolved not to give judgment on individual methods of birth
control but merely to indicate the general principles of reference)
was fully maintained even in the last somewhat hectic days of
their labours. This also was a way of showing respect to the
normal development of the theological discussion which was taking
place elsewhere, and of which the Fathers were evidently kept
informed. The new text of Schema 13, with its corrections and the
expensio modorum, was distributed in two volumes on 2 and 3
December,[29] and was voted upon in the following days: the
chapter on marriage was voted on 4 December and received
2047 *placet* against 155 *non placet* and 7 abstentions.

Conclusion

Thus ended the Conciliar phase of our problem. But the work
of the Pontifical Commission did not end here, for it was asked
by the Council to study the 'practical solutions'.

The Pope also awaited and requested results. He had said
this several times during 1965,[30] and a few days before the
Council debate, in an interview he granted to the *Corriere della
sera*, 3 October, he had made particular reference—in words
which betrayed all his anxiety about this problem—to the work of
the Commission:

'We are faced with so many problems! They are so numerous
and we have so many answers to prepare! We wish to speak to
the world, and we have to decide day by day on matters which will
have consequences throughout the centuries. We must answer the
questions of the modern man, the modern Christian, and there are
some questions, such as those concerned with the problems of the
Christian family, which we find particularly difficult. Take
birth control, for example. The world asks for our opinion and
we have to find an answer. But what answer? It is impossible
to keep silent, but to speak is most difficult. The Church has

---

[29] *Schema Constitutionis pastoralis de Ecclesia in mundo huius temporis. Textus
et correctiones admissae necnon expensio modorum partis primae*, Typis Polyglottis
Vaticanis 1965, 256 pp. *ibid., Expensio modorum partis secundae, ed. cit.*, 1965,
155 pp. The 'reflections' (*modi*) on the chapter on marriage are found in this
second volume, pp. 5–44; the report refers only very discreetly to the amendments suggested by the Pope, in the final note (p. 44), directing the reader to
nos. 5, 71, 98 and 107 of the *expensio Modorum*, where these are 'earnestly and
reverently' considered.

[30] Cf. above, note 12.

never, for centuries, had to face such questions. And this is a matter which is extraneous to the life of priests, even causing some natural embarrassment. So, the Commissions meet and the piles of reports and studies mount up. No doubt the question is being studied. But at the end of it all it is we who have to decide. And we are alone in our decision. It is harder to decide than to study. But we must say something. What . . . ? We need God's help to enlighten us.'[31]

When the Council ended he had a new opportunity of speaking on this problem, 12 February 1966, when he received the members of the Centro Italiano Femminile. On this occasion he frankly reminded them that the great congress had left certain problems still unsolved, and he tried to explain the reasons for the long and complicated work undertaken by the Commission: 'It was not possible, within the Council, to complete a thorough examination of this question, especially in all that concerns the grave and complex problem of the principles relating to procreation . . . It was not possible to study all the problems for which Christian husbands and wives, and parents, await and desire an answer. Some of these, because of their complexity and delicacy, could not easily be discussed in such a large assembly; others required, and still require, profound study, for which, as is well known, a special Pontifical Commission has been set up, charged to under-take the study of these problems in all their varied aspects, scientific, historical, sociological and doctrinal. The Commission is strengthened by numerous consultations with bishops and other specialists. We beg you to await the results of these studies, accompanying them with your prayers: the Magisterium of the Church cannot propose moral principles unless it is certain of interpreting the will of God, and in its efforts to arrive at this certainty the Church is not dispensed from study and research, nor from the examination of the numerous questions which from every part of the world are proposed for her consideration: these operations are sometimes long and difficult.'[32] The Pope then

[31] The text is to be found also in the book written by the journalist to whom the interview was granted: A Cavallari, *Il Vaticano che cambia*, Milan, Mondadori, 1966, p. 51.

[32] PAUL VI, *Mulieribus quae interfuerunt* . . . , a speech to the Thirteenth Congress of the Centro Femminile Italiano, 12 February 1966: *A.A.S.* 58 (1966), pp. 218-19. The Pope's state of mind at the end of November 1965

proceeded to give some general principles of Christian conduct in
marriage, principles which are derived from the belief that
marriage 'finds in human love, in accordance with the purpose and
will of God, the fundamental law of its moral purpose'.

Less than a month later, 7 March, the Holy Father strengthened
and enlarged the Commission by appointing seven cardinals and
nine bishops to join and direct it (actually Binz and Reuss were
already members, but among the newcomers must be mentioned
Dearden and Carlo Colombo) under the presidency of Cardinal
Ottaviani and the Vice-presidency of Cardinals Heenan and
Doepfner.[33] On 13 April there began in Rome the last working
session of this Commission: after a few days during which a select
group examined the work already done and the documentation
relative to the work still before them, the members of the doctrinal

is clear from what he said to A. Wenger (cf. *op. cit.*, IV, pp. 198-9) in the course
of an Audience granted to him on the evening of 26 November, the day on
which the difficulties which had arisen in the Mixed Commission with regard
to the Papal amendment had been smoothed out: 'There are no longer any
difficulties on the part of the Commission and consequently none on the part
of the Council, but the problem of the regulation of births remains unsolved.
Nothing has been decided. We have not wished to close the door upon the
Commission's research. And it was equally necessary that the Commission's
document should not close the door on Us, one way or another.'

[33] The Press immediately drew attention to the fact that the two Vice-
Presidents represented the two opposing tendencies: Cardinal Heenan the
'traditionalist' outlook and Cardinal Doepfner the movement for reform. In
fact, we have already referred to Cardinal Heenan's interventions, both within
and outside the Council. The general impression that Cardinal Doepfner was
a 'progressive' was increased by the publication, at the time of his nomination,
of a document which was at first attributed to him personally (cf. *The Tablet*
of 12 March 1966: later on it was published in very many other Catholic
periodicals in various languages). At one point it said: 'It is of decisive importance, for the good and holy growth of Christian marriage, that the young
married couple should place themselves deliberately, from the start of their
married life, under God's direction. In present day circumstances, it may
happen that after some years of marriage they will find themselves in a difficult
situation in which it would be irresponsible on their part to have another child,
at least for a certain time, while their conjugal unity is and remains of supreme
importance for the interior stability of their marriage and the perfecting of
their conjugal love. When this husband and wife, who seek to build up their
marriage in a spirit of mutual Christian responsibility and care for the well-
being of their children, believe that in such a difficult situation they cannot
avoid having recourse to "unnatural" means, they may not be accused, simply
and starkly, of abusing their marriage. Nevertheless, bearing in mind the
actual facts which are today the subject of frequent and earnest discussions
among theologians and moralists, and taking into account the declarations
hitherto made by the Church, the doctrinal and pastoral authorities of the

section[34] debated for four weeks (18 April–14 May) the general and particular problems now awaiting a solution (the natural law and moral principles, the competence of the Magisterium in this matter, the morality of interference with human faculties and in particular with the sexual faculty), step by step comparing their reports with the information of a medical, psychological and sociological order which was presented by some members of the Commission, specialists in their own fields. Then followed, until 19 June, a period of intense and careful editing, examination and comparison of the various reports, in preparation for the meeting with the cardinals and bishops which was held from 19–26 June, after which the results achieved were presented to the Supreme Pontiff. The press almost immediately announced that these results were largely favourable to the ideas of the reformers.[35]

Church cannot simply approve of these practices in a general way. The responsible married couple who feel obliged to use contraceptive methods, not light-heartedly and habitually, but rather unwillingly as a last resort, may be allowed to believe that by doing so they do not forfeit the right to share in Holy Communion. They will recognize very humbly that they are only on the way towards reaching that maturity of conjugal love which is in perfect harmony with God's will, and that they must in all honesty try to correspond wholeheartedly to God's loving appeal.'

In a letter to Cardinal Heenan (cf. *The Tablet*, 30 April 1966) Cardinal Doepfner explained that the document, published 'through an indiscretion', did not emanate from him personally; it had been drawn up by his pastoral Office ('naturally not without my knowledge') in order to give some guidance to priests giving instruction about marriage to engaged couples. In order to understand these directives, concluded the letter, it was of course necessary to see them in their context, generally ignored or distorted by the Press. They were the expression of a subjective judgment concerning the conduct of married persons who honestly try to live according to God's law, but who suffer from difficulties of conscience because of the actual circumstances of their lives.

[34] The members of the Commission invited to these meetings were: Bishop Reuss, the Monsignori Onclin, Abbo, Lambruschini; the Canons Anciaux, Delhaye, de Locht; the Professors Auer, van Melson, Görres; the Fathers Ford, Fuchs, Häring, de Lestapis, Labourdette, Perico, Sigmond, Visser, Zalba and Don Goffi. Hellegers represented the medical profession and Barrett the sociologists; other doctors, psychologists and sociologists belonging to the Commission intervened from time to time. Among the 'invited experts' were present, on certain occasions, Noonan, Semmelroth, Valsecchi and Egenter. De Riedmatten acted as permanent Secretary.

[35] The principal reports drawn up by the Commission are today known, because of an unjustifiable 'release of documents' in April 1967, resulting in their publication in an American Catholic paper, *The National Catholic Reporter*, and in the English Catholic weekly, *The Tablet* (cf. pp. 449–54, 478–85, 510–13 respectively in the numbers issued 22 and 29 April and 6 May). The

Nevertheless, and in spite of the urgency of the problem, the waiting period was to be still further prolonged.[36] The Pope announced this himself, in a speech he made, 29 October 1966, to a meeting of the Italian Society of Obstetrics and Gynaecology. After having recalled that, in conformity with what he had himself said in his first reference to this subject, 23 June 1964, 'the thought and the rule of the Church are not changed: they are those of the traditional teaching', Paul VI observed that 'the Ecumenical Council, lately held, has contributed certain elements for the formation of opinion, most useful for the integration of Catholic doctrine on this important theme but not such as to change its essential terms'; he then affirmed that the conclusions reached by the Commission could not yet be considered as final, but needed 'supplementary studies': 'We have thought it necessary to undertake an objective study of the new proposals and elements for forming an opinion. This seemed to us to be our duty, and we have tried to do this in the best way by appointing a wide, varied, highly competent international Commission which, in its various sections and lengthy discussions, has completed a great work and passed on to us its conclusions. But these do not yet seem to us definitive, because they present grave implications with

text of the interview granted by Fr de Reidmatten, 4 July 1966, to Italian Television, which was of a more general content, may be seen in *Il Regno* II (1966), pp. 450–541 (French version in *La Documentation Catholique* 63 (1966), pp. 1411–14). Certainly the wide publicity given to the reports of the Commission, and particularly to that of the 'progressive' majority, must have influenced the development of the whole problem because of the great authority of its authors: see, for example, the importance given to it by Cardinal Raúl Silva Henriquez in a recent interview on birth control ('La Iglesia y la regulación de la natalidad', *Mensaje* 16 [1967], pp. 362–3).

[36] This urgency was pointed out again by the group of lay Catholics who had signed the Message to the Council to which we have already referred (note 11) in a further message they sent in May 1966: *Second address to the Magisterium of the Church on the Subject of Family Problems*, Rome, *pro manuscripto*, 1966, 7 pp. This time five hundred people signed the document. Its central concept consists in the affirmation that the integrity of biological processes is only of secondary significance. We quote the most important assertions: that 'the foundation of all authentically Christian morality lies in respect and love for the human person, endowed with the gifts of freedom and reason, created in the image of the living God. This fundamental idea, upon which a dialogue with the contemporary world may be based, was unequivocally presented by

numerous other questions, also of considerable importance, whether of a doctrinal, pastoral or social order, which cannot be isolated and set apart but require logical consideration in the context of the question that is now the object of study. This fact indicates, once more, the enormous complexity and tremendous gravity of the subject of birth control; our sense of responsibility demands more supplementary study to which, with great respect for those who have already given it so much attention and labour, but with an equally keen sense of the obligation of our apostolic office, we are now resolutely giving our attention. This is the reason why we have delayed giving our answer and why we shall still have to defer it for some time longer.' He concluded by re-affirming once more the validity, for practical purposes, of the traditional rules: 'Meanwhile, as we said in our above-mentioned speech, the rule until now taught by the Church, integrated by the wise instructions of the Council, demands faithful and generous obedience. It may not be considered as if it were no longer binding, or as if the Magisterium of the Church were now in a state of

the Council as the basis for the doctrine on marriage; it implies man's responsibility for the preservation and active realization of true human values, including those of a physical nature. It is in the light of this principle that we must consider in their due importance the various aspects of the problems of fertility, and particularly the moral judgment of the physiological integrity of the reproductive factors. What is the significance of this integrity, in the total sum of the values of married life, based upon conjugal unity and responsible parenthood? The Council refers to personal values and, in emphasizing their transcendent character, does not subordinate them to the demands of permanent conformity with the biological order. In present conditions, in fact, it is no longer possible to consider the total preservation of this biological order as an indispensable condition of human integrity. Certainly, some directives were given, in other periods, in very strict terms, but they belong to a certain historical background, and moreover they are inspired by an interpretation, then generally accepted, of the natural law which is seen today to be defective. The theological concept upon which these directives are based, that of a God who is lord and master of our bodies, requires a very discreet interpretation, in order not to become tainted with anthromorphism and a dualist philosophy of mankind. Moreover, the increasing acknowledgement of the legitimacy of several important interventions in human biological processes, such as the transplantation of organs for various motives, indicates that the notion of the respect due to biological

doubt, whereas it is in a moment of study and reflection concerning what has been put forward as deserving most attentive consideration.'[37]

Meanwhile, however, still among theologians and especially since the Council, an active discussion is being carried on. This remains for us to examine in the last chapter of our survey.

integrity is not so absolute as to make it impossible for it to be subordinated to the principle of the welfare of the human person, understood in its complete sense. Some recent trends in theology, which seek to use anthropological data to justify the demand that man shall submit himself unconditionally to the obligation of preserving the integrity of his biological structures in general, and particularly in the sexual sphere, must be received at least with reserve. We must also express our reserves about a theology which, not distinguishing sufficiently between various fields of knowledge, has evolved a new 'determinism' contrary to the more personal values, and gives the authority of absolute moral law to what are merely psychological standpoints, valid only in their own sphere. On the other hand, many objective data in themselves show the impossibility of making the biological integrity of human functions an absolute moral principle.'

[37] PAUL VI, *Ad Gynaecologicae atque obstetriciae disciplinae peritos* (speech to the Congress of the Italian Society of Obstetricians and Gynaecologists) 29 October 1966: *A.A.S.* 58 (1966), pp. 1168–70. See also the reference to measures of birth control 'in conformity with the requirements of the moral law', contained in the encyclical *Populorum progressio*, no. 37 (note 39 refers to *Gaudium et spes*, nos. 50–51 and note 14): *A.A.S.*, 15 April 1967, pp. 275–6.

THE VARIOUS POSITIONS ASSUMED SINCE THE COUNCIL

When we examine the position assumed by Catholic theologians since the Council we see that, amid all the wealth of thoughtful teaching and pastoral counsel offered to the faithful on the subject of marriage and sexuality, it still left open the problem of the legitimacy of the various methods of birth control.

I. *The unreservedly negative attitude*

Few theologians now are still opposed to all possible innovation, and among these we must first of all mention those already known to us who had intervened, sometimes on several occasions, in the earlier discussions.

First come the two well-known American moralists who declare decidedly in favour of the definitive character of the earlier thesis:

> J. F. Ford, S.J., 'Footnote on contraception', *America* 114 (1966), pp. 103–7. The article is a reply to R. A. McCormick, S.J., 'The Council on contraception', *ibid.*, pp. 47–8. Ford expresses the same views again in 'More on the Council and contraception', *ibid.*, pp. 553–7.
>
> J. J. Lynch, S.J., 'The contraceptive issue: moral and pastoral reflections', *Theological Studies* 27 (1966), pp. 242–65.

In January he replied briefly to the above mentioned article by his fellow Jesuit McCormick, which seemed to him too generic in its treatment of the question. The eminent moralist, member of the Pontifical Commission for the family and procreation, maintains that in fact the Council appealed explicitly to *Casti Connubii*, thus satisfying a wish expressed by the Pope himself, and in this way specified authoritatively which ways of birth control were condemned by the Magisterium. The question which still remained open was not this but that of the relative importance of the purposes of marriage. A few months later, Lynch added his weight to this argument, in a longer and more fully annotated article in which all contraceptive measures, including the use of the pill, are still peremptorily forbidden. This view is based on the traditional principles concerning the nature of copulation, the limited and indirect power which man has over his generative function, and also on the teaching of the Magisterium, which was not modified by *Gaudium et spes*: in fact this Constitution refers to the condemnations of Pius XI and Pius XII. Pope Paul's speech of 23 June 1964 is significant only in having left open to theological discussion the question of oral contraceptives (but these too, in Lynch's own opinion, are illicit). As for the duties of confessors— the Jesuit concludes—they must in no case allow themselves in this matter to be influenced by the principle of probability: the Church is in no state of doubt, even if the Pope delays his reply. In fact, the discussion still continuing offers a useful opportunity for a re-consideration of the foundations of the traditional doctrine, certainly not for weakening the certainty of its content.

In Europe McReavy, in one of his customary replies (which, however, makes no explicit reference to Vatican II), asserts that it is not for the Church or the State to decide on the permissibility of the various contraceptive means, the intrinsic purpose of the conjugal act being unalterable.

L. L. McReavy, 'Existential objections to the traditional teaching on contraception', *The Clergy Review* 51 (1966), pp. 56–60.

Equally well known, and equally conservative, are three other scholars: Zalba, de Lestapis and Peinador:

M. Zalba, S.J., 'De Dignitate matrimonii et familiae fovenda', *Periodica de re morali, canonica et liturgica* 55 (1966), pp. 381–429; 'Circa ordinem rectum in usu matrimonii Episcopi per orbem quid tradiderint', *ibid.*, 56 (1967), pp. 61–87.[1]
S. de Lestapis, S.J., 'Control de natalidad y Vaticano II', *Revista*

---

[1] See, by the same author, an article written shortly before: 'Num Ecclesia doctrinam suam mutaverit', *Periodica de re morali, canonica et liturgica* 54 (1965), pp. 461–89, in which he examines certain doctrines which assert a change of opinion on the part of the Magisterium (with regard to periodic continence, castration for choral purposes, the value and significance of sexual pleasure, the right to revolt, usury etc.) whereas, in his opinion, these were merely

de Fomento Social 21 (1966), pp. 143–55; 'Regulación de natalidad
y antropologia', *Razón y fe* 173 (1966), pp. 579–96.

A. Peinador, C.M.F., 'Estado actual de las opiniones sobre
moralidad y responsabilidad en materia matrimonial', *Salman-
ticensis* 14 (1967). pp. 3–44.

G. Martelet, S.J., *Amour conjugale et renouveau conciliare*, Lyons,
Mappus, 1967, p. 48.

For Zalba (the only Roman moralist who continued to raise
his voice after the Council), the condemnation pronounced by
Pius XI and Pius XII, explicitly referred to also in *Gaudium et
spes*, can never be withdrawn. He admits that it is true that it
could only be arrived at '*satis obscure*', that is, by the light of
reason alone, and that even Holy Writ contains no precise and
indisputable norms concerning this question, nevertheless it is in
the power of the Magisterium to decide on it (as it has in fact
already decided), if not with a 'definition of faith', at least with an
authoritative declaration which demands 'internal assent'. Zalba
quotes not only from *Casti Connubii* and Pius XII's Speech to
the Midwives but also from *Gaudium et spes* and Paul VI's speech
of 23 June 1964 (from which some wish to conclude, '*quod vix
suaderi poterit*' ['which is hardly convincing'], that at least the
question of the pill has remained open), but he maintains that this
speech must be understood in the context of the irrevocable
teaching of the Magisterium which has declared illicit 'every
human interference in the natural biological process which is
intended for procreation'. Moreover, this doctrine (as Zalba tries
to prove in the second article we have mentioned) was put forward
not only by Pius XI and Pius XII but also previously and during
the same period—besides being stated in numerous replies and
resolutions of the Holy Office and the Sacred Penitentiary—in the
collective documents of the episcopates of various nations: of
Belgium (2 June 1909), Germany (1913), France (7 May 1919),

contingent changes within an essential continuity of doctrine. See also Zalba's
course of instructions, edited 'for private use' (*Adnotationes de castitate*,
Rome, Pont. Univ. Gregor., 1965–66, 135 pp.) in which the eminent moral
theologian, reiterating some of his earlier pronouncements on this theme,
rejects with closely reasoned arguments the theses put forward by the innovators
regarding contraception and anovulant drugs: since he makes no mention of
the chapter on marriage in *Gaudium et spes*, we think these instructions must
have been prepared before the Council.

the United States (27 September 1919), India (17 December 1957), Canada (13 November 1958) and France (3 March 1961).

De Lestapis, however, makes a careful study of the position of the reformers. He shows that the two tendencies (legitimization or condemnation of contraception) presuppose two different anthropological points of view. These agree in affirming dialogue to be a fundamental need of the human person, and that the essential value of sexuality lies in ordering and expressing this dialogue between husband and wife in a perfect incarnate, total and definitive manner, but they differ in what follows: whereas the former group stops short at this point and leaves the married couple free to choose the sexual expression of their love according to their own judgment, provided that they do not deprive it of adequate fecundity and do not make pleasure an end in itself, the latter group instead carries the principle of the incarnation of love still further and believes that the bio-physical structure of genital activity constitutes the necessary objective guarantee of the human and Christian authenticity of that love.[2] This second anthropological consideration is that which underlies the age old teaching and practice of the Church concerning contraception and which—in the opinion of the French sociologist—has received further confirmation in the doctrine of the Council. Periodic continence, therefore, is the only method which does not alter the objective structures of sexuality and so does not run the risk of 'profaning and de-humanizing' love. It makes use of 'a periodic alternation of intercourse and abstention, opportunely suggested by the female body itself'.

Peinador's article also very adequately surveys the whole problem in the light of the arguments put forward in an attempt to resolve it in a new manner, but his spirit is more polemical than critical. First of all, as regards the teaching of the Council, the Spanish moralist points out that the doctrine is the same in *Casti Connubii*, in Pius XII's speeches and in the Pastoral Constitution *Gaudium et spes*. Although it is true that the Sacred Synod

---

[2] At this point de Lestapis opportunely quotes the conciliar speech (29 December 1965) by Cardinal Giovanni Colombo, the Archbishop of Milan, in which he asserted that 'mutual and total self-giving between husband and wife, which is also the symbol of a generous intention of procreation, cannot be complete in the spirit if it is not complete also in the flesh' (cf. *La Documentation Catholique* 62 [1965], p. 1892).

does not intend to propose practical solutions for the cases entrusted to the Commission for its consideration, this obviously does not authorize any doubts about the former teaching of the Magisterium or encourage new interpretations.

To believe the contrary, to cast doubts on the clear and categorical affirmations of the Magisterium, adducing the pretext of 'historical development' and 'changed circumstances' would mean revoking the guarantee of certainty possessed by all papal and conciliar teaching. To those who have recourse to the principle of compromise, or of the lesser evil, Peinador replies that this principle never justifies a positive action which is intrinsically evil; nor may one accuse the traditional attitude of 'physicism', or of having considered the individual apart from his general human environment. The biological structure of an act may have in itself no value as a norm, but nevertheless it clearly reveals a divine intention which may not be ignored, even in a more global anthropological concept; nor can it be set aside by any fundamental option. The principle of total effect may not be quoted here because, in the case under consideration, the intention of responsible parenthood does not necessitate the sacrifice of the biological structure of the conjugal act, for the married couple may always resort to the 'natural' method of absolute or periodic continence.

Martelet is well aware of the strength of the reformers' position ('which cannot be contested with superficial arguments') and therefore makes a shrewd use of their own theses, starting with the Council's 'personalist' doctrine of married love and procreation. In resolving our problem, he says, 'the touchstone should always be, as the Council says, the dignity of the human person and of his actions, and only this'. But this does not mean that there is no connection between 'nature' and morality. Undoubtedly 'man has the right, and even the duty to control his nature and become its master', but 'his true victory over nature is never expressed by scorn of her'; in fact, man 'is the creature who can only dominate nature by consenting to obey her laws, not only *with* his body but also *in* his body', even in the harmony of his sexual duties he must take into account 'the structures, functions and rhythms which condition his life in this sphere'. For this reason contraception, unlike periodic continence, seems 'unnatural', not so much because (as was said in *Casti Connubii*) it deprives the conjugal act of procreative capacity (in fact in itself it would not always possess this capacity) but rather because 'it prevents the sexual function from being procreative in the very act in which it might become so', or 'imposes a pause on this function at times when the function would not naturally observe a pause'. Is this 'unnatural' character of contraception sufficient to render it illicit? This may not, in fact, be affirmed by those who think of the function as something apart from the persons involved: in fact, 'nature has not in herself any power over them', and still less power has their procreative duty over their liberty, which it should instead serve. But if the procreative duty is considered as a mission which is imposed upon husband and wife, 'as a consequence of their love', then contraception appears not only biologically unnatural but morally illicit: in fact, it impedes the procreative capacity of the married couple 'in the very act in which this capacity provides its most profound expression of the unifying power of love'. In short, it is nothing but a falsehood: 'we cannot truly assert that we respect love's mission with regard to life if, while we speak of love in words which themselves seem charged with life, we try violently to exclude this life from love'. One can understand the 'weaknesses of conjugal love', but they are still weaknesses, 'evils that should be carefully avoided'; to recognize that they are errors 'is not to condemn the persons but to enable them to develop', for we know well that 'married people cannot achieve in one day a virtuous conduct which is as difficult as it is truly necessary'.

But together with these familiar voices others also were raised against the innovators, by theologians whom we now mention for the first time. We give their names in chronological order:

M. Piñon, O.P. 'The issues in birth control', *Philippiniana Sacra* I (1966), pp. 156–74.

P. M. C. Davies, 'Love and contraception in Christian marriage', *The Irish Theological Quarterly* 33 (1966), pp. 327–51.

M. A. Genevois, O.P., Les normes données par Pie XII sur la limitation des naissances', *Angelicum* 48 (1966), pp. 204–24.

M. Brugarola, S.J., 'Sobre el articulo del Padre Häring: "Matrimonio y familia en el mundo ed hoy",' *Illustración del Clero* 59 (1966), pp. 273–87.

G. De Rosa, S.J., 'Dignita del matrimonio e della famiglia e sua valorizzazione', in *La Chiesa e il mondo contemporaneo nel*

Vaticano II, Turin, Elle Di Ci, 1966, pp. 679–804.

B. Russo, S.J., 'Il matrimonio nella chiesa prima e dopo il Vaticano II', *Palestra del clero* 46 (1967), pp. 725–40.

J. Kuničič, O.P., 'In procreatione regulanda minus rectae viae', *Divus Thomae* (Piac.) 70 (1967), 81–107.

The first two articles condemn all contraceptive practice on grounds of reason, but vary considerably in their tone. Piñon's article is merely a heated (and here and there ingenuous) protest against all artificial control of births because this would mean legitimizing sexual licence: he rejects the pill also because this induces married couples to take the 'line of least resistance', and leads to the 'glorification of physical pleasure'; periodic continence (which the author proposes as the Christian solution) is approved of chiefly because it teaches self-control. There is no other way in which Christian couples can learn to control themselves, and they must not think that, because they are married, they have an indisputable right, in all circumstances, to enjoy conjugal intimacy. Women must not refuse, as too many do today, to suckle their babies, as this also is a way in which nature herself limits and spaces births, for it is well known that as a general rule the woman who is suckling her child does not become pregnant.

On the other hand, Davies' arguments are more subtle: his condemnation of contraception is based on the presupposition, which he endeavours to prove, that procreative marital intercourse is the only totally significant expression of the love between husband and wife; therefore contraceptive measures are objectively immoral because they contradict the inner meaning of marriage and of conjugal love, and by so doing impede the spiritual progress of the married couple. One may say that this is a very difficult ideal, and the Irish theologian recognizes this and consequently admits the principle of observing tolerance in certain circumstances (sometimes, he says, a rigid adherence to the imperfectly understood rule imperils the spiritual, or even the physical, well-being of the faithful)—but nevertheless it is the only ideal which the Church, as mistress of all truth, can and must set before her children.

Genevois, De Rosa and Russo base their negative position not so much on rational grounds as on the teachings of the Church. Genevois is guided by the doctrine of Pius XII: after summarizing its main points he concludes that the rules the Pope laid down (including those concerning the use of the pill) 'appear so solid, so firmly anchored in Christian tradition and the natural law, that we are amazed that the hypothesis of their revision should ever have been contemplated': any future progress made will be merely in the better understanding, in a new light, of this doctrine.

The two Neapolitan Jesuits, however, base their substantially negative attitude on the Council texts, although they leave some loopholes still open. After a careful summary of the Council's work De Rosa concludes his examination of the origin and development of the chapter on marriage with the assertion that note 14 'is of great importance for an understanding of the Council's opinion on the morality of family life'. Nevertheless, in his comments on the individual paragraphs of the definitive Council text, the Jesuit considers that it confirms the condemnation of contraceptive practices expressed by the two Popes, 'authoritatively, even if not infallibly'. That is, it condemns 'practices such as the interruption of the conjugal act before its natural conclusion, the use of mechanical appliances by the man or woman, or of chemical means and drugs, intended to prevent the fertilization of the female ovule by the male seed'.

For Russo also the teaching contained in *Gaudium et spes*, when closely studied, not only does not contradict but positively confirms that of Pius XI and Pius XII: therefore the only permissible means of birth control remains that of periodic continence. However, after having affirmed the probable legitimacy of the use of the pill during lactation, in as much as it 'tends to obtain that sterility which nature herself desires', he seems less sure of being able to solve the problem of 'whether the onanistic act effected during periods which should normally be infertile should be considered as equivalent, from the moral point of view, to the same act effected at other times'.[3]

Finally, the opposition of Brugarola and Kuničič takes the form of polemical attacks on the arguments of the other party. Brugarola disapproves in particular of an article by Häring, of

[3] In a thoughtful review of the first edition of this present book (in *Palestra del clero* 48 [1968]), Russo reiterates his aversion to the use of contraceptive measures, quoting in support of his opinion from *Gaudium et spes*, but also pursuing some theological reflections which were already present in his previous article. It is in the context of these reflections that the Neapolitan Jesuit has asked me some pointed questions, to which I shall reply on another occasion.

which we shall speak later on, and which he discusses point by point—but his argument goes further than the particular occasion demands. First of all, he says, 'there exists an essential difference between the method of periodic continence, which does not interfere with any biological process, and the other methods which violate or disturb the physiological processes in order to prevent generation'. Now, 'even if it is legitimate to interfere with other organs of the human body, for the total good of the individual (for example, by a surgical operation), it is not legitimate to interfere with structures and acts which are essentially intended not only for the good of the individual but for the good of the human species'. Moreover, in the opinion of this author, Vatican II has already resolved the problem: in fact, 'every conjugal act which includes natural or artificial onanism, or in connection with which anovulant pills are used, is without the *integral* meaning (required by the Council) of mutual self giving, or of human procreation, because it includes some reservations'. As for the pill, Brugarola maintains that its use forms part of that 'artificial control of births' which Paul VI condemned in his speech to the United Nations.

The long article of Kuničič is a closely reasoned reply to the article by García-Vicente on treatment with progestational pills (to which we have already referred) and to Janssens's article, soon to be discussed here, in favour of the general legitimization of contraceptive methods.[4] The reply to both is strongly negative. Concerning Janssens, who is of more interest to us, the Zagreb

---

[4] The same number of the review which publishes the article by Kuničič has another by S. Gozzo, O.F.M., 'Il peccato di Onan e l'esegesi moderna', *Divus Thomas* (Piacenza) 70 (1967), pp. 45–80, which examines at length the various interpretations of the biblical account and expresses the opinion that 'onanism, together with the violation of the levirate law, was the sin of Onan': it was therefore also Onan's contraceptive act, in itself, which God punished with death. The author bases his interpretation, above all, on the particular meaning of the verb šiḥet (to waste the seed), on the fact that Juda was not punished (although he had disappointed Tamar) and on the teaching of the Church. We think however that Gozzo failed to understand the kernel of Dubarle's exegesis: for the French Dominican also it was not his failure to fulfil the levirate obligation which brought about Onan's punishment (in fact, Juda also was not severely punished for this) but his having had recourse to contraception in a marriage which contained the formal obligation that the husband was to beget a child. As for the Church's teaching, Gozzo refers merely to *Casti Connubii*, but it still has to be shown whether this exegetical interpretation given by the Pope is to be considered definitive, especially as he does not put it forward directly but as part of a quotation from St. Augustine.

theologian first of all complains of his 'radical opposition' to the teaching of Pius XI and Pius XII, and then makes a critical analysis of his doctrinal arguments. He points out, for example, that it is impossible to have recourse to the principle of the total good, in order to justify contraception for the sake of the total good of the married couple and their family, for this principle, in fact, serves only to legitimize mutilations effected for the good of the body whereas 'values of a higher order, such as the preservation of fidelity and love, can and must be safeguarded by other means'. In the case in point these means are: 'chastity, penitence, the spirit of mortification, etc.'. Nor is it permissible to make love the final justification which would give positive value even to coitus deprived of its biological end, for love, although it must inform the married couple's acts, does not justify a copulation which is robbed of its intrinsic generative purpose. That this purpose is indeed proper to it is clear from its own biological structure. This biological structure, although not in itself constituting an ethical norm, still remains a means by which one may discern the purpose desired by God and which, as it is a natural law, one is obliged to obey 'always and for ever'. Moreover, in Kuničič's opinion, *Gaudium et spes*, in spite of the specious and tendentious interpretations of certain theologians, fully confirmed the traditional doctrine.

As far as we know, these are the post-conciliar articles which showed marked opposition to the innovating tendency.[5] They

---

[5] To complete our survey let us refer also to some brief but purely negative opinions which were heard after the Council. BONAVENTURA DA GANGI, CAP., 'La illiceità dell' onanismo riaffermata dal Vaticano II', *Perfice munus* 61 (1966), pp. 104-6 (cf. *idem*, 'Pillola cattolica', *ibid.*, pp. 308-9) writes that 'the Council has specifically reaffirmed the illegitimacy of conjugal onanism, according to the traditional doctrine of the Church' and that 'whoever doubts the illegitimacy of onanism would be opposing the supreme authority of the Magisterium of the Church, which spoke clearly and definitely through Pius XI and Pius XII', so that 'onanism is illicit now and always and till the end of the world'. And the same opinion is held by E. GARRIGOU, 'Immoralité de la contraception', *L'ami du clergé* 76 (1966), pp. 207-8. Similar comments are found in F. G. ESPOSITO, *Matrimonio 'società d'amore'*, Rome, Coletti, 1967, pp. 143-6, 153-7: and in P. C. LANDUCCI, 'Pillola e onanismo', *Palestra del Clero* 46 (1967), pp. 544-8. We must here mention also the interesting and well informed talk given by G. CERIANI to the fifteenth 'Settimana Nazionale di aggiornamento pastorale', held in Catania in September 1965: 'Orientamenti teologici sulla morale della procreazione', in *Matrimonio e Famiglia nella communità cristiana*, Milan, Massimo, 1966, pp. 124-68: here the criticism of the new trend is quite unyielding.

show a fairly united front in which, however, it is possible to distinguish various intermediary shades of opinion. Categorical refusals appear side by side with oppositions which leave some loopholes still open; with writers who are quite convinced that the traditional thesis is no longer tenable there are others who recognize the difficulty of demonstrating this (among them is Zalba himself), or admit the logical strength of the new position (as do Lestapis and Martelet); it is also symptomatic that those who are most in favour of the latter, like the two Jesuit Fathers just mentioned, adopt a more flexible and enquiring attitude, presented more as an exploratory line of thought than as an apodictic assertion. Finally, some of the new articles in favour of the traditional teaching contain the pastoral advice that a greater indulgence should be shown, in practice, to married couples, and that the whole problem should be viewed in the wider context of married life and all its obligations.

II. *The attitude of those who think a reform of doctrine is possible*
Now let us speak of those theologians who, although not yet showing themselves decidedly in favour of an explicit legitimization of the use of contraceptive methods for an adequate regulation of births, still think that some change in the formulation of the doctrine may be possible. In any case they share the conviction that the traditional doctrine cannot be considered definitive.
The first group of these writers base their hopes of a possible revision on a careful study of the conciliar text on the subject of marriage. We shall refer, not so much to those theologians who, in commenting upon it, forbear to form any judgment (declaring themselves to be awaiting the authoritative decision of the Roman Pontiff),[6] as to those who, examining the problem very closely,

[6] For example, A. LEITE, O Concilio Vaticano II e alguns problemas matrimoniais: *Brotéria* 82 (1966), pp. 330–9, esp. p. 338; S. NAVARRO, C.M.F., 'El matrimonio y la familia en la Constitución pastoral sobre la Iglesia en el mundo contemporaneo', *Claretianum* 6 (1966), pp. 167–220, esp. p. 194; M. SANCHEZ, O.P., 'Matrimonio y Concilio', *Studium* 6 (1966), pp. 257–73, esp. pp. 267–9; and also Z. HERRERO, 'Algunos puntos conciliares en torno a la doctrina sobre el matrimonio', *Archivio Teológico Agustiniano* 2 (1967), pp. 319–46. See particularly, for the careful study of conciliar documents in the context of the current theological discussions, the already mentioned work by D. TETTAMANZI, 'Dignità del matrimonio e della famiglia e sua valorizzazione', in *Commento alla Costituzione pastorale sulla Chiesa nel mondo contemporaneo 'Gaudium et Spes'*, Milan, Ed. Massimo, 1967, pp. 291–340.

affirm that the Council deliberately left the way open for some change. We put forward first of all the names of some writers, most of whom are already known and whose opinions are undoubtedly most valuable, because of the attention they have always given to this question.

J. L. Thomas, S.J., 'What did the Council conclude on contraception?', *America* 114 (1966), 294–6.

J. Snoek, C.SS.R., 'Matrimonio e familia na *Gaudium et Spes*. Um primeiro balanço', *Revista Ecclesiástica Brasileira* 26 (1966), pp. 121–7.

R. Juan de Castro, 'Concilio Vaticano II. Dignidad del matrimonio y de la familia', *Teologia y Vida* 7 (1966), pp. 50–66.

A. Fz. Diaz-Nava, S.J., 'El matrimonio en la constitución pastoral sobre la Iglesia en el mundo actual', *Sal Terrae* 54 (1966), pp. 343–62; cf. 'Regulación de la natalidad en las publicaciones católicas 1966', *ibid.*, 55 (1967), pp. 209–29.

A. Arza, S.J., 'El problema teologico y moral de la fecundidad', *Estudios de Deusto* 14 (1966), pp. 467–521.

J. A. da Silva Soares, 'Perspectivas conciliares sobre o matrimonio e a familia', *Itinerarium* 13 (1967), pp. 265–87.

Ph. Delhaye, 'La communauté conjugale et familiale d'après Vatican II', *Revue Diocésaine de Namur* 20 (1966), pp. 413–26; republ. in *Aux sources de la morale conjugale*, Gembloux, J. Duculot, 1967, pp. 157–73; 'I problemi di matrimonio', in *Concilio vivo*, Milan, Ancora, 1967, pp. 647–58.

V. Heylen, 'La note 14 dans la constitution pastorale *Gaudium et Spes*, p. 11, no. 51', *Ephemerides Theologicae Lovanienses* 42 (1966), 555–66.

D. Quartier, 'Het verantwoord ouderschap volgens Vaticanum II', *Collationes Brugenses et Gandavenses* 12 (1966), pp. 161–8: cf. *ibid.*, 'De verantworde Methodes van Geboortenregeling', *ibid.*, 13 (1967), pp. 126–35.

It is hardly necessary to say that all these authors point out the new doctrinal context offered by the Council, with its personalistic view of marriage, its exaltation of married love and the important part assigned in this to sexuality, and the formal acknowledgment of the duty of responsible parenthood concerning which, in the last resort, the husband and wife are themselves the judges. And all dwell also on the question of the methods of birth control.

Thomas finds that an objective examination of the Conciliar document shows that it has left the problem of contraceptive measures at the point which it had reached at the beginning of the last session: obviously the Pope, in putting forward his amendments, had no intention of obliging the Fathers to resolve a problem which he had previously withdrawn from their competence. Snoek goes even further: the Council has not only left this question open, as regards both progestational drugs and contraceptive measures, despite the request of some Fathers (cf: the 'fine speech' of Cardinal Colombo) that it should pronounce against the latter, but has also suggested the principles for a new solution, adopting an 'anthropological' view of the problem which has meant abandoning 'the criterion of biological integrity as such', and which will lead to a re-interpretation of the teaching of Pius XI and Pius XII. He mentions the latter only in a note, and in connection with a quotation from Paul VI. A similar and contemporary judgment is that offered by de Castro, also from South America. He considers it is ingenuous to maintain that the Council has reaffirmed the traditional doctrine; the problem was, instead, 'deliberately left open', and it is clear, 'in the light of the Council and of present day theological studies, that the immutability of the doctrine expounded in *Casti Connubii* may no longer be defended with the certainty of ten years ago'. In Spain, Diaz-Nava adopts the same standpoint. After pointing out that the criterion for judging the virtue of sexual intercourse is no longer exclusively based on its bio-physiological elements, he considers that the use of hormonal contraceptives (he does not mention others) presents a problem which the Council has not resolved and causes 'grave doubts to arise' among representatives of both trends of thought.

Arza's exposition is still more lengthy, as is that of the Portuguese Silva Soares: both are anxious to adopt the 'personalist' and 'total' concept offered by the Council, which discards mere biological criteria in favour of a totality of values which married couples must continually estimate and safeguard in a responsible manner.

It is therefore now necessary to expound the new objective criteria for the legitimacy of birth control methods, and the question is still open: this is affirmed, with all the weight of their authority, by the two Belgian theologians, both, as we already know, members of the Council's Sub-Commission for marriage. 'Until now', wrote Delhay, 'the physiological integrity of the marriage act was considered all-important, but now it has been realized that it is difficult to insist upon this.' The Council has therefore indicated new principles, such as 'the dignity of the human person and a framework of genuine love. More value is also attached to the significance of mutual self-giving and responsible parenthood which coitus should have.' In conclusion, observes Heylen in his careful analysis of the Conciliar discussions on this problem, 'every translation or interpretation [of note 14] which insinuates that the teaching of Pius XI and Pius XII is reaffirmed by the Council as certain and unalterable, correspond in no way to the real sense of the text'. In fact, the Magisterium is now 'trying to discover the exact scope of earlier teaching with regard to contraceptive methods'.

This conclusion is put forward by Quartier, in his clear exposition of the Conciliar text and of its vicissitudes: he also points out that in the meantime the Council has substituted for the old ethical criteria of physiological integrity, the new and much broader criteria of respect for the human person in its complex totality.[7]

[7] Heylen's attitude seems equally progressive, judging from his comments on the chapter on marriage, published in two works written in collaboration on *Gaudium et spes* in *La Chiesa nel mondo contemporaneo*, Brescia, Queriniana, 2nd ed., 1967, pp. 159–92. Cf. also, on the same subject, his 'Concilie en huwelijksmoraal', *Pastor Bonus* 12 (1966), pp. 65–71.

The novelty of the Council's new presentation of the moral principles which govern the sexual conduct of married people is also made clear in the comments on Vatican II by J. RATZINGER, *Problemi e risultati del Concilio Vaticano II*, Brescia, Queriniana, pp. 130–4, in which the Tübingen theologian observes that, in spite of the Council's silence on the actual problem of birth control methods, the principles it indicated are nevertheless such that matters may no longer be left as they are: in fact, it is no longer the same whether a man is bound to consider if his act is 'against nature', or whether he is bound to consider if it fulfils his obligations to other men, to whom he is now united by marriage, and also his obligation to respond to the World of God in Person, who in his love for the Church, realized in Christ, has set the model for all married love.

Moreover, observes J. M. DIAZ MORENO, S.J., 'Ante la urgencia de un problema', *Sal Terrae* 54 (1966), pp. 402–6, in his comments on the directives put forward by Mgr Reuss and Cardinal Doepfner, 'moral theology and its pastoral applications are capable of legitimate evolution, and in fact the living and vital teaching office of the Church, in contact with the human realities of life, may suggest new points of view which, in various temporal or geographical situations, determine the precise and transcendental significance of Christian needs'.

From these well-known theologians other authors, more deeply engaged in pastoral work and in writing for a more general public, have obviously derived their conviction that a study of the Council's deliberations suggests a more open-minded attitude. We cannot review all these writers here and shall therefore speak only of those written in Italian, also because these were the first contributions in Italian which favoured the new trend. We mention particularly the articles by priests of the Centro Dehoniano of Bologna and those by Mgr A. Corti, Ecclesiastical Consultant to the Secretariat for the Family in the Milan Diocese:

> L. Lorenzetti, 'È possibile una revisione della dottrina della *Casti Connubii* circa le pratiche contraccettive?', *Settimana del Clero*, 14 August 1966, p. 4 (cf. 'Lettere al Direttore', *ibid.*, 23 October 1966); P.D., 'Amore coniugale e regolazione delle nascite', *ibid.*, 8 January 1967, p. 4. Cf. also T. Goffi, 'È il Signore solo che salva nelle tribolazioni della carne', ibid., 5 March 1967, p. 4.
>
> A Corti, *Famiglia e Concilio*, Milan, Opera della Regalità, 1966, 103 pp., expecially pp. 40–1; cf. idem, 'La Morale della procreazione. Visione retrospettiva e nuove prospettive', *Riflessi* 18 (1966), pp. 36–47; *Matrimonio e vita coniugale*, Milan, Ancora, 2nd ed., 1967, pp. 85–91.

Pope Paul's speech of 29 October 1966 offers some theologians another opportunity to assume this attitude of hopeful expectation which we are now examining. Among them are the Jesuits Perico and González, and to their contributions may be added an editorial of the review *Il Regno*, of the Centro Dehoniano of Bologna, and a longer article by a Brazilian theologian.

> G. Perico, S.J., 'Perché il Papa non parla', *Aggiornamenti sociali* 17 (1966), pp. 643–6. The article was amply commented upon by G. de Rosa, S.J.: 'Un silenzio responsabile', *La Civiltà Cattolica* 117 (1966), IV, pp. 352–5.
>
> N. González, S.J., 'La nuova espera', *Razón y fe* 174 (1966), pp. 407–11; 'Il futuro della famiglia cristiana', *Il Regno* II (1966), pp. 620–1.
>
> R. Mascarenhas Roxo, 'Teologia e métodos contraceptivos', *Revista Ecclesiástica Brasileira* 27 (1967), pp. 69–82.

According to Perico, the reason for the Pope's prolonged silence is to be found in the vastness of the research still to

be undertaken, particularly as regards the problem of birth
control, and among the 'inevitable questions' which still await
an answer, the illustrious Jesuit (member of the Pontifical Commission for the study of procreation and the family) mentions
several which explicitly refer to our theme: 'granted that procreation is the end of marriage, can it be said that its procreative
meaning must be extended to every individual matrimonial act?
To what extent is the conjugal act intangible in its biological
structure and mechanism? Could it not be considered as a "part",
at the service of the "whole" for the purpose of greater conjugal
harmony? Once the recourse to periodic continence as a means of
avoiding progeny has been legitimized, in what way, on the moral
plane, does this technique of avoidance differ from the technique
which aims at preventing the fertilization of the egg and the
fertilizing encounter of the two germs of life? Can one speak
of intrinsic wickedness in connection with this type of intervention? Is there in scripture, in tradition, or in the official
teaching of the Church a precise and unequivocal attitude towards
these problems?'

These are precisely the questions which the traditional attitude,
based upon *Casti Connubii* and the teachings of Pius XII, will
not allow to be raised and considers already resolved: but the
doctrinal discussion still goes on. In fact, González observes, the
debate has reached such a point that one might expect the Pope
to issue a document which, wisely associating itself with earlier
teachings, yet 'authoritatively ratified the new attitude assumed
by the Christian people which showed considerable elements of
authenticity and was certainly endowed with a symptomatic
universality'. If such a document has not yet appeared, it is not
so much because of an insuperable uncertainty about certain
questions but rather because of the present-day absence of a
'comprehensive formula for the interpretation of human sexuality'
which may take the place of earlier formulae, now irretrievably
discredited. In any case, write the editors of *Il Regno*, 'a Pope who
publicly admits that he has not yet found the hoped-for doctrinal
certainty, gives us cause not for grief but for edification'. Nor
must we look back wistfully to past certainty, which concealed
a very limited knowledge of the various aspects of the problem.
Now, as it is, 'if one thing is obvious in the attitude of Paul VI,
it is precisely this awareness that it is necessary to offer a new

doctrinal presentation, to satisfy the anxiety of men of good will who find the doctrine hitherto presented no longer adequate'.

Moreover, observes Mgr Roxo, the Council, as Pope Paul also mentioned in his speech of 28 October, has offered new elements for a moral judgment, different from those furnished by previous teaching. This earlier doctrine made almost everything depend on the safeguarding of the procreative intention of the conjugal act; the constitution *Gaudium et Spes*, however, presents the conjugal act as 'the peculiar expression and realization of that communion of love' in which marriage is now said to consist, and relates the problem of contraception to the principle of the total good at stake, and to the practice of responsible parenthood, thus showing itself much more concerned with the real and existential interests of the husband and wife. These presuppositions might even lead to a new solution of the problem of contraceptives, and some writers have indeed already formulated a solution, basing it on the principle that 'the objective physiological structure of the conjugal act must be subordinated to the greater good of conjugal intimacy'. But if we proceed to study the individual measures used, the question becomes very delicate: it is clear that *coitus interruptus* is condemned, for indeed, in the light of conciliar doctrine it is seen to be 'the most condemnable of contraceptive measures'; on the other hand, although the use of progestational pills does not impair the physical integrity of coitus, it attacks the very source of life, with physical consequences which are still unknown; local contraceptives, when they leave copulation at least psychologically unimpaired, seem finally to be the means which show most respect for the values at stake, but they present the danger of a mechanization of the act which may be to the detriment of its human significance. Even periodic continence may present the grave danger of a 'mathematical control of love'. It is therefore not surprising, concludes Roxo, that the Pope has still further deferred a solution. Although 'all men's hopes are turned towards a favourable reply', we understand the difficulties which still arise. It is, moreover, providential that the expectation should be long drawn out, if this period of waiting may be of use as 'a historical experience in search of a solution'.

Thirdly, there were other theologians who hoped for a revision of doctrine, basing their hopes not so much on the conciliar declarations of Paul VI as on an examination of the discussion still in course and of the considerations underlying the new theses:

D. O'Callaghan, 'Dilemma in birth control', *The Irish Ecclesiastical Review* 105 (1966), pp. 232–45; 'The evolving Theology of Marriage', *The Clergy Review* 51 (1966), pp. 836–49 (re-edited also in *Catholic World* 204 (1967), pp. 326–34).

M. Huftier, 'Morale chrétienne et régulation des naissances', *L'ami du clergé* 77 (1967), pp. 193–208, 209–12.

A. Valsecchi, 'Amore e fecondità nel matrimonio. La regolazione delle nascite', *Bollettino diocesano di Ravenna e Cervia* 57 (1967), pp. 83–119; cf. 'Morale del matrimonio', in *Preparazione al Matrimonio*, Milan, Ed. Ancora (1967), pp. 89–108.

L. Rossi, 'Il dibattito odierno sull' antifecundazione', *Anime e Corpi* 5 (1967), Supplement to no. 20, pp. 5–56; cf. idem, 'Pastorale dell'onanismo', *ibid.*, pp. 207–14.

R. H. Springer, S.J., 'Notes on moral theology: Christian love and sexuality', *Theological Studies* 28 (1967), pp. 322–30.

In his two articles (very similar in content) O'Callaghan presents an intelligent survey of the questions under discussion, and lays particular emphasis upon the affirmation that procreation is not a duty incumbent upon every individual act, but incumbent upon the whole of married life. This loosening of the link between procreation and the individual act of coitus may well be the start of a process which may lead to complete detachment from the contrary concept associated with Augustinian doctrine. How to explain such a development, given the position taken up by the Magisterium, is a problem for the solution of which the Irish theologian chooses neither of the hypotheses he mentions: that which denies that the Church has the power to interpret in these details the natural law, or that which, while acknowledging her competence in this field, considers the pronouncements uttered until now to be without a definitive character. Yet this development is clearly to be expected: indeed, at least for the use of pills in extreme cases, O'Callaghan already considers applicable the permissive thesis now very widely accepted by theologians, and which is presented by Rossi, Professor of Moral Theology at the Seminary of Lodi, in his careful bibliographical notes, frequently accompanied by shrewd (and sharp) critical references to the position of the 'traditionalists'.

A close examination of Christian doctrinal tradition, from its persistent Augustinian premises to the present-day demand for revision (which stems from a new social and cultural context and a more profound awareness of the human and Christian mystery of sexuality and conjugal love) is proposed also by Huftier. It now becomes more clear how one should consider the concepts of the 'natural' and the 'unnatural', and this means that one should no longer accept as the only and overriding term of reference the physiological development of the conjugal act. Instead there is being formed a broader idea of 'nature', which the Magisterium itself, if one studies its pronouncements from *Casti Connubii* to the most recent speeches of Paul VI, is taking more and more into consideration. Therefore methods of birth control will have to be judged much less in their material content and much more according to considerations of the maturity and responsibility of the married couple and the values which they propose to achieve. This is the conclusion to which we ourselves came during our course of lectures to the clergy of Ravenna—and it was our study of the present-day theological discussions, which can no longer be brought to a halt, which led us to this attitude of hopeful expectancy.

Springer has arrived at the same conclusions. He has taken Lynch's place on the staff of the American Jesuit Review and has effectively introduced a new direction of thought. He considers some examples of the problem of birth control in order to demonstrate the present state of confusion and disarray among Catholics; he stresses also anxieties of a pastoral order, pointing out the danger of scandal among Christian people for opposite reasons, whether the Pope confirms or alters the doctrine of *Casti Connubii*. Yet, he observes, although the teaching of Vatican II on marriage and the family decided nothing on the question of methods of birth control, it did assign greater importance to love between husband and wife, and entrusted to the sense of responsibility of the parents themselves the decision about the size of their families, thus establishing the pre-conditions for a possible change of judgment concerning means of birth control: the Pope's pronouncement will necessarily take this trend into consideration. So it may be concluded that *Casti Connubii* is a theology which now belongs to history; it is an integral part of tradition, but as theology it is not adequate for the world of today and all its problems. It is hard to believe, as some still persist in saying, that the Magisterium could merely re-affirm earlier teaching'.[8]

Finally, a note of expectant hope appears in the formulation which some authors present of their own personal hypotheses. This is true of Pendergast, Di Marino and Chirico:

> R. S. Pendergast, S.J., 'Some neglected factors of the birth control problem', *Sciences Ecclésiastiques* 18 (1966), pp. 207–27.
> A. Di Marino, S.J., 'Un'ipotesi in materia di castità coniugale', *Rassegna di Teologia* 8 (1967), 15–19. 'Continuità e sviluppi nella dottrina della Chiesa sulla castità matrimoniale', *ibid.*, pp. 193–201.
> P. Chirico, S.S., 'Tension, morality and birth control', *Theological Studies* 28 (1967), pp. 258–85.

The hypothesis put forward by the first of these, a Professor at the Loyola University of New Orleans, is that the question of contraceptives is among those for which the Magisterium, not having at its disposal any explicit divine revelation in this connection (it is very improbable, the Jesuit writer admits, that even the story of Onan refers to it), is not in a position to prepare a solution that can be definitive in its doctrinal content. This is, in fact, a question in which revealed doctrine is mingled with conclusions deduced from it by human reason. When, for example, Pius XI speaks of the 'natural creative power' of the conjugal act, he is in reality describing sexuality in terms of the common doctrine of the moralists of his age which had received no specific confirmation

---

[8] A more or less decidedly progressive attitude is seen also in those authors who merely report the various positions assumed during the discussion, without apparently wishing to form their own conclusions. We restrict ourselves to mentioning a few Italian contributions: G. VIMERCATI, 'Il Concilio e la regolazione delle nascite', *La famiglia italiana* 22 (1967), pp. 25–36; P. LIGGERI, *Famiglia e demografia nella 'Populorum progressio'*, Ed. di Vicenza, 1967, pp. 32–6; G. CONTI, S.J., 'Regolazione delle nascite', *La Rivista del catechismo* 5 (1968), pp. 108–18; F. BERSINI, S.J., 'Regolamentazione delle nascite: pratica pastorale in attesa della parola del Papa', *Perfice munus* 43 (1968), pp. 149–62. See also the progressive attitude of some reviewers of this present volume (1st ed.), in the light of the 'ten years of theological pronouncements' which it surveys: L. LORENZETTI, in *Settimana del clero*, 10 December 1967, p. 4; A. COSTI, in *Il Regno* 12 (1967), pp. 483–4; G. PERICO, in *Letture* 23 (1968), pp. 67–9, *Aggiornamenti sociali* 19 (1968), pp. 235–8, and in *La Civiltà Cattolica*, 1968, I, pp. 504–5; L. ROSSI, in *La famiglia* 2 (1968), pp. 190–2.

from revelation. In the light of modern knowledge can it still be said that the individual conjugal act has a 'natural procreative power'? And if it has, in what sense? The Pope's affirmation, therefore, is no more incapable of revision than was man's former knowledge of the proper nature of sexuality. This does not mean that contraceptives may today appear legitimate: in fact, the modern knowledge of sexual activity as the means of dialogue between husband and wife may well lead to their exclusion as constituting a grave violation of this symbolism. But this new requirement is not so binding—and just as it does not exclude the use of progestational drugs (which do not impair the symbolic value of copulation) so, in Pendergast's opinion, it might also permit the use of certain local contraceptive measures (for example intra-uterine devices).

The hypothesis put forward by Di Marino, Professor of Moral Theology at the Jesuit Faculty of Naples and Vice-President of the Association of Italian Moralists, however, is more casuistic, but nevertheless highly personal. He is certain that the deliberate frustration of the fertility of copulation by means of any inter- ference with its physical structure is sinful. Nevertheless he considers that it is gravely sinful only when the husband and wife have 'here and now' the duty to procreate: in the latter case, in fact, the deflection of the sexual act from its natural result in progeny is total. On the contrary, when the interference with the natural order is only partial, it does not constitute, even objectively, a grave sin, but belongs to the 'grey region' of slight sinfulness when the contraceptive measures are used by married couples whose sense of responsibility urges them not to generate other children, and who are moreover incapable of observing a rule of continence. 'They should therefore seek to avoid procreation with the calmness and earnestness proper to those who wish to make progress in love and chastity, but without feeling the anguish of those who think they have gravely sinned and so rendered themselves unworthy to receive the sacraments of the Church.'

Similar to this in its conclusions, but with a firmer theological basis, is the hypothesis put forward by Chirico (which appeared, like the above-mentioned article by Springer, in *Theological Studies*). He examined first of all the hypothesis of a 'conflict' and 'tension' of moral values in which the Christian may often find himself, and in which he cannot be required to conform to an absolute ideal but only to that which is actually practicable. This is true also of the conflict between different values which is sometimes present in the recourse to contraceptive techniques. These are always blameworthy, because of the 'personal harm' they do to the married couple by weakening their respect for life: certainly, the American theologian explains, *one* contraceptive act does not reduce respect for life to the point of making a person a murderer, just as *one* lie spoken in a moment of necessity does not make a man a liar; but a long series of these acts and a moral climate which accepts contraception as a normal human activity and a normal means of birth control, has the result of diminishing respect for human life. This is why contraception can never be an ideal solution. But if it is resorted to in a situation of conflict, in which the husband and wife find themselves morally incapable of fulfilling all the duties of their matrimonial life (love, responsible parenthood, domestic peace, etc.) it seems to be a lesser evil which cannot be considered grave: if one does all one can in one's own situation, this does not mean turning one's back on God, or committing a grave sin, provided, of course, that the husband and wife live in permanent expectation of the moment when it will be possible for them (perhaps even through an acquired capacity of continence free from other dangers) to obey the whole moral law in their own situation.

So we see that the attitude of expectant hope of some doctrinal revision, with its many manifestations in both form and content, represents a phenomenon of very wide distribution even in the brief spell of time that has passed since the conclusion of the Council.

III. *In favour of reform*

Equally numerous is the group of thinkers and theologians who declare themselves outspokenly in favour of some change of attitude on the part of the Church. Besides those already well known to us there are some new writers, and new treatments of this subject appear by the side of reviews and summaries of earlier articles.

Let us first consider the contributions of laymen. It has not been possible to sift all the material published by Catholic writers, and therefore we restrict ourselves to mentioning Italian contributions:

P. Raineri, 'Osservazioni sul problema della regolazione delle nascite', *Il Gallo* 20 (1966), pp. 158-9.

M. and M. Pittau, *La regolazione delle nascite e la liceità dei suoi mezzi*, Cagliari, Editrice Sarda Fossataro, 1967, p. 326. Cf. also the critical review of this volume by O. La Pietra in *Sessuologia* 8 (1967), 182-4.

G. Zoppis, *Limitazione responsabile delle nascite*, Gubbio, Tipografia Eugubina, 1966, p. 139; *Spiritualità e sessualità*, Gubbio, publ. by author, 1967, p. 100; *Limitazione delle nascite, problema risolto?* Gubbio, Tipografia Eugubina, 1968, p. 34.

'Matrimonio, morale e regolazione delle nascite', *La Famiglia* I (1967), pp. 363-70. This is a document prepared by the 'Jacques Maritain' study circle of Rimini and other groups and circles of Emilia and the Romagna.

E. Minoli, 'La Coppia coniugale oggi: rischi e prospettive di salvezza', *Studium* 64 (1968), pp. 4-11.

Dr Raineri's note is brief but to the point. He supports the thesis already put forward by other writers that 'the duty of procreation is incumbent upon married life as a whole and cannot be strictly applied to every individual conjugal act', and he points out the incoherence of the official position which only permits birth control at the cost of a contradiction (as in the choice of infertile periods) between the material and intentional content of an act. He also presses the accusation of 'physicism' launched against the earlier doctrine and demonstrates that every biological function has 'a merely instrumental and subordinate significance' so that it is quite erroneous 'to recognize in biological processes (considered as unalterable) absolute and guiding principles'.

The treatise by the two Pittaus (a married couple, the husband a professor of philosophy and the wife a doctor) is lengthy and very fully annotated. They reject the legitimization of the use of progestational pills because of their positive and well-founded doubt that their function may be not anovulant but abortifacient.[9]

[9] Starting from this doubt about the pill's effect, these two authors reproach me (pp. 319-21) for having declared that the legitimacy of the pill was 'already practically admitted' during a 'round table' conference held in Milan, 22 February 1966, in the Great Hall of the Istituto Zaccaria, and reported by, among other papers, the Review *Asclepeio*, January–February 1966, pp. 15-17 (from which the Pittau couple draw their information). In fact, the reporter for that review did not accurately define my opinion when he attributed to me the affirmation that 'the moral legitimacy of the pill seems practically already admitted', although immediately afterwards he recorded the very real doubt

On the other hand, they consider that all contraceptive measures, if used for the purposes of responsible parenthood, are in general to be considered legitimate, on the basis of the various arguments now familiar to us, which they are at pains to quote from various authors.

Dr Zoppis deserves special mention, also because his painstaking studies trace in a very lively manner the gradual development of his thought towards the new position which he has now adopted. The first of the monographs mentioned above, which includes and re-edits other pamphlets previously written by this doctor on the subjects of sexuality and birth control, is written to defend the legitimacy of oral contraceptives, with the usual already familiar arguments used by various authors. In reality, many of his most original reflexions, especially those of the psycho-spiritual significance of sexuality, and on the purposes of love and integration which are proper to marriage, might be used also in logical justification of other means of birth control. And this point is indeed reached by the author in his two following monographs, and especially in the last, in which with great precision of terminology he concludes that all means to prevent fertility which are not in themselves illicit (as any attempt at abortion would be) 'are characterized by their purpose, that is, receive their meaning from their end; they are evil if used for selfish purposes, and good if used for human fulfilment'. Therefore, 'it is not so much a question of respecting the physical integrity of a copulation or of not altering the biophysical order of the organism, as of finding out whether the means adopted to avoid progeny are such as to perfect or impede the human and Christian development of conjugal life'. This judgment can in the final instance only be formed by the married couple themselves. But at this point we fail to understand certain reserves expressed by the author, apparent also in his last article, and based upon a certain biblical

which I myself had expressed concerning the possible anti-implantation effect of oestro-progestational drugs; he would have recorded more accurately what I had said (and so spared me the criticism of the Pittaus) if he had reported that the moral legitimacy of the pill, *when it is certain* that its effect is above all anovulatory, is doctrinally very probable, but that there are various reasons for forbidding its practical use (such as the doubt to which we have already referred, which however is quite unfounded, at least as regards some oestro-progestational drugs) and above all the warning given by Paul VI against the applicability of this thesis.

exegesis (the value of which we are inclined to doubt) concerning the positive significance of sexuality, the expression of which is pedantically described as intended as a 'remedy for concupiscence', and so would in any case be incompatible with the requirements of a perfect spiritual self-giving.[10]

The various themes already studied in the writings mentioned above (some of which are explicitly referred to) reappear in a concise form in the document prepared by Catholic groups and societies of Emilia and the Romagna. The natural law should be looked upon not as consisting in a 'physical mechanism created for men and animals alike' but in relation to 'the general significance and purpose of man and the particular significance and purpose of an individual person or of a married couple'; the responsibility for human generation must be assigned to the whole sexual activity of married persons, not to a single act, which moreover is now seen by scientists to be generally infertile (the contrary of what had been previously asserted); a 'codification of licit and illicit methods' must not be drawn up on the basis of conformity or nonconformity to a 'static and abstract moral order'; instead, these methods must be judged 'according to the use made of them for the purpose of maintaining true human values, such as physical and spiritual well-being, harmony between husband and wife and in the family circle, and the responsibly controlled preservation and increase of the human species on earth'. All these considerations lead the compilers of this document to conclude that the moral judgment, before distinguishing between the various methods, must consider the 'inner significance of each method'; with the acceptance of periodic continence 'not a new method but a principle has been introduced and affirmed'; 'the maxim: "the end does not justify the means" is valid only for those means which in and by themselves destroy a personal good; every other kind of means is something which man uses for the sake of personal

---

[10] See a brief study by another Italian doctor, already known to us for his research in connection with anovulants: G. BONOMI, *Amore o contraccezione?* Turin, Gribaudi Ed., 1967, p. 102. Adopting many of Dr Chauchard's opinions (and even the title of his book) the author categorically rejects every contraceptive technique, and proposes as a legitimate means of birth control only periodic continence. He considers copulation without ejaculation to be praiseworthy ('a true act of conjugal love', through which husband and wife learn a complete control of their sexuality, thus placing it at the service of their total good).

well-being and so is good in relation to this purpose'. These conclusions, it is true, are reached by lay people but, as they frequently point out, their own experience, especially as it seems to be the general experience of Christian people, must be considered with the greatest respect 'in view of the formulation of a new moral theology and a new pastoral doctrine of the family'.

These new moral standpoints, based on the affirmation that natural fertility no longer satisfies 'the general needs of the human race', are asserted also by Minoli. In order to preserve the 'honesty' of the conjugal act, that is, to free it from the danger (always foreseen in traditional Christian teaching and today perhaps more present than ever before) that it may degenerate into selfishness and eroticism, and in order to make it instead a fitting means of increasing the married couple's growth in moral virtue, in these new demographic conditions of today the procreative obligation, which must still purify and determine the sexual union, must perforce count for much less. Therefore a new and immense task awaits Christian husbands and wives, unless they wish to destroy, perhaps in a single generation, a morality that has been built up over the centuries. It is necessary that sexual activity, in which the procreative purpose has now ceased to be the primary unifying factor, must find in conjugal love a purpose which will give it honesty and fulfilment. It is necessary 'that it should be an expression of love and nourished by love, and that this love should grow in intensity and quality and be more and more quickened by that special charity which is the gift of the sacrament'. One thing then seems certain: 'in the new morality of married life the defence against the dangers inherent in sexual activity will no longer consist so much in sanctions imposed from without and determined by the definition of the physical structure of the conjugal act (though obviously it must always be partly determined by this) but will consist more in an internal sanction, provided by the intention, the spirit, the sentiment and the end to be attained'. And it is equally certain that, in the context of this 'internal morality, the scope for superficial solutions is diminishing'.

There have been some well-informed writings on this subject from lay people, and from various countries. As we cannot review them all, we restrict ourselves to mentioning the most significant.

Great interest was aroused by two articles written by the well known married couple, H. and L. Buelens.

H. Buelens (with G. Buyse and P. Leemans) in *De Maand* 9 (1966), pp. 137–40.
H. and L. Buelens, 'Huwelijk en vruchtbaarheit. Voor een Eerlijke Onzerkerheidspastoral', *De Maand* 9 (1966), pp. 464–70.

In the first article the author, after praising the Council's doctrinal presentation of the problem of marriage, and in particular of birth control, demands further clarification, of a pastoral nature, which shall put forward explicitly, as a moral criterion for judging means of birth control, no longer the 'former determinist argument' but one based on the dignity of the human person and the requirements of genuine human love. He adds, however, that among these requirements must not be included (despite the arguments of a new theology which is as 'unilaterally theoretical' as that which preceded it) the demand that copulation must be biologically complete in order to be totally expressive of love. In the second article the two authors expound once more their theory, which they consider sufficiently supported by moral doctrine and therefore—to avoid an unedifying recourse to tutiorism (the preference for the 'safer' doctrine)—should be put into practice. The article was however written before Paul VI's speech of 29 October 1966, which is referred to at the end in an editorial note.

The publication of replies received to an enquiry addressed to Christian married couples throughout France aroused great attention:

3000 *foyers parlent . . . Une enquête de Clair Foyer sur la régulation des naissances*, introduced by P. and M. Lambert, Paris, Les Editions Ouvrières, 1966, 295 pp.

This is a document of great human interest because of the variety and drama of the situations therein described, but it is also of considerable doctrinal value because of the moral reflections, in favour of reform, which several married couples express in their replies.[11] May it not then be said that a vast movement is now directed, in sensitive and alert Catholic lay circles, towards the new outlook with regard to contraception? A very significant trend is seen also in the document signed by five hundred lay people in May 1966,[12] and even more clearly in the fourth Resolution approved of by the Third World Congress of the Lay Apostolate (Rome, October 1967) which, among other questions, mentions 'the social duty of married couples to ensure responsible parenthood' and the 'very lively sense among lay Christians of the need for the Magisterium of the Church to take up a definite position concerning this problem, concentrating on fundamental moral and spiritual values and leaving the choice of scientific and technical measures to ensure responsible parenthood to the parents themselves, who will decide according to their Christian faith and with the assistance of expert medical and scientific advice'.[13]

The reflections of another layman are chiefly concerned with a particular topic. The writer, J. T. Noonan, justly considered a great expert on the subject of birth control, attempts to establish an analogy between the problem of contraception and that of

[11] An indirect reply to this enquiry is that recently put forward by M. and Mme RENDU (members of the Pontifical Commission for the family and for births): *L'Eglise nous a-t-elle trompés? Témoignages des foyers sur la régulation des naissances*, Lyon, Ed. Mappus, 1967, 296 pp. These testimonies defend the traditional doctrine of the Church (and in particular the method of periodic continence) as the only teaching which can safeguard the fundamental spiritual values of marriage and can fulfil the purpose of authentic conjugal love.

[12] The text is partly quoted in note 36 of the preceding chapter.

[13] Cf. *L'Osservatore romano*, 20 October 1967, p. 3, where the text of the concluding motions is given in French. The following footnote appears at the end of the above mentioned resolution: 'The President of the Ecclesiastical Commission of the Third World Congress of the Lay Apostolate, in answer to a query about a point relating to responsible parenthood, declares that the text interprets the actual sentiment expressed by lay Catholics, who appeal trustfully to the Magisterium of the Church. As regards the particular words "leaving the choice of . . . measures . . . to the parents themselves, who will decide according to their Christian faith", it is obvious that they are to be interpreted in the sense clearly indicated by the Second Vatican Ecumenical Council in nos. 50b and 51c of the Constitution *Gaudium et spes*, that is, "Christian faith enlightened by the teaching authority of the Church".' A more detailed report of the work of the Congress on the theme of the family (commented upon by F. FRANCESCHETTI) may be read in *Presenza pastorale* I (1968), pp. 144-56.

usury[14] and suggests a new interpretation of the text of *Gaudium et Spes*:

> J. T. Noonan, jr., 'Authority on usury and on contraception', *Tijdschrift voor Theologie* 6 (1966), pp. 26–50. '*Tokos* and *Atokion*. An examination of natural law reasoning against usury and against contraception', *Natural Law Forum* 10 (1956), pp. 213–35. 'Contraception and the Council. A fresh analysis, a new framework?', *Commonweal* 83 (1967), pp. 657–62.

This study first of all throws into a clearer light the equally contingent nature of the arguments adopted by Christian teachers to support both these condemnations. With reference only to those arguments which are theoretically most important, that is, those which are based on considerations of the unalterable 'nature' of things, it is pointed out that they appear to be conditioned by the actual knowledge available at that moment of the facts under examination: thus, contraception is rejected in the name of the 'natural fecundity' of sexuality, just as, before the fifteenth century, usury was condemned in the name of the 'natural sterility' of money. But no one can fail to see the partiality of this conception which speaks of money as a '*res sterilis*' and reduces sexual activity to a mere procreational function.

This comparison may also be used to illustrate the relative character of the condemnations themselves, not only of their arguments, but even of their content. Consider that the condemnation of usury, which reached its highest point at the very moment when this practice was becoming a widespread social phenomenon, boasted of its justification, in numerous and precise biblical and patristic texts, many more than those used today to condemn contraception. Moreover, the theologian of that age could defend the prohibition of usury by referring to the stern condemnations pronounced by three Ecumenical Councils (Lateran II and III and Vienne), by numerous local Synods and by the papal Magisterium, which had a crushing force in comparison with those used today against contraceptive practices. No Ecumenical Council has ever

---

[14] Before writing his history of the Church's doctrine on contraception, which we have already reviewed, Noonan had studied the history of the doctrine concerning usury: *The Scholastic Analysis of Usury*, Cambridge (Mass.), Harvard University Press, 1957.

pronounced judgment on these, and of the very few condemnations issued by local Synods and handed down by tradition, the two most important (Ancyra in 314 and Worms in 830) are apocryphal, and one has to wait for Pius XI and Pius XII to find papal documents on contraception (and these, moreover, were soon challenged in the well-known speeches by Paul VI and in the discussions in the Council itself). Nevertheless, the condemnation of usury has been progressively abandoned by the Magisterium and by moral theologians. How did this change of attitude come about? Noonan comments that it would be too easy, and also un-Christian, to impute to the Church such a gross error of judgment; can one avoid the difficulty by referring to the opposition to that rule shown by many Christians of that period, in an attempt to prove that, in spite of her stern language, the Church did not attempt to impose the rule by force? The true interpretation is suggested when we consider those absolute values which the Church was trying to protect and to confirm: the prevention of the exploitation of the poor, the appeal to the miserly to share their wealth, and a more equal sharing of capital for the good of the whole community —values which, in the society of that day (on the threshold of the radical changes in economic and financial affairs) could only be saved by such a peremptory intervention. But later on it proved to be quite possible to protect these values more efficiently by new regulations, more in keeping with the changed economic and social conditions. The same thing can and must happen with regard to the condemnation of contraceptive measures. In the gradual formulation of this condemnation, and until its culmination in recent times (at the very moment when their use was becoming universal) the Church was thinking only of the values which were imperilled, and which could not be defended in any other way: the values of procreation, of the protection of innocent life, the personal dignity of the wife and the spiritual significance of sexuality. But the rule needs to be re-examined as soon as it is found that those values—in a Christian community well aware of their enormous importance—may be equally well safeguarded, or even more easily and wholly realized.

We have now to wait for this transition, concludes the Professor of Notre-Dame University, which there is every reason to think may not now be long delayed. In fact (he explains in *Commonweal*) Vatican II has already established the pre-conditions.

It has in fact placed the problem of contraception in a new context, for it has made procreation a responsible task and conjugal intercourse the expression of conjugal love which, besides having a procreational purpose, has an independent and essential value of its own. There result from this new approach certain new criteria by which to judge the conjugal act of coitus: these criteria are no longer sought, according to the tradition which is derived from St Thomas, in the nature of the act itself considered apart from the persons involved in it, but in the persons themselves, of whose capacity for generating love the individual act is an expression. It may be said that *Gaudium et Spes* has used this argument to reinforce the assertion of the necessity of preserving the physical structure of copulation intact, as a full and unreserved expression of the gift of love. Certainly this assertion by the Council constitutes a valid objection to the legitimization of contraceptive measures 'which destroy the physical integrity of intercourse'. Yet such a criterion is less rigid than that pronounced in *Casti Connubii*, and this is proved, Noonan observes, by the fact that the conciliar Constitution does not adopt as its own the encyclical of Pius XI but merely quotes from it in a note (with a cf.) and associates it with the speech by Paul VI. In conclusion, everything combines to convince the learned American scholar that the Council considered the existing condemnations to be at least partially susceptible to revision.

Among the professional theologians certain 'minor' contributions deserve notice, not so much for their authors' names as for their length:

G. Baum, O.S.A., 'Birth control: what happened?', *Commonweal* 81 (1965), pp. 369–71.

L. Beirnaert, S.J., 'Régulation des naissances et sexualité humaine', *Etudes* 324 (1966), pp. 21–31.

P. van Leeuwen, O.F.M., 'Huwelijk en gezin in Vaticanum II', *Theologie en Zielzorg* 62 (1966), pp. 47–61.

E. Schillebeeckx, O.P., 'Het huwelijk volgens Vaticanum II', *Tijdschrift voor Geestelijk Leven* 22 (1966), pp. 81–107.

T. Beemer, *Morale coniugale e controllo delle nascite*, IDO–C dossier no. 66–3

P. de Locht, *La morale conjugale à la lumière du Concile*, Brussels, Centre-nationale de Pastorale familiale, 1966, 24 pp.

F. Böckle, 'Literatur zu Ehefragen', *Diakonia* 2 (1967), pp. 187–92.

In Baum's brief article, which appeared immediately after the conclusion of the Council, it is interesting to note that he finds confirmation of his belief that there had been a modification of principles in his study of the conciliar declarations on birth control, in the light of the processes by which these declarations were finally formulated, and of which he is the first to give a precise account. In fact he concludes that 'since the Church is sharply divided on this question, and since the solution is in no way contained in divine revelation, even the authoritative principles which the Pope, as universal teacher, will in due time propose cannot be a definitive and final interpretation of the divine law, binding in all circumstances, but will rather offer an indispensable and valuable guide to Christian consciences'.

Shortly afterwards appeared the lengthier article by the moral theologian Beirnaert, of *Etudes*. After having recalled the social and cultural reasons which make the regulation of births not a 'historical incident' but the result of the acknowledgment of certain personal values (of parents and of children) previously ignored, Beirnaert observes that nevertheless it presents 'one of the most difficult problems concerned with human sexuality': the question is how to achieve this regulation without impairing the sexual expression which is said to have the specific purpose of procreation. In reality, however, a careful study of human sexuality shows that it is not only 'naturally' fertile, but also 'naturally' infertile. This presents the solution for our problem, that is, the regulation of its natural fertility through that of its equally natural infertility, by means of 'technical interventions' which control the latter and maintain it as long as this may be necessary. It is true that some objections may be raised against these artificial interferences. Leaving aside the objection which is based on the so-called intangibility of biological processes (this being a taboo without any objective foundation), there still remains the difficulty that contraceptive conduct, by eliminating all need for continence, may lead to the prevalence of the hedonistic instinct and to a disrespectful attitude towards the sexual act. The Jesuit recognizes that this is a serious difficulty, which can not be overcome by periodic continence. In fact this method, because it merely follows 'the natural rhythm of fertility and infertility', cannot in itself preserve that dialogue between persons which is the proper character of human sexuality, and which must instead satisfy other individual and mutual needs in the daily life of every married couple. The conclusion is that the temporary control of infertility, not only for the purpose of responsible and orderly procreation but also in order to satisfy every couple's individual need for sexual expression, should be 'entrusted primarily to the married couple themselves'. 'Every attempt to draw up *a priori* a sort of objective scale of values between the various methods seems to conflict with the fact that everyone of these acquires its significance only in relation to the persons themselves, their psychology and their mutual relations.' To avoid the danger of vulgarizing conjugal intercourse the choice of one particular means more than another seems of no avail; the only solution is the personal determination to make of all sexual intercourse, fertile or infertile as it may be, and by whatever means it has been made infertile, the means to express an authentic communion between man and wife.

The three Dutch theologians adopt very much the same standpoint. They are van Leeuwen and Schillebeeckx (both members of the Council Sub-Commission on marriage) and Beemer. Beginning with a clear historical analysis of the conciliar text, van Leeuwen then proceeds to deal with the three main opinions which today divide theologians in their attitude to contraceptive means: these are those who are totally faithful to *Casti Connubii*, and believe that the same principles and therefore the same condemnation should apply also to the new methods recently discovered; then there is the intermediary group which believes that the traditional doctrine will be maintained but with some more or less significant modifications. Lastly comes the group of the reformers, for whom 'the rule of *Casti Connubii*, especially in all that concerns the so-called natural integrity of the individual act, no longer possesses a sufficiently convincing force', so that 'it is no longer possible to make a distinction of absolute value between means which are against nature and means which are not against nature'. For the time being all three opinions 'may continue to appeal to explicit expressions or veiled suggestions on the part of the Council'. The second group 'seems that which, with its cautious affirmations, is most in harmony with the words Paul VI uttered in 1964, which are now quoted in the conciliar text'. But even this opinion 'can be held only temporarily': the most coherent opinion is that of the third and last group.

Schillebeeckx's comment is summary but conclusive. If 'sexuality in the truest sense is not a biological fact but a specifically human activity', then we can understand the 'fine, profound and complete formula' used by the Council by way of a guiding principle, that is, that 'husband and wife must respect, in a context of true love, the *human* meaning of sexuality, as a symbol which expresses the real mutual gift of love, and also its intention of effecting a procreation worthy of man'. This means that 'biological ends cannot form ethical principles', because the biological purpose acquires 'a personalist content which, because of the human nature of the sexuality of which it is only a particular moment, may not serve as a norm'. It may be said that 'matrimonial intercourse in which the procreation of children has been fundamentally and radically eliminated from the personal sexual relationship must be condemned as contrary to its meaning. But this negative judgment must not for this reason be applied to the individual conjugal acts: every one of these in fact, even if rendered infertile, may still be capable of expressing the integral meaning of human sexuality as a symbol which expresses conjugal love and a fertility worthy of man. This conclusion springs from a general concept of man which may evoke and become modified in time by Christian people, and it is the duty of the Magisterium to propose this, without binding itself to 'forms which express a concept of man now superseded'. In this light, the reference made by the Council, regarding methods of birth control, to *Casti Connubii*, 'the content of which is no longer quite clear', has a merely relative value.

In his contribution Beemer asks for a new pastoral attitude, but not one which (as proposed by some theologians in recent years) 'may assign relative degrees of subjective sinfulness to actions contrary to the rules'; instead it should be a new pastoral attitude determined to change objectively the rule itself in all that concerns means of birth control. Moreover, the arguments adduced to support the old condemnation are gradually being proved inadequate and the same inadequacy now impairs the most recent argument, which bases that condemnation on the fact that birth control measures 'annul the peculiar human significance of sexual self-giving'. There is indeed no real difference between mechanical means, which are still condemned, and oral means, which very many theologians now consider permissible.

A new sense of responsibility is therefore required of the Christian man and wife, and this time of waiting for the Church to give its verdict is, for them ,'a privileged period of adult responsibility'. This is the opinion of de Locht, who says that that for a long time now we have restricted ourselves to a concept of nature that was too exclusively biological, without recognizing that man, even in the field of sexuality and procreation, has wide powers of intervention in his own bodily functions, for the sake of 'complete sexual fulfilment'. Certainly, the physical integrity of conjugal intercourse constitutes a 'true value' for the person, and the married couples themselves moreover desire this, but it is not an absolute value in itself. Even the condemnation uttered by Pius XI may be thought to have been based on a consideration of the greater importance of other values, felt to be permanent and absolute, such as procreative generosity and the overcoming of all conjugal selfishness. 'It would therefore gravely impoverish the moral development of husband and wife if attention were to be concentrated on one point only, that is the respect due to the biological structure of intercourse, without harmonizing it with all the other requirements of conjugal life.' Moreover, this same particular value 'is not respected if, because of its too automatic application, it compromises other requirements: it is an over-simplification of morality to decide every question according to this criterion, considered as enjoying absolute and general priority, whatever its consequences may be as regards fidelity, healthy fecundity and the very survival of the home. What is needed therefore is 'a clear-sighted responsibility', and a 'heart always alert to new needs'. 'The attribution of an absolute priority to a rule which concerns a relative value, in order to give it precedence over all others, is an attempt to evade the obligations of human responsibility.'

This tendency appears to be in line with the thought of the Council, and it is on this consideration that Böckle bases his arguments. The Council has attached more importance to responsible parenthood than to the problems of birth control', and as for the methods of control, 'it deliberately makes no mention of the traditional difference between natural and unnatural methods'. This is highly significant, and points to its awareness that the problem of the permissibility of the various contraceptive methods must be stated in a manner different from that traditionally used:

in fact, if the sexual act, as a *human act*, in its objective active structure, is, as used to be said, always and essentially procreative, then all contraceptive practice is opposed to this ('and in my personal opinion', adds Böckle, 'even periodic continence becomes very questionable') 'but if, with good reason (as many moralists have now agreed), we set aside the traditional definition of the act, then the intrinsic sinfulness of contraceptive practice as such becomes doubtful: the positive exclusion of the biological possibility of procreation is no longer sinful in itself, and the method by which this is obtained must be judged from other standpoints'.

As for the interventions forbidden by the Magisterium, 'one must remember that these condemnations are not based upon revealed truths infallibly ascertained, but upon purely rational reflections on human sexuality', that is, from the philosophical, psychological, sociological and biological information which 'always make up our human knowledge, limited and fallible'. It is therefore possible that a further study of this knowledge may lead to modifications or corrections of the rules previously laid down: this is what is happening with regard to the doctrine that is set out in *Casti Connubii*.[15]

Moreover, for some time past, as Dayez observes, there has been a debate in the Church on the question of the means of contraception and 'the crux of the problem lies in the question as to whether every contraceptive method (*coitus interruptus*, contraceptive appliances, chemical products, surgical sterilization) is evil in itself and therefore absolutely forbidden'. The Council, however, 'did not condemn new attempts to solve the problem which put forward the suggestion that for objective reasons (the mutual harmony and the growth of conjugal love, the welfare of children, etc.) recourse may be had to contraception'. Conse-

---

[15] Obviously we cannot refer to all the numerous recent writings on the theology of the natural law and the competence of the Magisterium to deal with this. We quote merely the book edited by F. BÖCKLE *Das Naturrecht im Disput*, Düsseldorf, Patmos-Verlag, 1966, which also contains a more specific study of matrimonial morality; F. X. KAUFMANN, *Dei Ehe in sozialanthropologischer Sicht* (pp. 15-60); G. ERMECKE, 'Kirche und Naturrecht', *Theologie und Glaube* 57 (1967) 56-61; we shall deal, a little later on, with the opinions of Fr. DAVID, to whom Ermecke is here replying. The problem of natural law is also the fundamental theme of recent essays by Dr. J. RÖTZER, 'Eheliche Liebe als gesamtmenschlicher Auftrag', *Die neue Ordnung* 21 (1967), pp. 1-15 (cf. pp. 305-13) and 'Empfängnisregelung: nur eine Frage der Technik?', *Theol. praktische Quartalschrift* 115 (1967), pp. 164-76.

quently, according to the Belgian moralist, 'considering the extent of doctrinal research today, the evolution of ideas which is now apparent, and the positive and reasonable doubt cast on the affirmation that every contraceptive method is in itself sinful, it would seem that a confessor may no longer, before granting absolution, require that the penitent should give up a contraceptive method which he considers justified by grave reasons affecting the welfare of his marriage'.

Finally, one must mention the 'major', or at least the more lengthy contributions to the discussion which are in favour of the new attitude.

We record first of all the writings by the Jesuit, Fr David, who had been one of the first to state and resolve the question in its new terms. He published his articles in a small volume, adding some passages from his previous contributions.

J. David, S.J., *Neue Aspekte der kirchlichen Ehelehre*, Frankfurt, Verlag Gerhard Kaffke, 1966, 119 pp. The author re-edits in this book (translated into French: *Nouveaux aspects de la doctrine catholique du mariage*, Tournai, Desclée, 1967, 159 pp.) also some articles which had appeared in preceding months: 'Neue Aspekte und neue Akzente der kirchlichen Ehelehre', *Orientierung* 30 (1966), pp. 3–7; 'Ehe und Familie nach dem zweiten Vatikanischen Konzil', in E. Sieves, *Vollendung ehelicher Liebe*, Recklinghausen, Paulus Verlag, 1966, pp. 155–74;, "Kirche und Naturrecht', *Orientierung* 30 (1966), pp. 129–33.

The German Jesuit's first and constant aim (discernible despite a certain prolixity of style) is to give a historical context to the various concepts of marriage, and particularly to the concept of its procreational purpose, which Christian tradition has elaborated during the centuries. In this way it becomes possible to distinguish between valid propositions and those doctrines which are contingent and capable of development. Among the latter is that view of sexuality which, on the basis of incomplete physiological information and in the total absence of a psychological study of this reality, considers every conjugal act to be 'naturally' procreative. It is not surprising that Pius XI, in *Casti Connubii*, the first document issued by the Magisterium on the subject of marriage, also referred to this concept. In fact, because of the close relationship which it established between sexuality and the procreative duty, it served him as a solid defence against the pan-sexualistic literature of the time, which exclusively emphasized the elements of pleasure to be found in sexual acts and advocated 'trial marriages' or 'compassionate marriages', or even free love. But in a historical and therefore contingent context, there are now emerging the principles of a Christian doctrine of sexuality, which, even if it sees its essential purpose as procreative, still assigns to it an equally profound intention with regard to the development of the individual personality and the married couple's mutual relationship of knowledge and love. This is seen in recent years in the approval granted by the Magisterium to periodic continence, and by many theologians to the use of the pill—and these approvals imply the admission and acknowledgment of the personal meanings of sexuality and of the value of its physical expressions even without immediate purpose of procreation. So the old 'physiological' concept is now superseded, as moralists follow the light of which Pius XI had caught a glimpse but which he had not the courage to follow himself, and there is set up against the ever present pan-sexual and selfish temptations the much more solid bulwark of a more comprehensive concept of sexuality and married life.

The Council did not lack the courage to follow this light, and David attributes particular significance to some speeches made in the autumn of 1964 (Maximos IV, Léger, Suenens, Alfrink and Reuss), and for the results already attained gives credit to Bishop Reuss and to the theologians Häring and Janssens. The Council teaching is clear in its main lines: it recognizes that 'marriage is first of all a relationship of love between a man and woman, and its value exists and may be expressed even independently of procreation and progeny; in particular the bodily union of husband and wife is the expression and exercise of their love, esteem and personal regard and cannot be reduced to the formula (still adopted by Pius XI) of "procreation and pleasure". This sexual union between man and woman, considered in its entirety, has an essential connection with procreation even when this is not clearly defined.' This concept, so much broader and more complex than that which preceded it, 'explains why there is a steady increase in the number of moralists who while certainly maintaining that the essential purpose of marriage, and especially of the sexual life of husband and wife, is the procreation of children, attribute this purpose to their sexual life in its entirety and not specifically to every individual act'. Consequently, they establish another basis for the discussion of the legitimacy or illegitimacy of individual acts and the moral judgment on the occasional use of contraceptive devices. In this light there appear to be only two conditions which are indispensable for the legitimization of these measures: 'that in their conjugal life as a whole there should exist a genuine desire for offspring and that nothing should be done which deprives or substantially impairs the character and significance of an authentically personal union in love'. Every other kind of distinction drawn between one contraceptive measure and another constitutes 'over-subtle casuistry' and would moreover be based on facts of 'natural law' concerning which neither the Magisterium nor theology has any specific competence to form a judgment.

This is, in fact, a final aspect of Fr David's above-quoted contributions: his close study of the question of the Church's competence to decide questions concerning natural law. When the question at issue is one of pure natural law, such as can only be resolved by the use of reason applied to the 'nature of the object', without any guarantee from revelation, it cannot find in the Church (Magisterium and theology) a decisive solution. If in such cases the Magisterium formulates some rules, it does so more with a predominantly pastoral intention, than with the aim of pronouncing dogmas to which may be attached the guarantee of infallibility. This is true also of the problem of contraceptive measures, for the solution of which the only means at our disposal is rational reflection on the 'nature' of the conjugal act, so that the ecclesiastical authority itself has, in order to prepare a solution, summoned the aid not only of theologians but also of representatives of the various other branches of knowledge which are concerned in this. 'But then,' asks Fr David, 'how could one base on their affirmations, which have a merely human authority, a doctrine which should have a binding theological sanction?' That is why, if one asks to what extent a contraceptive device substantially alters the natural significance of copulation, the answer—to this as to other similar questions—is supported by the authority of a study in which all branches of human knowledge have collaborated, and because of which moral theology as such 'must give up making many assertions in the elaboration of which she has only a very doubtful competence'.[16]

The position of Mgr Reuss is among the most significant, and the Auxiliary Bishop of Mainz made it very clear in his post-conciliar writings:

> J. M. Reuss, 'Zeugungsziel und eheliche Vereinigung', *Der Seelsorger* 36 (1966), pp. 249–59. 'Zur derzeitigen Ehepastorale', *Diakonia* I (1966), pp. 234–6. In French: 'Où en est la pastorale du mariage?', *Choisir* 85–86 (Dec. 1966).

The central affirmation of the first article, written in reply to the articles (already reviewed here) by Demmer, Krauss and Günthör, is that, although it must be admitted that the intrinsic purpose of sexuality as a whole is procreative, it may nevertheless not be asserted that the procreative purpose is an intrinsic end, or indeed a primary end, of every individual copulation. In fact if copulation is considered in its empirical and physical reality (and no other method can be used to acquire a metaphysical understanding of its meaning) it must be concluded that it very rarely presents all the conditions which render it capable of generating life. It is pointed out that not only actual procreation but even the possibility of procreation is very frequently absent. The only element of procreativity which is present in every copulation is the emission of semen, but this emission is not copulation, and just as it is not sufficient to render it fertile so it is not sufficient to define it as necessarily directed towards generation. Therefore copulation, as a human act, includes procreativity only to a very restricted degree. On the contrary, the achievement of union between husband and wife is 'a possibility always available in every copulation, and so it is this integrating purpose, rather than procreativity, which characterizes every act of coitus'. So the procreative purpose 'cannot be in any sense the final purpose of conjugal intercourse unless it can be said (which is absurd) that an end which can be said only in a very limited sense to be the immediate end of the conjugal union defines this union much more truly than an end (the integrating purpose) which belongs to it in

---

[16] On this aspect of David's doctrine and showing the same trend of opinion, are the shrewd observations of A. ZIEGLER, in his review of David's book in *Orientierung* 31 (1967,) p. 23.

every instance'. Consequently, one cannot say that the procreative end is essential to every copulation, and therefore condemn every intervention to render it sterile, and this conclusion weakens the only valid argument which has been put forward against the use (when other reasons require it) of contraceptive measures.

These reflections, concludes Mgr Reuss, are offered as a personal contribution to the discussion while the 'authoritative decision' of the Pope is still awaited. But, practically speaking, what is to be done in the meantime? This is the question, no longer doctrinal but pastoral, which he faces in the second article mentioned above. Here he explicitly asserts that the doubt as to whether all contraceptive measures are illicit when used for grave reasons, is 'a positive and reasonable doubt' in the Church today. The proof of this was seen in the attitude of the Council, which 'not only did not condemn the tentative solutions proposed by theologians during the discussion, but, when the time came to vote, several times rejected some amendments which aimed at the inclusion in the conciliar text of formulations favourable to the traditional doctrine'. Therefore, to married couples who find it is impossible to practise periodic continence and ask whether it is permissible to use, for grave reasons, other contraceptive methods, the confessor may, according to Mgr Reuss, reply as follows:

'If you really find yourself in this situation you do not sin if you have recourse to contraceptive measures. You must however try to find the method which most befits the dignity of your union. This is my personal opinion. I assume before God the responsibility for it. This opinion, based on a knowledge of your particular situation, is valid only for you. You must not generalize it.' 'This reply given by a priest', concludes Reuss, 'must not be taken to mean that the contraceptive method is actually admitted by ecclesiastical authority. It expresses what the priest can say in this intermediate situation in which we find ourselves.'

And now we come to the familiar name of Janssens: in fact the moral theologian of Louvain, who had in 1959 been the first to affirm the permissibility of progestational treatment after childbirth and in the period immediately preceding the menopause, and in 1963 had encouraged the new trend of thought concerning the general use of the pill, now returns to the discussion with an article which further extends his reflections on the use of all other contraceptive measures:

L. Janssens, 'Chasteté conjugal selon l'encyclique *Casti Connubii*
et suivant la constitution pastorale *Gaudium et Spes*', *Ephemerides
Theologicae Lovanienses* 42 (1966), pp. 513–54. This reappears
in a book: *Mariage et fécondité. De Casti Connubii* à Gaudium et
Spes, Gembloux, J. Duculot, 1967, 120 pp. See also idem,
'Les grandes étapes de la doctrine chrétienne du mariage',
Revue Diocésaine de Namur 20 (1966), pp. 387–411.

As in his previous article Janssens here, too, presents an
ample historical synthesis of Christian concepts of sexual activity.
During the last centuries it is obvious that these concepts have
undergone a certain evolution in fact; whereas the old doctrine
maintained that only sexual intercourse with a procreational
purpose is without sin, a new concept begins with St Thomas
Aquinas who affirms more and more explicitly that the conjugal
act may be justified even if it has no generative intention, but has
other motives: the 'payment of the debt of marriage' (*redditio
debiti*), the prevention of the danger of adultery, the satisfaction of
concupiscence in legitimate enjoyment, and the preservation and
expression of mutual love. These motives are recognized as valid
even in *Casti Connubii*, and that is why Janssens finds the encyclical
illogical when it proceeds to condemn contraceptive measures
because, it maintains, the 'nature of the act' is procreative. Since
it has already said that the purpose of intercourse is not exclusively
procreative, does the reference to its 'nature' suffice to prove that
the physical integrity of the act is absolutely intangible and
indispensable? The doubt which even then was quite rightly
aroused received obvious confirmation in the developments which
followed Pius XI's encyclical. On the one hand there appeared an
increased awareness (thanks to a 'personalist' trend whose new
approach to the problem was prompted by the 'phenomenological'
movement) that conjugal love is not merely a subjective motive for
copulation but instead constitutes its intrinsic and probably
hitherto neglected meaning, and on the other hand it has been
admitted that parenthood must be responsible and must be regulated according to the different values at stake in family life.

In the light of these developments which the Council itself
acknowledged, one understands why the Constitution no longer
contains any reference to the 'nature of the act' as being essentially
procreative, but instead, in order to resolve the difficult problems
presented by the conflicting needs of conjugal love and responsible

parenthood, proposes as a guiding principle 'the nature of the human person and of his acts', which no longer requires, as obviously as the former criterion, the physical integrity of every individual copulation.

In fact, we must now consider copulation as an 'act of the human person' and no longer as a 'natural' act having its own intangible structure. Obviously, the respect of this bodily structure still represents an ideal because of its natural capacity to express the personal values which are at stake, but it has been the cause of much ambiguity. Sexual intercourse although perfect in its physical structure, may still fail to express the value of mutual self-giving, or that of satisfactory procreation. Therefore another moral criterion must be invoked which shall be less ambiguous and of more universal validity, in order to judge of the virtue of the single act of coitus. This means that the true character of conjugal intercourse 'seems to be perfectly respected when the husband and wife, in the whole of their shared sexual life, aim at that degree of procreation which objectively accords with the conditions of their family life and when, in every conjugal act, they try to further their mutual love and to safeguard the values of the whole of married life'. Can this purpose be attained in the case of contraceptive intercourse? Janssens does not exclude this possibility, that is, that the real meaning of copulation, as an act of the human person, may be respected 'even if, in extreme circumstances, the husband and wife, without giving way to selfish or hedonistic desires, have recourse to certain sexual relations in which a deliberate intervention on their part has prevented conception, that is, of course, when they can find no other means of preserving the fidelity of their love and at the same time safeguarding the essential values of the whole of their conjugal and family life'.

Like Mgr Reuss, Fr Häring explicitly deals with the doctrinal problem of the permissibility of contraception, as well as with the pastoral problem of actual conduct during this intermediate period of waiting:

B. Häring, C.SS.R., 'Ehe und Familie in der Welt von heute', *Theologie der Gegenwart* 9 (1966), pp. 1–13. The article appeared, a short time previously, in Italian: Eng. trans. 'Marriage and the Family in the World Today' in *Road to Renewel*, London, Geoffrey

Chapman, 1967, pp. 147–69. Idem, 'Um die Ehefrage. Eine
mögliche Lösung?', *Theologie der Gegenwart* 9 (1966), 77–79.
Idem, *Il matrimonio nelle prospettive del Vaticano* II,
Vicenza, Favero Editore, 1966, 61 pp.; 'Il silenzio del Papa e
il disagio dei confessori', *Settimana del clero*, 18 Dec. 1966, p. 4.

The doctrinal problem is the main theme of his comments on
the chapter on marriage in *Gaudium et Spes*, and his position is
further explained, regarding the more practical aspect of contraceptive measures, in the second of his above-mentioned articles.
The Redemptorist is convinced that the Council did not intend to
contradict the teaching of *Casti Connubii*, and yet 'one would be
blind indeed if one failed to see that this chapter goes far beyond
the limits of Pius XI's encyclical in certain points of decisive
importance'. The limitations of *Casti Connubii* are due to the
fact that 'it pronounces an opinion on the problem of contraceptive
measures without having previously given a frank and conscientious judgment on the permissibility of birth control in general'.
It therefore associates in the one condemnation all kinds of
contraceptive measures (whether motivated by sound reasons or
not) and in its general attitude to this question its limited viewpoint is seen in the doctrine that 'the whole question lies in the
formal structure and purpose of individual conjugal acts'. The
conciliar document, however, makes it clear that 'the fundamental
problem of conscience, which must be resolved with great respect
for the vocation of parenthood, lies in the question as to whether
here and now God wishes a new creature to be generated'. Consequently, the first criterion to be observed in the choice of a
permissible method is whether this satisfies the requirements of
generous and responsible parenthood; only afterwards can one
examine the problem of actual ways of achieving birth control,
but one must be guided, in the study of this problem, not by 'a
kind of biological ontology' but by a 'personalistic approach'.
Therefore it is chiefly the good of the human person which must
be put first when one considers the advisability of the various
methods. Those methods are illicit which destroy or impair the
integrity of mutual love (this seems to be the case with *coitus
interruptus*), or which eliminate the possibility of a future fecundity
when this might be considered reasonably desirable. On the
other hand, some other measures, such as pills or the use of the
cervical diaphragm, do not seem to frustrate these intentions.

In any case 'the principle of conjugal morality must be decided from the point of view of human persons and not based on purely biological considerations'.

As for rules of actual conduct before the Pope pronounces judgment, the confessor must 'point out what is sure and certain', writes Häring in the last of the above-mentioned articles. Naturally, 'he cannot advise or permit methods disapproved of by the Magisterium', but on the other hand 'he must not show himself particularly intransigent when it is a question of points still being discussed by moral theologians and conscientious and enlightened lay people' and he may also respect good faith, especially in situations of grave difficulty and conflict between different values and obligations.

Finally we must mention three very important contributions from three Italian writers, the first being a critical essay entirely devoted to our problem by a young priest of the diocese of Turin, and initially presented as a thesis for a Degree in Philosophy at the Catholic University of the Sacred Heart. It is symptomatic of the mentality now common to younger thinkers, and may be said to make a valid contribution to what has been called the 'tradition of the future'. The other two treatises are by Professors of Moral Theology at the Seminaries of Lodi and Florence respectively.

P. Balestro, *Sesso e persona. Verso una nuova etica sessuale?*, Milan, Bompiani, 1967, 220 pp. The 3rd edition is already published. The author has included some of its themes also in 'La castità coniugale', *La Famiglia* 2 (1968), pp. 17–27.

L. Rossi, *Morale sessuale in evoluzione*, Turin, Gribaudi, 1967, 414 pp.: chaps. 9, 10 and 11 deal with our theme (pp. 265–376).

E. Chiavacci, *La Costituzione pastorale sulla Chiesa nel mondo contemporaneo*, Rome, Ed. Studium, 1967, 497 pp.; cf. pp. 197–249.

Balestro's thesis, largely influenced by theological writings of recent years, begins with a historical summary intended to show the origins (not in revelation but derived from 'a certain interpretation of revelation') of the 'division between conjugal love and sexual intercourse', and then proceeds to examine the actual problem of our own time. Balestro first of all studies the principal phases of the discussion on the use of progestational drugs and then proceeds to distinguish the various doctrinal trends concerning the general use of contraceptives. Certain more general concepts are already apparent: the superseding of the exaggeratedly 'physical' notion of nature, the 'watchful and constant' study of the historical context of moral principles, and the pre-eminence assigned to the element of love in sexuality and Marriage. The conclusion which the author deduces is, as is to be expected: in situations in which 'procreation, given the actual circumstances, is not a duty, whereas other intentions remain still present (such as, for example, the need in those particular circumstances to express conjugal love as a mutual bond between husband and wife), this conjugal love is accepted as the purpose of union and all their acts are intended to express it. If married life requires an expression of love, but in those particular circumstances does not permit a procreative act, the husband and wife will use those means or devices which truly further this intention at that moment of time.' The question of which means to adopt 'is not really within the competence of the moralists. They may of course indicate the means which are always to be condemned, such as, for example, those which constitute a threat to human life, those which unjustifiably impair the personal integrity of the husband and wife, etc.'

After presenting a detailed and well-informed survey of the most recent discussions on contraception, which enables him to trace the various principles put forward successively by the theologians who wish to demonstrate that the attitude of *Casti Connubii* is now out-dated, Rossi defines his own personal attitude, based on certain fundamental distinctions in Catholic moral doctrine between direct and indirect volition and the arguments derived from these. His conclusion is that 'even if the pill and the practice of onanism were always to produce evil effects, we still could not for that reason alone assert that they were intrisically illicit, for absolute and intrinsic sinfulness, precisely and technically speaking, is found only in "willing evil" and not in merely causing it—for this latter effect might be legitimized, at least for very grave reasons, by the principle of the lesser evil.' In fact, Christian morality permits many kinds of behaviour (the author gives a list of several) in which an action considered evil in itself is no longer condemned if used as a means to achieve certain ends. 'This does not mean that the end justifies the means but only that those particular actions cannot be called evil unless they are intended for certain evil purposes.' Even the traditional argument, therefore, when it attempts to judge the morality of an action, is much more concerned than is apparent at first sight with what is deliberately willed. It asserts implicitly, moreover, that 'sometimes it is the specific purpose intended which legitimizes the use of the particular method adopted'. Rossi does not doubt that this is true, in certain circumstances, also of the use of contraceptives: here even more than in other cases, 'the means must be judged by its intention'.

The attitude of Chiavacci is based on the concept of a fundamental option or purpose, several times referred to by other writers also, in connection with this problem. 'So the moral judgment must not dwell on the individual act of intercourse but be inspired by a consideration of the whole conjugal life, and the whole complex of sexual activity which expresses it, if it wishes to judge each action only as part of a whole and unique fundamental purpose.' It follows that in practice the conjugal act must always preserve its capacity to express total mutual self-giving, and must not impair the future procreative capacity inherent in the fundamental purpose. Not only abortion must be condemned, but also all those degenerate practices which destroy the symbolic integrity of the act, and also every method which, like permanent sterilization, will prevent future generation. Instead, those practices may be permitted which effect a sterilization restricted to a single act of intercourse and so do not interfere with the fundamental purpose, always provided that the symbolic integrity of the act be safeguarded. This 'hypothesis' seems moreover to the author the only one capable of adequately interpreting the sense of the Conciliar document itself, which simply states that, in sexual activity, the integral meaning of mutual self-giving and human procreation must be safeguarded in a context of genuine love.

It is therefore quite obvious now that, since the conclusion of the Council, a large and highly competent group of theologians and moralists have shown an eager expectation of some modification of the Church's teaching on birth control. In the light of the discussions and developments which have inspired this hope, we may presume to believe that it would be very difficult now to go back upon this authoritative opinion.

IV. *The most recent articles on the problem of the pill*

To complete our survey, we must now mention some articles, dealing with the moral problem of oestro-progestational treatment for contraceptive purposes, which have appeared since the Council. We shall not refer to opinions on this question expressed in articles dealing with the morality of contraceptive measures in general (of which the 'pill method' is only one of many) but only to more or less specific studies of this particular aspect, justified by the assertion that there exists a real difference between this method and others because this method alone does not impair the 'natural process' of copulation.

We must first of all speak of those articles which restrict themselves to reviewing the discussions still continuing, but which show a general tendency to adopt the more permissive line. For example, there are:

Eugenio da Veroli, 'Le discussioni teologiche sulle "pillole",' *Digest religioso* 12 (1966), pp. 27–35.

Z. Herrero, O.S.A., 'La regulación de nacimientos', *Archivio Teologico Agustiniano* I (1966), pp. 71–85.

P. Alfieri, 'Considerazioni medico-morali sugli steroidi ormonali ovariostatici', *L'attualità medica* 31 (1966), VI, pp. 19–28.

A. Sini, 'Limitazione delle nascite e matrimonio canonico. Brevi osservazioni', *Justitia* 19 (1966), pp. 350–66.

M. F. Sánchez Jménez: 'Paternidad responsable y Vaticano II', *Sal terrae* 55 (1967), pp. 183–208.

L. Azzolini, S.J., 'La "pillola cattolica", il magistero della Chiesa e il probabilismo', *Rassegna di Teologia* 8 (1967), pp. 202–7.

L. Rossi, 'Pillola e maternità: la parola al moralista', *Anime e corpi* 5 (1967), pp. 133–40. (The article is prefaced, pp. 129–33, by medical information supplied by G. B. Garbelli.)

The first two articles merely summarize the theological discussion. Herrero's is particularly precise and well-informed, written to show that the very nature of the arguments successively put forward has led inevitably to the adoption of the more advanced position, which the author himself seems inclined to support. An equally frank résumé of the debate is provided by Sánchez

Jménez who, in spite of the very general title of his article, deals only with the problem of anovulants. Alfieri's report, as is to be expected from a doctor, deals particularly with the medical aspects, but without ignoring the terms of the moral problem, and he puts forward the hypothesis that 'the proclamations of Pius XII, although now of binding force, are not to be thought of as immutable'.

Sini is more interested in the juridical implications of the debate and still feels 'almost insuperable doubts' about the legitimacy of a generalized use of the pill within the context of the *jus conditum*, since by their use there would be excluded from conjugal intercourse 'not only *proles in se ipsa*, but *proles in suo principio*'. These doubts would be dissipated if one could accept the new thesis which asserts that the chief end of marriage is the expression of perfect union between husband and wife, but in that case 'there would seem to be no longer any significance in the choice of one contraceptive method rather than another'. Finally we must mention the articles by Azzolini and Rossi which are written from the point of view of pastoral direction. Azzolini, while admitting the legitimacy, in theory, of the use of progestational drugs, denies its applicability in practice. Rossi, starting from the terms of the theological discussion, suggests— between the two extremist parties of the 'blind conservatives who think only of Pius XII's pronouncements' and the 'superficial reformers who already behave as if the change in doctrine were not only possible and desirable but already a *fait accompli*'—an attitude of responsible silence when dealing with married couples who use the pill 'with a good conscience, finding themselves in grave danger with regard to their marriage'.[17]

Other contributions show a more decided attitude. We refer first of all to two articles which are almost totally condemnatory in their references to the contraceptive use of progestational drugs:

K. Hörmann, 'Moraltheologische Sonderbehandlung der Sterilization?', *Theologisch-praktische Quartalschrift* 114 (1966), 31-4.
A. Osuna, O.P., 'Los modernos progestogenos y su valoración

---

[17] After a brief summary of the question, *Morale del matrimonio*, ed. P. LIGGERI, Milan, Istituto La Casa, 1966, pp. 17–22, expresses an attitude of hope and expectation of some change in the traditional doctrine.

ética', *La Ciencia Tomista* 93 (1966), 537–79; 'Opiniones actuales que propugnan la licitud del uso de anovulatorios con fines anticonceptivos', *ibid.*, 94 (1967), pp. 161–232.

P. Chauchard, in *Pour ou contre la pillule et le planning familial*, Nancy, Berger-Levrault, 1967, 80 pp.

The principle of the total good which legitimizes therapeutic sterilization can also legitimize, in Hörmann's opinion, anovulatory treatment for a woman threatened with violence, or incapable of supporting a pregnancy until its proper term because of some defect irremovable by any other means. In both cases this would be merely suppression of an 'abnormal' fertility, which could not be considered direct sterilization. But if the intervention is effected in the case of a 'healthy procreative capacity' and with a view to 'unimpeded sexual activity', it may not be justified by the principle of the total good. In this hypothesis the resultant copulation would be deprived of its 'full content', and therefore, at least in the long run, would be harmful to the total good of the person. Moreover, in the much more categorical opinion of Osuna, this would constitute an 'abuse of the powers which God has given man over his body', as in fact is clearly pointed out in the documents emanating from the Magisterium which deal with this matter. In fact, 'the whole sexual order, including its organs, functions and the free use of its faculty, is structurally directed to the propagation of the species' and therefore cannot be sacrificed for the sake of the individual person or individual act of copulation. The negative verdict of Dr Chauchard is based upon the now familiar consideration that progestational drugs, like every other contraceptive measure, cause a physiological, psychological and moral deviation from 'nature' in both husband and wife, and particularly in the wife.

Finally we come to the opinions which are decidedly favourable to the new trend; the last two of these, both from Brazil, are particularly well reasoned:

Q. de la Bedoyère, 'Sterilization and human reason', *New Blackfriars* 48 (1966), pp. 153–6.

D. X. Burt, O.S.A., 'The anovulants and mutilation', *Augustinianum* 6 (1966), pp. 301–10.

B. Leers, O.F.M., 'O método da pílula. Uma reflexâo teológica', in *Moral conjugal e regulaçāo da natalidade*, Petrópolis, Editôra Vozes, 1966, pp. 48-121.

B. B. Dos Santos, 'Contrôle dos nascimentos e uso dos contraceptivos', *Revista Ecclesiástica Brasileira* 27 (1967), pp. 83-94.

G. Perico, S.J., 'La "super-pillola",' *Aggiornamenti sociali* 18 (1967), pp. 551-6 and *La Civiltà Cattolica*, 1967, IV, pp. 261-4.

The first two authors start from the principle of the total good, which they believe can be applied to the case under discussion. Burt, although he does not consider the permissive solution to be certain, thinks that contraceptive anovulatory treatment, in the context of a reasonable control of fertility, may be a legitimate extension of the application of this principle, by analogy with what has already happened in the case of transplantations.

Leer's exposition is very lengthy. He thinks that the problem of the pill, like all other new moral problems, should be studied in the context of the 'moment in history' in which it has arisen, and which with its new insights and useful 'circumstantial' knowledge suggests the absolute moral principles by which it must be resolved. It would, therefore, be mistaken to judge this problem in the light of historical concepts which are now being superseded, like those with a 'pessimistic' or 'merely physical' foundation, elaborated in past times with regard to marriage and sexuality. The new concept must therefore be illuminated by these realities which our own times are discovering: for example, the new notion of marriage as a 'specific union of two persons of different sex, which finds its consummation in its sexual expression'. Sexuality, as the means of this community between two persons, finds fulfilment in its procreative function. This new aspect enables us to understand the asserted legitimacy of periodic continence, and also justifies the use of the pill: 'the justification of periodic continence in marriage, in certain circumstances and for the duration of these, seems also applicable to the method of the pill'. The distinctions between the various methods were drawn by moralists who relied too mechanically on superseded concepts: sterilization was judged by its physical data and not, as instead it must be judged, in relation to the whole person and all the values involved; 'nature' is described almost solely in its biological expressions instead of in the complexity of its truly human elements. Nor is approval of the pill blocked by the pronouncements of the Magisterium, for in fact the teaching of the Church also is based on contemporary concepts and may therefore, in these fields, be capable of development and modification. In fact, as Leers points out, 'in putting forward the arguments against contraceptive measures . . . Pius XI concentrated his attention on the procreative purpose and value of marriage and on the procreative intention of sexuality'.

The last article, by Dos Santos, after a brief survey of the problem and an exposition of the moral principles known to be involved in it, concludes that the use of pills 'permits married couples to control their periods of natural infertility, prolonging their duration: this prolongation, which is in perfect harmony with the significance of the sexual act, is the specific expression of conjugal love harmonized with the requirements of responsible parenthood'. But when he examines recent hormonal preparations intended to prevent the implantation of the fertilized ovum (the 'pill for the next day') or to effect its premature discharge from the uterus (the 'pill for the next month') Perico does not hesitate to condemn these as abortifacients. As regards anovulant drugs, he points out that the moral judgment concerning these 'is not yet defined' but that nevertheless 'they may not be classed with contraceptives properly so-called: they do not interfere directly with the conjugal act, they do not mutilate its generative elements and they do not neutralize any process or function closely bound up with the procreative act'.

These are the latest contributions to the discussion on the pill,[18] which started in 1957 and produced all those abundant reflections and discussions which we have reviewed and which we must now try to summarize.

---

[18] We have not been able to examine: F. BERNARD, *Limitation ou régulation des naissances. Comment s'aimer sans pillule*, Paris, Les Edit. Ouvrières, 1966, 86 pp.; and O. MARCHAL, 'La pillule. Pourquoi Paul VI doit dire oui', in *Spécial* (Brussels), 30 June 1966, pp. 26–35.

CONCLUSION

WE now propose to make a few final observations in order to conclude our survey of this debate which has lasted for ten years. As we review the development of the discussion, we shall speak first of all of the problem of the 'pill', before passing on to the consideration of contraceptive measures in general.

I. *The question of the 'pill'*

The first step in a new orientation of the problem of the pill was taken when it became more and more evident that a decision as to what was licit or illicit could not be based on the distinction between the therapeutic and non-therapeutic uses of the pill. In fact, from the beginning of the debate it was becoming the general practice, if not of all moralists, frequently of a majority among them, to legitimize the use of progestational treatment to which a therapeutic purpose could hardly be attributed, or was out of the question, as for example in treatment to regularize the female cycle, or during lactation, or when the threat of violent assault was imminent. It seemed, therefore, more and more likely that the conclusion would be reached that the cure of a pathological condition is not the only justification for the use of progestational drugs. Pius XII's speech of 12 September 1958 seemed to put forward this use as the only possibility, but his position must now be said to be at least in this matter superseded by almost all moral theologians. Moreover, in the light of present day knowledge, one must not forget that clinical treatment hardly ever raises the moral problem of ovulatory inhibition, partly because it may be administered by means of progestational drugs which do not have this effect (like those derived from progesterone) and partly because very frequently the intervention takes place during the second phase of the female cycle, that is, when the ovule is already discharged.

In the sphere of moral teaching new and various arguments for the permissibility of the use of pills apart from therapeutic

205

treatment were now advanced. These arguments were twofold:

(a) In a more restricted and somewhat casuistic context, which was none the less very interesting, a closer study was made of the problem of sterilization, that is, of the question as to whether every intervention, deliberately intended to effect a state of temporary biological sterility, should be considered for this very reason illicit when not undertaken for reasons of health. Some writers suggested in this connection a more extended application of the principle of the total good, seeing this to be valid even when the total good, for which the 'part' is sacrificed, is not physical health, but some other personal good; others, instead, tried to find a truly ethical concept of sterilization, which they sought to define (as we have pointed out several times) not on the basis of merely biological data but in relation to an accompanying desire for sexual activity and its legitimate and rightful expression. In reality, it was not always possible to ascertain clearly the scope of the moral applicability of these new concepts. They were extremely useful in justifying certain procedures (above all, the use of progestational drugs in self-defence) but they also prepared the way for the use of pills to regularize fertility. One might ask why what was declared to be permissible for a nun in the Congo, for the sake of personal spiritual values, could not be permitted also to a married woman when the prevention of ovulation would have brought about an equally good result (the possibility of regulating births without the grave difficulties and dangers of total abstinence). Was it not possible that in family life also the right and duty to procreate might not always be present, so that in this case also sterilization might have a merely biological significance? These questions could be answered without great difficulty, by making opportune and specific distinctions and giving adequate explanations, but in the meantime certain future developments were already being prepared, even in this first stage of reflection.

(b) Another sort of study, more general and theoretical, was concerned with the concept of 'nature' and the 'natural' moral obligations incumbent upon the procreative faculty, especially in women. This concept was implicit even in the preceding discussion on sterilization (and in fact was apparent in the moral judgment which defined artificial sterilization as the effecting of a sterility 'not already intended by nature'), but now this subject was more openly discussed in the controversy about the permissibility of using progestational drugs to regularize the female cycle, or during lactation, or in the period preceding the menopause. The essential problem was always the same: what limits does 'nature' set to man's power of controlling his procreative faculty? It was very easy to deduce the reply from a consideration of the biological order and so to present normal biological manifestations as moral principles. From this standpoint it could be considered permissible to suspend the ovulatory cycle, to reduce every cycle to a uniform length (or even to the standard duration of twenty-eight days), or to inhibit ovulation during the puerperal and pre-climacteric cycles. In fact, in these three cases, since the intention was merely to reproduce (artificially) the biological situation which was considered to be normal, it was believed that the moral 'natural' obligations were respected. In reality, however, this presentation of the case was not as conclusive as it might seem at first sight, for it was somewhat hazardous to attempt to discern a precise biological pattern in a sphere as biologically multifarious and 'disordered' as sexuality. Moreover, this attitude had no decisive effect on the debate concerning the permissible uses of the pill. In fact, some writers were quick to point out that, by administering the pill in order to prevent ovulation for the purpose of a reasonable control of births, one was merely reproducing (even if by artificial means) the same wastage of ovules which was already biologically intended. Indeed (the scientific basis of this observation is not certain), one was making sure of a better biological result because in this way the whole supply of ovules was preserved for the moment of generation. These ethical considerations are obviously based mainly on 'physical' data and in any case leave the problem still unsolved. In fact, because of their limitations they prepare the way for more 'metaphysical' considerations.

It was precisely on this plane and with relation to this question that the problem was now studied: must there be complete harmony between the 'natural' moral order and the spontaneous biological process? Only a negative answer to this question seemed to us to be legitimate, and the principles which could be formulated on the basis of this negative answer could finally be considered adequate. But the questions which still remained unanswered were very urgent. What is properly meant by the 'natural' moral order? Does it mean that ovulation must regularly take place (one might say, uselessly, at least in most cases) about every twenty-eight days, or should ovulation take place only when it is needed and when it is adequate to fulfil the purpose of generous and prudent procreation which God has assigned to marriage? Further, if a woman were to succeed at some future date (the hypothesis is not entirely unfounded and in any case is useful to illustrate our question) in initiating the ovulatory process by an act of her will only on those occasions when it is her duty to procreate, would such a 'voluntary and deliberate' process of ovulation be called unnatural? And is it therefore unnatural to procure this result by means of opportune medical assistance, such as is permitted in the rational control of other physical functions such as digestion, sleep, etc? In short, the regularization of the female capacity for generation (which a providential alternation of fertile and sterile periods seems already to provide in an adequate manner), in order to ensure responsible procreation, may entail an alteration in the physical organism, but is it for that reason to be considered a 'disorder' from the moral point of view? Is it not instead a re-ordering of the reproductive function to its proper end? It is true that we have until now been restricted by a somewhat abstract concept of nature, always based on a consideration of the reproductive function in itself, rather than on this function as a capacity of the person responsible for it. But at least this presentation of the question avoided the former exaggeratedly 'physical' criteria, and personal needs now begin to take precedence over the requirement of an integral biological structure. One understands, therefore, that the opinion which maintained, in certain conditions, the legitimacy of the contraceptive use of oestro-progestational pills, at first timidly suggested by a few, has been steadily gaining ground and may today be claimed to be the opinion of most moralists, provided, of course, that the limits set by medical and psychological science for such treatment are respected.

II. *On contraception in general*

Meanwhile, however, the discussion had become much more extended and now included the whole question of contraception, without any further distinction between the various methods: this development must have been foreseen as inevitable, although initially nearly all the moralists who spoke in favour of the pill had affirmed a qualitative difference between this method and other contraceptive measures which interfered with the actual process of copulation.[1]

The first critical attacks on the traditional position attempted to demonstrate the extreme weakness of the rational argument produced in its defence, based on the necessary procreational intention of every conjugal act, and so a distinction was made, which later on became widely accepted, between the fertility of an individual act and the fertility of the marriage as a whole. This led to the conclusion that not the individual act but the expression of the sexual instinct as a complex whole contained within itself the intrinsic intention of fertility (a fertility worthy of man), which could not be thwarted for the whole of married life. As for the individual act, this must satisfy the need for the expression of the love between husband and wife, which sexuality is intended to foster. At first several writers attempted to use this need of expression as a pretext for insisting upon that physical integrity of intercourse which the procreative purpose was no longer in itself considered sufficient to impose (copulation, they said, must be integral in order to have a totally integrating effect on the married couple), but the weakness of this argument also was soon evident. In what sense can it be said that in order to be an adequate expression of conjugal love copulation must necessarily require the integrity of the physical union? Would this new formulation not lead us back once more to the founding of sexual morality on purely physical data?

These speculations were accompanied by a series of studies which attempted to illustrate the Christian attitude to this question. The biblical and patristic condemnations seemed now much less categorical than had been thought before, and an attentive historical survey showed that traditional teaching, although opposed to contraceptive practices, did not formulate an irrevocable doctrine. This is because it is now seen to have been based on reasons today considered unacceptable or, more generally, dependent on sexual concepts in which the influence of imported notions of anthropology was much stronger than that of original Christian thought. As for the declarations of the Magisterium, especially those of Pius XI and Pius XII, they were now placed

[1] We ourselves pointed out this difference when, two years ago, we concluded our article: 'La discussione morale sui progestativi. Rassegna bibliografica', *La Scuola Cattolica* 93 (1965) pp. 157*–216*.

in their historical context and shown to be based on an outdated conceptualization of sexuality. It also became apparent that these pronouncements were intended primarily to answer an urgent pastoral need to erect a new bulwark in defence of profound values of married life which could not otherwise be safeguarded.

The Council document also dwelt much on these values, already partly acknowledged by the Magisterium when it affirmed the legitimacy of the deliberate use of sterile periods. The union of married couples, in which sexuality is used as an honourable means of promoting conjugal love, demands that the husband and wife shall constantly cherish that community in love which is the very structure of marriage, and which makes the sexual acts themselves mature expressions of this union, and they must pledge themselves to achieve the generous and responsible procreation which is the crown of their union, using sexuality honourably for this purpose. It then became clear that the conjugal act, even when freed from the binding principle of biological integrity, still possessed an intrinsic principle of its own which made it incumbent upon husband and wife to judge the moral meaning of their acts according to the expression, in them and in their marriage as a whole, of those values (of genuine love and responsible parenthood) with regard to which the principle of biological integrity was seen to be of merely relative importance. It became also apparent that contraceptive measures were not in themselves illicit but required to be continually re-examined in a clearly understood ethical context (of expressive spontaneity, mutual respect, control of the sexual instinct, innocuity, aesthetic considerations, etc.). It was also clear that the capacity of any one of these measures to satisfy these needs could only with great difficulty be judged in the abstract, and that the married couple themselves were more fitted to judge of it than were the moralists: it was indeed much more the proper subject for detailed anthropological study (to be undertaken by psychologists, sociologists and philosophers) than for theological discussion as such.

Here of course we come to those careful examinations of the concepts of nature and of the natural law which were now being undertaken and which, as we have seen, had already produced some convincing results in the debate on the pill. It is above all a question of what we mean by 'nature' and 'natural'; we must acquire a less conservative notion of human nature, one which will take into account its historical development under the influence of the new insights which are gradually enlightening our knowledge of its various and complementary aspects (for example, we must consider the difference between our own concept of sexuality and that held by men of former civilizations); we must give primacy to the human person and to man's more characteristically spiritual values, rather than to biological mechanisms and processes which in themselves can never have any absolute value—and this means that the notion of the necessity of the physical integrity of copulation must be abandoned (as no longer sacrosanct) when it is impossible otherwise to procure a proportionate personal good, of authentic value, for the married couple. We must assign to man a more active and extended control over his natural functions in order that he may promote his personal development in a more ordered evolution of society.

Therefore, for the sake of an adequate control of births, it is more 'unnatural' to submit to the determinism of biological processes than to control them and direct them in a responsible manner to that end. These are a few notes on the content of a natural law, regarding sexuality and fertility, which has never been sufficiently explored. But it is also a question of competence: in answering these questions what help can we expect from revealed truth and from theology? For example, how can a theologian judge the good or evil effect of the contraceptive use of a condom in coitus on the expression of the married couple's mutual love, except on the basis of medical, biological, sociological and rational arguments, the validity of which is not within the competence of Christian doctrine to judge? And the same may be said of every other similar problem. It is, therefore, clear that many solutions given in the past by moral theologians, and not with relation to marriage only, are not properly speaking within their competence, and this admission renders the Christian moralist of our own age more humble, for if he wishes to remain within his own sphere he has fewer certainties to offer his fellow believers.[2]

---

[2] To express these doubts about the precise competence of the Magisterium to judge of the morality of individual contraceptive techniques by no means signifies—as G. Rossino recently reproaches me with saying (*Perfice munus* 43 (1968), pp. 62–4) in his review of the first edition of this volume—that 'the Church may not deal with the specific theme of the practice of marriage': I

Finally, we wish to offer our colleagues and fellow believers two last words of practical advice, even if they seem superfluous. First of all, no one must harbour the illusion, or the fear, that Christian morality for married people is becoming lax: every time the discussion turned on the values to be safeguarded, as theologians have pointed out in recent years whenever the sexual conduct of married couples has been under review, the relevant principles have appeared more and more authoritative, and the moral law more binding. Moreover, no one must doubt the good faith of the more 'progressive' moralists: they have had more to lose by the new trend of thought than any other Christians, especially as in the past they were all, except the youngest group, pledged to defend in all honesty and loyalty the position then generally held.[3]

have tried to explain this more clearly in 'Magistero e contraccezione', *Settimana del clero*, 17 March 1968, p. 4.

[3] We also have done this in our article: 'Le virtù della vita coniugale', in *Enciclopedia del Matrimonio*, Brescia, Queriniana, 1960, pp. 487–552.

APPENDIX A

The encyclical *Humanae Vitae*

The transmission of life

1. The most serious duty of transmitting human life, for which married persons are the free and responsible collaborators of God the Creator, has always been a source of great joys to them, even if sometimes accompanied by not a few difficulties and by distress.

At all times the fulfilment of this duty has posed grave problems to the conscience of married persons, but, with the recent evolution of society, changes have taken place that give rise to new questions which the Church could not ignore, having to do with a matter which so closely touches upon the life and happiness of men.

I. New aspects of the problem and competency of the Magisterium

New formulation of the problem

2. The changes which have taken place are in fact noteworthy and of varied kinds. In the first place, there is the rapid demographic development. Fear is shown by many that world population is growing more rapidly than the available resources, with growing distress to many families and developing countries, so that the temptation for authorities to counter this danger with radical measures is great. Moreover, working and lodging conditions, as well as increased exigencies both in the economic field and in that of education, often make the proper education of an elevated number of children difficult today. A change is also seen both in the manner of considering the person of woman and her place in society, and in the value to be attributed to conjugal love in marriage, and also in the appreciation to be made of the meaning of conjugal acts in relation to that love.

Finally and above all, man has made stupendous progress in the domination and rational organization of the forces of nature, such that he tends to extend this domination to his own total being: to the body, to psychical life, to social life and even to the laws which regulate the transmission of life.

3. This new state of things gives rise to new questions. Granted the conditions of life today, and granted the meaning which conjugal relations have with respect to the harmony between husband and

wife and to their mutual fidelity, would not a revision of the ethical norms in force up to now, seem to be advisable, especially when it is considered that they cannot be observed without sacrifices, sometimes heroic sacrifices?

And again: by extending to this field the application of the so-called 'principle of totality', could it not be admitted that the intention of a less abundant but more rationalized fecundity might transform a materially sterilizing intervention into a licit and wise control of birth? Could it not be admitted, that is, that the finality of procreation pertains to the ensemble of conjugal life, rather than to its single acts? It is also asked whether, in view of the increased sense of responsibility of modern man, the moment has not come for him to entrust to his reason and his will, rather than to the biological rhythms of his organism, the task of regulating birth.

Competency of the Magisterium

4. Such questions required from the teaching authority of the Church a new and deeper reflection upon the principles of the moral teaching on marriage: a teaching founded on the natural law, illuminated and enriched by divine Revelation.

No believer will wish to deny that the teaching authority of the Church is competent to interpret even the natural moral law. It is, in fact, indisputable, as our predecessors have many times declared,[1] that Jesus Christ, when communicating to Peter and to the apostles his divine authority and sending them to teach all nations his commandments,[2] constituted them as guardians and authentic interpreters of all the moral law, not only, that is, of the law of the gospel, but also of the natural law, which is also an expression of the will of God, the faithful fulfilment of which is equally necessary for salvation.[3]

Conformably to this mission of hers, the Church has always provided—and even more amply in recent times—a coherent teaching

---

[1] Cf. Pius IX, Encyclical *Qui Pluribus*, Nov. 9, 1846; in *Pii IX P. M. Acta*, I, pp. 9-10; St Pius X, Encyc. *Singulari Quadam*, Sept. 24, 1912; in AAS IV (1912), p. 658; Pius XI, Encyc. *Casti Connubii*, Dec. 31, 1930; in AAS XXII (1930), pp. 579-581; Pius XII, Allocution *Magnificate Dominum* to the Episcopate of the Catholic world, Nov. 2, 1954; in AAS XLVI (1954), pp. 671-672; John XXIII, Encyc. *Mater et Magistra*, May 15, 1961; in AAS LIII (1961), p. 457.

[2] Cf. *Mt.* 28, 18-19.

[3] Cf. *Mt.* 7, 21.

concerning both the nature of marriage and the correct use of conjugal rights and the duties of husband and wife.[4]

Special studies

5. The consciousness of that same mission induced us to confirm and enlarge the Study Commission which our predecessor Pope John XXIII of happy memory had instituted in March, 1963. That Commission which included, besides several experts in the various pertinent disciplines, also married couples, had as its scope the gathering of opinions on the new questions regarding conjugal life, and in particular on the regulation of births, and of furnishing opportune elements of information so that the Magisterium could give an adequate reply to the expectation not only of the faithful, but also of world opinion.[5]

The work of these experts, as well as the successive judgments and counsels spontaneously forwarded by or expressly requested from a good number of our brothers in the Episcopate, have permitted us to measure more exactly all the aspects of this complex matter. Hence with all our heart we express to each of them our lively gratitude.

Reply of the Magisterium

6. The conclusions at which the Commission arrived could not, nevertheless, be considered by us as definitive, nor dispense us from a personal examination of this serious question; and this also because, within the Commission itself, no full concordance of judgments concerning the moral norms to be proposed had been reached, and above all because certain criteria of solutions had emerged which departed from the moral teaching on marriage proposed with constant firmness by the teaching authority of the Church.

[4] Cf. *Catechismus Romanus Concilii Tridentini*, Part II, Ch. VIII; Leo XII, Encyc. *Arcanum*, Feb. 10, 1880; in *Acta Leonis XIII*, II (1881), pp. 26-29; Pius XI, Encyc. *Divini Illius Magistri*, Dec. 31, 1929, in AAS XXII (1930), pp. 58-61; Encyc. *Casti Connubii*, in AAS XXII (1930), pp. 545-546; Pius XII, Alloc. to the Italian Medico-Biological Union of Saint Luke, Nov. 12, 1944, in *Discorsi e Radiomessaggi*, VI, pp. 191-192; to the Italian Catholic Union of Midwives Oct. 29, 1951, in AAS XLIII (1951), pp. 857-859; to the Seventh Congress of the International Society of Haematology, Sept. 12, 1958, in AAS L (1958), pp. 734-735; John XXIII, Encyc. *Mater et Magistra*, in AAS LIII (1961), pp. 446-447; *Codex Iuris Canonici*, Canon 1067; Can. 1968, § 1, Can. 1076 §§ 1-2; Second Vatican Council, Pastoral Constitution *Gaudium et Spes*, Nos. 47-52.

[5] Cf. Paul VI, Allocution to the Sacred College, June 23, 1964, in AAS LVI (1964), p. 588; to the Commission for Study of Problems of Population, Family and Birth, March 27, 1965, in AAS LVII (1965), p. 388; to the National Congress of the Italian Society of Obstetrics and Gynaecology, Oct. 29, 1966, in AAS LVIII (1966), p. 1168.

Therefore, having attentively sifted the documentation laid before us, after mature reflexion and assiduous prayers, we now intend, by virtue of the mandate entrusted to us by Christ, to give our reply to these grave questions.

II. Doctrinal principles

A total vision of man

7. The problem of birth, like every other problem regarding human life, is to be considered, beyond partial perspectives—whether of the biological or psychological, demographic or sociological orders —in the light of an integral vision of man and of his vocation, not only his natural and earthly, but also his supernatural and eternal vocation. And since, in the attempt to justify artificial methods of birth control, many have appealed to the demands both of conjugal love and of 'responsible parenthood', it is good to state very precisely the true concept of these two great realities of married life, referring principally to what was recently set forth in this regard, and in a highly authoritative form, by the Second Vatican Council in its Pastoral Constitution *Gaudium et Spes*.

Conjugal love

8. Conjugal love reveals its true nature and nobility when it is considered in its supreme origin, God, who is love,[6] 'the Father, from whom every family in heaven and on earth is named'.[7]

Marriage is not then, the effect of chance or the product of evolution of unconscious natural forces; it is the wise institution of the Creator to realize in mankind his design of love. By means of the reciprocal personal gift of self, proper and exclusive to them, husband and wife tend towards the communion of their beings in view of mutual personal perfection, to collaborate with God in the generation and education of new lives.

For baptized persons, moreover, marriage invests the dignity of a sacramental sign of grace, inasmuch as it represents the union of Christ and of the Church.

Its characteristics

9. Under this light, there clearly appear the characteristic marks and demands of conjugal love, and it is of supreme importance to have an exact idea of these.

This love is first of all fully human, that is to say, of the senses and of the spirit at the same time. It is not, then, a simple transport of

[6] Cf. *I Jn.* 4, 8.
[7] Cf. *Eph.* 3, 15.

instinct and sentiment, but also, and principally, an act of the free will, intended to endure and to grow by means of the joys and sorrows of daily life, in such a way that husband and wife become one only heart and one only soul, and together attain their human perfection.

Then, this love is total, that is to say, it is a very special form of personal friendship, in which husband and wife generously share everything, without undue reservations or selfish calculations. Whoever truly loves his marriage partner loves not only for what he receives, but for the partner's self, rejoicing that he can enrich his partner with the gift of himself.

Again, this love is faithful and exclusive until death. Thus in fact do bride and groom conceive it to be on the day when they freely and in full awareness assume the duty of the marriage bond. A fidelity, this, which can sometimes be difficult, but is always possible, always noble and meritorious, as no one can deny. The example of so many married persons down through the centuries shows, not only that fidelity is according to the nature of marriage, but also that it is a source of profound and lasting happiness.

And finally, this love is fecund, for it is not exhausted by the communion between husband and wife, but is destined to continue, raising up new lives. 'Marriage and conjugal love are by their nature ordained toward the begetting and educating of children. Children are really the supreme gift of marriage and contribute very substantially to the welfare of their parents'.[8]

Responsible parenthood

10. Hence conjugal love requires in husband and wife an awareness of their mission of 'responsible parenthood', which today is rightly much insisted upon, and which also must be exactly understood. Consequently it is to be considered under different aspects which are legitimate and connected with one another.

In relation to the biological processes, responsible parenthood means the knowledge and respect of their functions; human intellect discovers in the power of giving life biological laws which are part of the human person.[9]

In relation to the tendencies of instinct or passion, responsible parenthood means that necessary dominion which reason and will must exercise over them.

In relation to physical, economic, psychological and social conditions responsible parenthood is exercised, either by the deliberate and generous decision to raise a numerous family, or by the decision,

[8] Cf. II Vat. Council, Pastoral Const. *Gaudium et Spes*, No. 50.
[9] Cf. St. Thomas, *Summa Theologica*, I-II, Q. 94, Art. 2.

made for grave motives and with due respect for the moral law, to avoid for the time being, or even for an indeterminate period, a new birth.

Responsible parenthood also and above all implies a more profound relationship to the objective moral order established by God, of which a right conscience is the faithful interpreter. The responsible exercise of parenthood implies, therefore, that husband and wife recognize fully their own duties towards God, towards themselves, towards the family and towards society, in a correct hierarchy of values.

In the task of transmitting life, therefore, they are not free to proceed completely at will, as if they could determine in a wholly autonomous way the honest path to follow; but they must conform their activity to the creative intention of God, expressed in the very nature of marriage and of its acts, and manifested by the constant teaching of the Church.[10]

Respect for the nature and purposes of the marriage act

11. These acts, by which husband and wife are united in chaste intimacy, and by means of which human life is transmitted, are, as the Council recalled, 'noble and worthy',[11] and they do not cease to be lawful if, for causes independent of the will of husband and wife, they are foreseen to be infecund, since they always remain ordained towards expressing and consolidating their union. In fact, as experience bears witness, not every conjugal act is followed by a new life. God has wisely disposed natural laws and rhythms of fecundity which, of themselves, cause a separation in the succession of births. Nonetheless the Church, calling men back to the observance of the norms of the natural law, as interpreted by her constant doctrine, teaches that each and every marriage act (*quilibet matrimonii usus*) must remain open to the transmission of life.[12]

Two inseparable aspects: union and procreation

12. That teaching, often set forth by the Magisterium, is founded upon the inseparable connection, willed by God and unable to be broken by man on his own initiative, between the two meanings of the conjugal act: the unitive meaning and the procreative meaning. Indeed, by its intimate structure, the conjugal act, while most closely uniting husband and wife, capacitates them for the generation of new

[10] Cf. Pastoral Const. *Gaudium et Spes*, Nos. 50, 51.

[11] *Ibid.*, No. 49.

[12] Cf. Pius XI, Encyc. *Casti Conubii*, in AAS XXII (1930), p. 560; Pius XII, in AAS XLIII (1951), p. 843.

lives, according to laws inscribed in the very being of man and of woman. By safeguarding both these essential aspects, the unitive and the procreative, the conjugal act preserves in its fulness the sense of true mutual love and its ordination towards man's most high calling to parenthood. We believe that the men of our day are particularly capable of seizing the deeply reasonable and human character of this fundamental principle.

Faithfulness to God's design

13. It is in fact justly observed that a conjugal act imposed upon one's partner without regard for his or her condition and lawful desires is not a true act of love, and therefore denies an exigency of right moral order in the relationships between husband and wife. Hence, one who reflects well must also recognize that a reciprocal act of love, which jeopardizes the disponibility to transmit life which God the Creator, according to particular laws, inserted therein, is in contradiction with the design constitutive of marriage, and with the will of the author of life. To use this divine gift destroying, even if only partially, its meaning and its purpose is to contradict the nature both of man and of woman and of their most intimate relationship, and therefore it is to contradict also the plan of God and his will. On the other hand, to make use of the gift of conjugal love while respecting the laws of the generative process means to acknowledge oneself not to be the arbiter of the sources of human life, but rather the minister of the design established by the Creator. In fact, just as man does not have unlimited dominion over his body in general, so also, with particular reason, he has no such dominion over his generative faculties as such, because of their intrinsic ordination towards raising up life, of which God is the principle. 'Human life is sacred', Pope John XXIII recalled; 'from its very inception it reveals the creating hand of God.'[13]

Illicit ways of regulating birth

14. In conformity with these landmarks in the human and Christian vision of marriage, we must once again declare that the direct interruption of the generative process already begun, and, above all, directly willed and procured abortion, even if for therapeutic reasons, are to be absolutely excluded as licit means of regulating birth.[14]

[13] Cf. JOHN XXIII, Encyc. *Mater et Magistra*, in AAS LIII (1961), p. 447.

[14] Cf. *Catechismus Romanus Concilii Tridentini*, Part. II, Ch. VIII; PIUS XI, Encyc. *Casti Connubii*, in AAS XXII (1930), pp. 562-564; PIUS XII, *Discorsi e Radiomessaggi*, VI (1944), pp. 191-192; AAS XLIII (1951), pp. 842-843; pp. 857-859; JOHN XXIII, Encyc. *Pacem in Terris*, Apr. 11, 1963, in AAS LV (1963), pp. 259-260; *Gaudium et Spes*, No. 51.

Equally to be excluded, as the teaching authority of the Church has frequently declared, is direct sterilization, whether perpetual or temporary, whether of the man or of the woman.[15] Similarly excluded is every action which, either in anticipation of the conjugal act, or in its accomplishment, or in the development of its natural consequences, proposes, whether as an end or as a means, to render procreation impossible.[16]

To justify conjugal acts made intentionally infecund, one cannot invoke as valid reasons the lesser evil, or the fact that such acts would constitute a whole together with the fecund acts already performed or to follow later, and hence would share in one and the same moral goodness. In truth, if it is sometimes licit to tolerate a lesser evil in order to avoid a greater evil or to promote a greater good,[17] it is not licit, even for the gravest reasons, to do evil so that good may follow therefrom;[18] that is, to make into the object of a positive act of the will something which is intrinsically disorder, and hence unworthy of the human person, even when the intention is to safeguard or promote individual, family or social well-being. Consequently it is an error to think that a conjugal act which is deliberately made infecund and so is intrinsically dishonest could be made honest and right by the ensemble of a fecund conjugal life.

Licitness of therapeutic means

15. The Church, on the contrary, does not at all consider illicit the use of those therapeutic means truly necessary to cure diseases of the organism, even if an impediment to procreation, which may be foreseen, should result therefrom, provided such impediment is not, for whatever motive, directly willed.[19]

Licitness of recourse to infecund periods

16. To this teaching of the Church on conjugal morals, the objection is made today, as we observed earlier (No. 3), that it is the pre-

[15] Cf. Pius XI, Encyc. *Casti Connubii*, in AAS XXII (1930), p. 565; Decree of the Holy Office, Feb. 22, 1940, in AAS L (1958), pp. 734-735.

[16] Cf. *Catechismus Romanus Concilii Tridentini*, Part II, Ch. VIII; Pius XI, Encyc. *Casti Connubii*. in AAS XXII (1930), pp. 559-561; Pius XII, AAS XLIII (1951), p. 843; AAS L (1958), pp. 734-735; John XXIII, Encyc. *Mater et Magistra*, in AAS LIII (1961), p. 447.

[17] Cf. Pius XII, Alloc. to the National Congress of the Union of Catholic Jurists, Dec. 6, 1953, in AAS XLV (1953), pp. 798-799.

[18] Cf. *Rom.*, 3, 8.

[19] Cf. Pius XII, Alloc. to Congress of the Italian Association of Urology, Oct. 8, 1953, in AAS XLV (1953), pp. 674-675; AAS L (1958), pp. 734-735.

rogative of the human intellect to dominate the energies offered by irrational nature and to orientate them towards an end conformable to the good of man. Now, some may ask: in the present case, is it not reasonable in many circumstances to have recourse to artificial birth control if, thereby, we secure the harmony and peace of the family, and better conditions for the education of the children already born? To this question it is necesssry to reply with clarity: the Church is the first to praise and recommend the intervention of intelligence in a function which so closely associates the rational creature with his Creator; but she affirms that this must be done with respect for the order established by God.

If, then, there are serious motives to space out births, which derive from the physical or psychological conditions of husband and wife, or from external conditions, the Church teaches that it is then licit to take into account the natural rhythms immanent in the generative functions, for the use of marriage in the infecund periods only, and in this way to regulate birth without offending the moral principles which have been recalled earlier.[20]

The Church is coherent with herself when she considers recourse to the infecund periods to be licit, while at the same time condemning, as being always illicit, the use of means directly contrary to fecundation, even if such use is inspired by reasons which may appear honest and serious. In reality, there are essential differences between the two cases: in the former, the married couple make legitimate use of a natural disposition; in the latter, they impede the development of natural processes. It is true that, in the one and the other case, the married couple are concordant in the positive will of avoiding children for plausible reasons, seeking the certainty that offspring will not arrive; but it is also true that only in the former case are they able to renounce the use of marriage in the fecund periods when, for just motives, procreation is not desirable, while making use of it during infecund periods to manifest their affection and to safeguard their mutual fidelity. By so doing, they give proof of a truly and integrally honest love.

Grave consequences of methods of artificial birth control

17. Upright men can even better convince themselves of the solid grounds on which the teaching of the Church in this field is based, if they care to reflect upon the consequences of methods of artificial birth control. Let them consider, first of all, how wide and easy a road would thus be opened up towards conjugal infidelity and the general lowering of morality. Not much experience is needed in order to

[20] Cf. PIUS XII, AAS XLIII (1951), p. 846.

know human weakness and to understand that men—especially the young, who are so vulnerable on this point—have need of encouragement to be faithful to the moral law, so that they must not be offered some easy means of eluding its observance. It is also to be feared that the men, growing used to the employment of anti-conceptive practices, may finally lose respect for the woman and, no longer caring for her physical and psychological equilibrium, may come to the point of considering her as a mere instrument of selfish enjoyment, and no longer as his respected and beloved companion.

Let it be considered also that a dangerous weapon would thus be placed in the hands of those public authorities who take no heed of moral exigencies. Who could blame a government for applying to the solution of the problems of the community those means acknowledged to be licit for married couples in the solution of a family problem? Who will stop rulers from favouring, from even imposing upon their peoples, if they were to consider it necessary, the method of contraception which they judge to be most efficacious? In such a way men, wishing to avoid individual, family, or social difficulties encountered in the observance of the divine law, would reach the point of placing at the mercy of the intervention of public authorities the most personal and most reserved sector of conjugal intimacy.

Consequently, if the mission of generating life is not to be exposed to the arbitrary will of men, one must necessarily recognize insurmountable limits to the possibility of man's domination over his own body and its functions; limits which no man, whether a private individual or one invested with authority, may licitly surpass. And such limits cannot be determined otherwise than by the respect due to the integrity of the human organism and its functions, according to the principles recalled earlier, and also according to the correct understanding of the 'principle of totality' illustrated by our predecessor Pope Pius XII.[21]

The Church guarantor of true human values

18 It can be foreseen that this teaching will perhaps not be easily received by all: too numerous are those voices—amplified by the modern means of propaganda—which are contrary to the voice of the Church. To tell the truth, the Church is not surprised to be made, like her divine founder, a 'sign of contradiction',[22] yet she does not because of this cease to proclaim with humble firmness the entire moral law, both natural and evangelical. Of such laws the Church was not the author, nor consequently can she be their arbiter; she is

[21] Cf. AAS XLV (1953), pp. 674-675; AAS XLVIII (1956), pp. 461-462.
[22] Cf. Lk. 2, 34.

only their depositary and their interpreter, without ever being able to declare to be licit that which is not so by reason of its intimate and unchangeable opposition to the true good of man.

In defending conjugal morals in their integral wholeness, the Church knows that she contributes towards the establishment of a truly human civilization; she engages man not to abdicate from his own responsibility in order to rely on technical means; by that very fact she defends the dignity of man and wife. Faithful to both the teaching and the example of the Saviour, she shows herself to be the sincere and disinterested friend of men, whom she wishes to help, even during their earthly sojourn, 'to share as sons in the life of the living God, the Father of all men'.[23]

III. Pastoral directives

The Church Mater et Magistra

19. Our words would not be an adequate expression of the thought and solicitude of the Church, mother and teacher of all peoples, if, after having recalled men to the observance and respect of the divine law regarding matrimony, we did not strengthen them in the path of honest regulation of birth, even amid the difficult conditions which today afflict families and peoples. The Church, in fact, cannot have a different conduct towards men than that of the Redeemer: she knows their weaknesses, has compassion on the crowd, receives sinners; but she cannot renounce the teaching of the law which is, in reality, that law proper to a human life restored to its original truth and conducted by the Spirit of God.[24] Though we are thinking also of all men of good will, we now address ourself particularly to our sons, from whom we expect a prompter and more generous adherence.

Possibility of observing the divine law

20. The teaching of the Church on the regulation of birth, which promulgates the divine law, will easily appear to many to be difficult or even impossible of actuation. And indeed, like all great beneficent realities, it demands serious engagement and much effort, individual, family and social effort. More than that, it would not be practicable without the help of God, who upholds and strengthens the good will of men. Yet, to anyone who reflects well, it cannot but be clear that such efforts ennoble man and are beneficial to the human community.

Mastery of self

21. The honest practice of regulation of birth demands first of all

---

[23] Cf. PAUL VI, Encyc. *Populorum Progressio*, March 26, 1967. No. 21.
[24] Cf. *Rom.*, 8.

that husband and wife acquire and possess solid convictions concerning the true values of life and of the family, and that they tend towards securing perfect self-mastery. To dominate instinct by means of one's reason and free will undoubtedly requires ascetical practices, so that the affective manifestations of conjugal life may observe the correct order, in particular with regard to the observance of periodic continence. Yet this discipline which is proper to the purity of married couples, far from harming conjugal love, rather confers on it a higher human value. It demands continual effort yet, thanks to its beneficent influence, husband and wife fully develop their personalities, being enriched with spiritual values. Such discipline bestows upon family life fruits of serenity and peace, and facilitates the solution of other problems; it favours attention for one's partner, helps both parties to drive out selfishness, the enemy of true love; and deepens their sense of responsibility. By its means, parents acquire the capacity of having a deeper and more efficacious influence in the education of their offspring; little children and youths grow up with a just appraisal of human values, and in the serene and harmonious development of their spiritual and sensitive faculties.

Creating an atmosphere favourable to chastity

22. On this occasion, we wish to draw the attention of educators, and of all who perform duties of responsibility in regard to the common good of human society, to the need of creating an atmosphere favourable to education in chastity, that is, to the triumph of healthy liberty over licence by means of respect for the moral order.

Everything in the modern media of social communications which leads to sense excitation and unbridled customs, as well as every form of pornography and licentious performances, must arouse the frank and unanimous reaction of all those who are solicitous for the progress of civilization and the defence of the supreme good of the human spirit. Vainly would one seek to justify such depravation with the pretext of artistic or scientific exigencies,[25] or to deduce an argument from the freedom allowed in this sector by the public authorities.

Appeal to public Authorities

23. To rulers, who are those principally responsible for the common good, and who can do so much to safeguard moral customs, we say: do not allow the morality of your peoples to be degraded; do not permit that by legal means practices contrary to the natural and divine law be introduced into that fundamental cell, the family.

[25] Cf. II Vatican Council, Decree *Inter Mirifica* on the media of Social Communication, Nos. 6-7.

Quite other is the way in which public authorities can and must contribute to the solution of the demographic problem: namely, the way of a provident policy for the family, of a wise education of peoples in respect of the moral law and the liberty of citizens.

We are well aware of the serious difficulties experienced by public authorities in this regard, especially in the developing countries. To their legitimate preoccupations we devoted out encyclical letter *Populorum Progressio*. But, with our predecessor Pope John XXIII, we repeat: no solution to these difficulties is acceptable 'which does violence to man's essential dignity' and is based only on an utterly materialistic conception of man himself and of his life. The only possible solution to this question is one which envisages the social and economic progress both of individuals and of the whole of human society, and which respects and promotes true human values.[26] Neither can one, without grave injustice, consider divine providence to be responsible for what depends, instead, on a lack of wisdom in government, on an insufficient sense of social justice, on selfish monopolization, or again on blameworthy indolence in confronting the efforts and the sacrifices necessary to ensure the raising of living standards of a people and of all its sons.[27]

May all responsible public authorities—as some are already doing so laudably—generously revive their efforts. And may mutual aid between all the members of the great human family never cease to grow: this is an almost limitless field which thus opens up to the activity of the great international organizations.

To men of science

24. We wish now to express our encouragement to men of science, who 'can considerably advance the welfare of marriage and the family, along with peace of conscience, if by pooling their efforts they labour to explain more thoroughly the various conditions favouring a proper regulation of births'.[28] It is particularly desirable that, according to the wish already expressed by Pope Pius XII, medical science succeed in providing a sufficiently secure basis for a regulation of birth, founded on the observance of natural rhythms.[29] In this way, scientists and especially Catholic scientists will contribute to demonstrate in actual fact that, as the Church teaches, 'a true contradiction cannot exist between the divine laws pertaining to the transmission

[26] Cf. Encyc. *Mater et Magistra*, in AAS LIII (1961), p. 447.

[27] Cf. Encyc. *Populorum Progressio*, Nos. 48-55.

[28] Cf. Pastoral Const. *Gaudium et Spes*, No. 52.

[29] Cf. AAS XLIII (1951), p. 859.

of life and those pertaining to the fostering of authentic conjugal love'.[30]

To Christian husbands and wives

25. And now our words more directly address our own children, particularly those whom God calls to serve him in marriage. The Church, while teaching imprescriptible demands of the divine law, announces the tidings of salvation, and by means of the sacraments opens up the paths of grace, which makes man a new creature, capable of corresponding with love and true freedom to the design of his Creator and Saviour, and of finding the yoke of Christ to be sweet.[31]

Christian married couples, then, docile to her voice, must remember that their Christian vocation, which began at baptism, is further specified and reinforced by the sacrament of matrimony. By it husband and wife are strengthened and as it were consecrated for the faithful accomplishment of their proper duties, for the carrying out of their proper vocation even to perfection, and the Christian witness which is proper to them before the whole world.[32] To them the Lord entrusts the task of making visible to men the holiness and sweetness of the law which unites the mutual love of husband and wife with their co-operation with the love of God the author of human life.

We do not at all intend to hide the sometimes serious difficulties inherent in the life of Christian married persons; for them as for everyone else, 'the gate is narrow and the way is hard, that leads to life'.[33] But the hope of that life must illuminate their way, as with courage they strive to live with wisdom, justice and piety in this present time,[34] knowing that the figure of this world passes away.[35]

Let married couples, then, face up to the efforts needed, supported by the faith and hope which 'do not disappoint . . . because God's love has been poured into our hearts through the Holy Spirit, who has been given to us';[36] let them implore divine assistance by persevering prayer; above all, let them draw from the source of grace and charity in the eucharist. And if sin should still keep its hold over them, let them not be discouraged, but rather have recourse with humble perseverance to the mercy of God, which is poured forth in the sacrament of penance. In this way they will be enabled to achieve the

[30] Cf. Pastoral Const. *Gaudium et Spes*, No. 51.

[31] Cf. *Mt.* 11, 30.

[32] Cf. Pastoral Const. *Gaudium et Spes*, No. 48; II Vatican Council, Dogmatic Const. *Lumen Gentium*, No. 35.

[33] *Mt.* 7, 14; cf. *Hebr.* 12, 11.

[34] Cf. *Tit.* 2, 12.

[35] Cf. *I Cor.* 7, 31.

[36] Cf. *Rom.* 5, 5.

fulness of conjugal life described by the apostle: 'Husbands, love your wives, as Christ loved the Church . . . Husbands should love their wives as their own bodies. He who loves his wife loves himself. For no man ever hates his own flesh, but nourishes and cherishes it, as Christ does the Church . . . This is a great mystery, and I mean in reference to Christ and the Church. However, let each one of you love his wife as himself, and let the wife see that she respects her husband'.[37]

Apostolate in homes

26. Among the fruits which ripen forth from a generous effort of fidelity to the divine law, one of the most precious is that married couples themselves not infrequently feel the desire to communicate their experience to others. Thus there comes to be included in the vast pattern of the vocation of the laity a new and most noteworthy form of the apostolate of like to like: it is married couples themselves who become apostles and guides to other married couples. This is assuredly, among so many forms of apostolate, one of those which seem most opportune today.[38]

To doctors and medical personnel

27. We hold those physicians and medical personnel in the highest esteem who, in the exercise of their profession, value above every human interest the superior demands of their Christian vocation. Let them persevere, therefore, in promoting on every occasion the discovery of solutions inspired by faith and right reason, let them strive to arouse this conviction and this respect in their associates. Let them also consider as their proper professional duty the task of acquiring all the knowledge needed in this delicate sector, so as to be able to give to those married persons who consult them wise counsel and healthy direction, such as they have a right to expect.

To priests

28. Beloved priest sons, by vocation you are the counsellors and spiritual guides of individual persons and of families. We now turn to you with confidence. Your first task—especially in the case of those who teach moral theology—is to expound the Church's teaching on marriage without ambiguity. Be the first to give, in the exercise of your ministry, the example of loyal internal and external obedience

[37] *Eph.* 5, 25, 28-29, 32-33.

[38] Cf. Dogmatic Const. *Lumen Gentium*, Nos. 35 and 41; Pastoral Const. *Gaudium et Spes.* Nos. 48-49; II Vatican Council, Decree *Apostolicam Actuositatem*, No. 11.

to the teaching authority of the Church. That obedience, as you know well, obliges not only because of the reasons adduced, but rather because of the light of the Holy Spirit, which is given in a particular way to the pastors of the Church in order that they may illustrate the truth.[39] You know, too, that it is of the utmost importance, for peace of consciences and for the unity of the Christian people, that in the field of morals as well as in that of dogma, all should attend to the Magisterium of the Church, and all should speak the same language. Hence, with all our heart we renew to you the heartfelt plea of the great apostle Paul: 'I appeal to you, brethren, by the name of Our Lord Jesus Christ, that all of you agree and that there be no dissensions among you, but that you be united in the same mind and the same judgment'.[40]

29. To diminish in no way the saving teaching of Christ constitutes an eminent form of charity for souls. But this must ever be accompanied by patience and goodness, such as the Lord himself gave example of in dealing with men. Having come not to condemn but to save,[41] he was indeed intransigent with evil, but merciful towards individuals.

In their difficulties, many married couples always find, in the words and in the heart of a priest, the echo of the voice and the love of the Redeemer.

To Bishops
Beloved and venerable brothers in the Episcopate, with whom we most intimately share the solicitude of the spiritual good of the People of God, at the conclusion of this Encyclical our reverent and affectionate thoughts turn to you. To all of you we extend an urgent invitation. At the head of the priests, your collaborators, and of your faithful, work ardently and incessantly for the safeguarding and the holiness of marriage, so that it may always be lived in its entire human and Christian fulness. Consider this mission as one of your most urgent responsibilities at the present time. As you know, it implies concerted pastoral action in all the fields of human activity, economic, cultural and social; for, in fact, only a simultaneous improvement in these various sectors will make it possible to render the life of parents and of children within their families not only tolerable, but easier and more joyous, to render the living together in human society more fraternal and peaceful, in faithfulness to God's design for the world.

[39] Cf. Dogmatic Const. *Lumen Gentium*, No. 25.

[40] Cf. *I Cor.* 1, 10.

[41] Cf. *Jn.* 3, 17.

Final appeal

31. Venerable brothers, most beloved sons, and all men of good will, great indeed is the work of education, of progress and of love to which we call you, upon the foundation of the Church's teaching, of which the successor of Peter is, together with his brothers in the Episcopate, the depositary and interpreter. Truly a great work, as we are deeply convinced, both for the world and for the Church, since man cannot find true happiness—towards which he aspires with all his being—other than in respect of the laws written by God in his very nature, laws which he must observe with intelligence and love. Upon this work, and upon all of you, and especially upon married couples, we invoke the abundant graces of the God of holiness and mercy, and in pledge thereof we impart to you all our apostolic blessing.

Given at Rome, from Saint Peter's, this twenty-fifth day of July, Feast of Saint James the Apostle, in the year nineteen hundred and sixty-eight, the sixth of our pontificate.

PAULUS PP. VI

INDEX OF MODERN AUTHORS

Abbo, 149n
Acker, 118n
Acland, 10, 21
Adjakpley, 138n
Albert, 80
Aldunate, 15, 16, 20, 21
Alfieri, 200, 201
Alfrink, 117n, 127, 129–30, 190
Alvarez, 138n
Anciaux, 12, 20, 21, 23, 149n
Andriessen, 84n
Anscombe, 100n
Apocada, 66, 67
Arza, 164, 165
Auer, 47, 48, 141n, 149n
Ayd, 57n, 58
Azzolini, 200, 201

Bailo, 57n
Balestro, 197–8
Baltazar, 104n
Barret, 149n
Baum, 102–3, 105, 183, 184
Beemer, 12, 13, 37, 81, 185, 186
Bekkers, 54
Beirnaert, 175, 183, 184–5
Bender, 31, 32, 33
Bernard, 204n
Bersini, 172n
Bertrams, 110, 190
Binz, 141n, 148
Böckle, 14, 21, 23, 61, 62, 63–4,
    97, 108–9, 183, 187–8
Boissard, 70
Bonaventura de Gangi, 162n
Bonomi, 1, 177n

Boschi, 15
Bouchaud, 95n
Bromley, 108n
Browne, 126–7, 136
Bruch, 97, 98
Brugarola, 158, 160–1
Brunec, 57, 58, 59–60, 71
Buelens, 80–3, 131n, 179
Burch, 1, 2
Burt, 202
Buyse, 179

Caffarel, 109, 110–11
Caletti, 131n
Callewaert, 83, 84–6
Caprile, 119n
Cardegna, 69–70
Castellano, 138n, 139
Cavallari, 147
Cavanagh, 46n
Ceriani, 64, 65, 162n
Charbonneau, 66, 67–8
Chauchard, 109, 110, 177n, 202
Chiavacci, 64, 65–6, 197, 199
Chirico, 172, 173–4
Cicognani, 143, 144
Colombo, C., 142, 148, 165
Colombo, G., 137–8, 156n
Concetti, 15
Conley, 102
Connell, 1, 3, 10, 17, 18, 20,
    49, 54n, 69, 70
Connery, 5, 6, 18, 21
Connolly, 11
Conti, 172n
Corti, 167

Coutelier, 109, 111–12, 113
Crotty, 11, 17, 20, 25

Daly, 107
D'Antonio, 104n
Daugherty, 104n
David, 89–90, 91, 92, 93, 188n, 189–92
Davies, 158, 159
Dayez, 38, 60–1, 69, 188–9
Dearden, 126, 132, 138, 141, 148
De Castro Reyes, 118n, 164, 165
De Contenson, 73–5
De Freitas Azevedo, 66
De Guchteneere, 13, 21, 131n
De Koninck, 69
De la Bedoyere, 202
De Lahidalga, 26, 66, 67
De Lestapis, 13. 56, 74, 75, 141n, 149n, 154, 156, 163
Delhaye, 117n, 119n, 132, 138n, 139, 149n, 164, 166
Delille, 11, 12
De Locht, 95n, 141n, 149n, 183, 186
Delorenzi, 56n
Demmer, 14, 21, 25, 34, 35, 61–4, 96n, 192
De Pauw, 69, 70
De Reitmatten, 141n, 149n, 150n
De Roo, 136
De Rosa, 119n, 121n, 144n, 158, 159
De Vine, 76
Dewart, 103
Diaz Moreno, 166n
Diaz-Nava, 49, 70, 164, 165

Di Christina, 11
Di Marino, 172, 173
Dionne, 69
Doepfner, 148n, 149n, 166n
Doms, 98, 99
Dos Santos, 203, 204
Drinkwater, 68, 105, 106
Dubarle, 75–8, 100, 109–10, 161n
Dummett, 68, 105, 106
Dupré, 99, 100, 131n

Egenter, 61, 62, 63, 149n
Egner, 113n
Ermecke, 61, 62, 63, 89, 91, 96n, 188n
Esposito, 162n
Eugenio da Veroli, 200

Farraher, 9, 10, 21, 25, 32
Felici, 125n
Ferin, 40, 131n
Ford, 11, 17, 19, 20, 21, 25, 34, 35n, 37, 38, 139, 141n, 149n, 153
Fortmann, 12
Franceschetti, 180n
Fuchs, J., 16, 20, 21, 23, 34, 35n, 57, 58, 139, 141n, 149n
Furlong, 8

Garbelli, 200
García-Vicente, 57, 58, 60
Garrigou, 162n
Garrone, 136
Genevois, 158, 159–60
Géraud, 138n
Gibbons, 1, 2–3, 4, 5, 8, 18
Glorieux, 125n
Goffi, 64, 65, 149n

Gonzales, 66, 67, 167, 168
Görres, 149n
Gozzo, 161
Grisez, 99, 100, 106
Grootaers, 119n, 131n
Guano, 122, 125, 126, 132, 136
Guindon, 69, 70, 71
Günthör, 57, 58–9, 63, 70, 94, 95, 96n, 192
Guzzetti, 15, 20, 24, 30

Häring, 13, 18n, 20, 23, 53, 65, 89n, 122, 126n, 149n, 190, 195–7
Hauschen, 132
Healy, 11, 21, 118n
Heenan, 54–5n, 126n, 136, 148, 149n
Heggen, 12, 47, 87
Hellegers, 149n
Hengsbach, 139
Herrero, 163n, 200
Hervas, 127
Heylen, 47, 48, 117n, 119n, 132, 138n, 142n, 143n, 145, 164, 166n
Hillen, 12, 13
Hofmann, 89, 91
Hörmann, 201, 202
Huftier, 170, 171
Hulsbosch, 83–4
Hürth, 27, 28, 29, 30, 31, 32, 34
Huygen, 81

Janssens, 4, 5, 6, 8, 18, 21, 24n
Johann, 118n
Juan de Castro, 164, 165

Kaufmann, 188n
Kelly, 11, 17, 19, 21, 25, 34, 35n, 37, 38, 49, 50

Kerns, 116n
Krauss, 96n, 192
Kriekemans, 81n, 131n
Kuničič, 159, 160, 161–2
Kutz, 101–2

Labourdette, 149n
Lambert, 179
Lambruschini, 27, 28–30, 32, 35
Landucci, 162n
La Pietra, 175
Larraín Acuña, 48
Laurentin, 119n
La Valle, 119n
Lawler, 104n
Leemans, 131n, 179
Leers, 202, 203–4
Léger, 127, 136, 190
Leite, 163n
Liebhart, 14, 23
Liénart, 112n
Liggeri, 172n, 201n
Lips, 81n
Loftus, 11
Lorenzetti, 167, 172n
Lumbreras, 70–1
Lynch, 1, 3–4, 8, 9, 10, 16, 17, 19, 20, 49, 50–1

Madden, 11
Marchal, 204n
Marks, 80
Marshall, 108n
Martelet, 60, 61, 69, 70, 155, 157–8, 163
Mascarenhas Roxo, 167, 168
Maximos IV, 127, 128–9, 190
McCabe, 105
McCormick, 10, 17, 25, 100n, 106, 118n, 153

McDonagh, 108
McReavy, 10, 11, 20, 54, 68,
   70, 71, 105, 106, 154
Mejia, 109
Mertens, 113n
Milhaven, 100n
Miller, 14
Minoli, 138n, 175, 178
Mondria, 66
Montaigne, 109, 112-3
Montervino, 15
Morris, 138n

Nalesso, 15, 20, 21, 23, 64
Navarro, 15, 16, 20 ,21, 25, 31,
   33, 163n
Neirynck, 12
Nicodemo, 136
Nolasco, 15, 18, 20, 21, 23
Noonan, 113-8, 149n, 180-3
Novak, 104n, 131n

O'Callaghan, 10, 17, 19n, 20,
   21, 25, 68, 107, 170
O'Donnell, 11, 25
O'Leary, 48n
Onclin, 149n
O'Reilly, 46
Orsenigo, 115n
Osuna, 201, 202
Ottaviani, 55, 126, 139, 143, 148

Palazzini, 5, 6, 15, 21, 27, 29,
   32, 33, 35
Pasetto, 19n, 64
Peinador, 31, 33, 66, 67, 70,
   154, 155, 156-7
Peiro, 33
Pendergast, 172-3

Perico, 15, 20, 21, 23, 24, 64,
   65, 141n, 149n, 167-8, 172n,
   203, 204
Petit, 138n
Philippe de la Trinité, 32, 33
Pierre, 69
Pincus, 1, 38
Piñón, 158, 159
Pittau, 175-6
Pleasants, 105n
Prignon, 138n
Proesmans, 12
Pyle, 46

Quartier, 46, 164, 166
Quay, 74

Raineri, 175
Ranke-Heinemann, 89
Ratzinger, 166n
Ray, 109
Rendu, 56, 69, 180n
Reuss, 38, 43-6, 48, 50, 52, 53,
   58-9, 60, 61, 62, 67, 68, 71,
   89n, 93-6, 127, 129, 130-1,
   137, 141n, 148, 149n, 166n,
   190, 192-3, 195
Ricoeur, 74
Rieterman, 118n
Roberts, 54n, 101
Rock, 1, 37, 40, 49, 131n
Rossi, 170, 172n, 197, 198-9,
   200, 201
Rossino, 211n
Rottinghuis, 12
Rötzer, 14, 61, 104n, 188n
Rouquette, 119n
Royo Villanova, 33
Ruether, 104n
Ruffini, 126, 136

Ruiz Amezcua, 68
Russo, 159, 160

Salazar, 15, 16, 21
Salvo, 15, 16, 17, 18
Sanchez, 97, 115, 163n
Sanchez Jménez, 200, 201
Savalle, 13, 37
Sbarigia, 57n
Schaumberger, 76
Schelfhout, 60, 61
Scherer, 98, 99, 138n
Schillebeeckx, 73, 78–80, 81, 84n, 86, 88–9, 132, 138n, 183, 185, 186
Schockaert, 13, 20, 23, 131n
Schöllgen, 97, 98
Schurr, 89n
Seelhammer, 47
Semmelroth, 149n
Sigmond, 149n
Silva Henriquez, 150n
Silva Soares, 66–7, 164, 165
Simonet, 74
Sini, 200, 201
Snoek, 15, 16, 20, 21, 23, 25, 34, 35, 46, 66, 67, 86, 164, 165
Springer, 170, 171–2, 173
Squillaci, 30
Stenger, 89n
Straven, 81n
Suenens, 55, 121, 122, 127–8, 136, 190
Sullivan, 104n
Suster, 89n
Svidercoschi, 119n

Teichtweier, 89, 92
Tesson, 8, 48
Tettamanzi, 119n, 163n
Thiéffry, 13, 20, 21, 23
Thomas, 105, 108n, 164, 165
Tissot, 118n
Trimbos, 131n
Turri, 113n

Umbricht, 56n

Valsecchi, 64, 65, 149n, 170
Vandenberghe, 75
Van der Marck, 9n, 38, 41–3, 46, 48, 50, 51, 52, 60, 61, 68, 71, 86–7
Van der Wey, 13
Van Dodewaard, 138n
Van Gansewinkel, 118n
Van Kol, 4–5, 6, 8, 18, 21
Van Leeuwen, 138n, 183, 185
Van Melsen, 149n
Van Ouverkerk, 87n
Villee, 1
Vimercati, 15, 21, 172n
Visser, 139, 141n, 149

Weber, 14, 21, 47, 53, 68, 89n, 98, 99
Wenger, 119n, 148n
Work, 138n

Zalba, 15, 16, 20, 21, 25, 33, 34, 35, 36, 49, 51–2, 56, 58–9, 70, 139, 141n, 149n, 154–6, 163
Ziegler, 89, 92, 93, 192n
Zoppis, 175, 176–7